WILLIE'S WILDCAT COOKBOOK

A COLLECTION OF
FAVORITE RECIPES FROM THE
NORTHWESTERN WILDCAT FAMILY

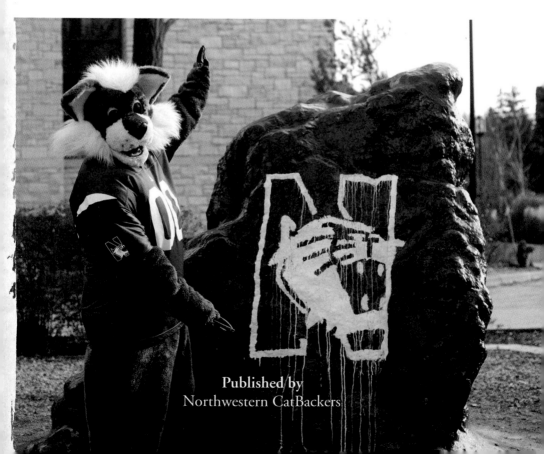

Published by
Northwestern CatBackers

Publisher's Cataloging in Publication Data

CatBackers of Northwestern University, Evanston, Illinois, pub.
Willie's Wildcat Cookbook—First Edition

x, 342p, includes index | 22.86 cm

Summary: Recipes from Northwestern University alumni, faculty, staff and
friends with an emphasis on Wildcat sports-related connections.

ISBN 978-0-615-52508-2 (pbk. : alk. paper)

First Edition

I. Cooking II. Cookbooks — Northwestern University

Library of Congress Control Number: 2011936290

CatBacker Board of Directors

Liz Kerr, President

Zoe Barron

Sandy Eszes

Stacy Fitzgerald

Marian Kurz

Bonnie Lytle

Sharon McGee

Bonita Paynter

Laura Phillips

Gwyn Rahr

Greta Sims

Bernice Valantinas

Tammy Walker

Mary Pat Watt

Bonnie Wefler

Jean Yale

Cookbook Committee

Helene Bak Slowik, Editor

Joann Skiba, Co-Chair

Don Skiba, Co-Chair

Bonita Paynter, Photography

Kathy Newcomb, Layout

Marian Kurz, Publicity, Co-Editor

Zoe Barron

Kelly Deiters

Susan Gaud

Jack Griffin

Jane Haeger

Liz Kerr

Joanne McCall

Linda Nagel

Greta Sims

Lu Sunkel

Bernice Valantinas

Carolyn Wangelin

Tammy Walker

Mary Pat Watt

Bonnie Wefler

Jean Yale

Marilyn Zilka

Acknowledgements

Special Thanks

Jim Phillips, Ph.D., Athletic Director

Laura Phillips

Northwestern Athletic Department

Pam Bonnevier

Julie Dunn

Jack Griffin

Maureen Harty

John Mack

Shon Morris

Mike Wolf

Cathy Stembridge,
Northwestern Alumni Association

Amanda Sloan

Dan Barron

Dave Eanet

Dave & Cindy Gaborek (Let's Tailgate)

Samir Mayekar,
NUMB Alumni Association

Adam Paoli

Joseph Slowik

Julie Sweica

Anne Uible

Rob Lichten

Joel Childs

Bob Kurz

Willie the Wildcat

Northwestern Coaches

Parents of Northwestern Student-Athletes

Northwestern Fans

Photos provided by Stephen Carrera,
NU Photographer

Tim Sonder,
Innovative Design & Graphics, Evanston

Bluestone, Evanston

Girl and The Goat, Chicago

Lou Malnati's, Evanston

McCormick & Schmick's, Skokie

Oceanique, Evanston

The Hilton Orrington Hotel, Evanston

The Spice House, Evanston

Wildfire, Glenview

Dedication

This cookbook is dedicated to the student-athletes past and present, who have worn a Northwestern uniform as a player, cheerleader, Lady Cat, or "Willie" on the fields, courts, strips, courses, mats, or pools of competition.

The Wildcat Nation is proud of you.

Go Cats!

All of the proceeds from Willie's Wildcat Cookbook will go to:

The Wildcat Fund

Thank you for your purchase of Willie's Wildcat Cookbook which helps support the Wildcat Fund! The Wildcat Fund is the top ongoing funding priority for Northwestern Athletics and helps provide scholarship and other vital support to our student-athletes. Your support of the Wildcat Fund helps provide the resources necessary for our young people to have the best experience possible, both on the field of competition and in the classroom.

Thanks again for your support of the Wildcat Fund and Northwestern Athletics.

Jack Griffin '90
Assistant A.D./Director of the Wildcat Fund

Willie's Wildcat Cookbook is special! This incredible project, a year in the making, was undertaken by the Northwestern CatBackers as a fundraising initiative. This cookbook contains so many wonderful things that will be enjoyed time and time again. The primary focus is a collection of recipes that are family treasures, fan favorites and tailgate fare. Former student-athletes, NU coaches – past and present, university staff, parents, and intensely loyal fans have all generously contributed to this cookbook.

However, the special features don't end there. This cookbook is a link to some of the history of Northwestern athletics. Within its covers you will take a tour of athletic facilities, and enjoy special photos of former stand-out players as well as a variety of particular places on campus that will be sure to evoke fond memories of Northwestern. How do Wildcat coaches motivate their players before facing an opponent? What do our players eat as part of their training tables before each game? What are historical facts relating to each of our 19 NCAA sports teams? This is all included as well.

Willie's Wildcat Cookbook will be a "go to" cookbook, treasured by Wildcat fans for years to come. All of the proceeds from *Willie's Wildcat Cookbook* will directly benefit the Wildcat Fund which provides scholarships for future student-athletes that will wear a Wildcat uniform.

We are grateful to the CatBackers for their vision, their passion for cooking and their support and undying loyalty to Northwestern athletics. We are all the beneficiaries.

Jim Phillips

James J. Phillips, Ph.D.
Director of Athletics and Recreation
Northwestern University

TABLE OF CONTENTS

Warm Ups

Appetizers

CROSS COUNTRY

Head Coach April Likhite (1998–2001 & 2007–present)
– *6th and 8th head coach*

• First season was in 1976.

• There are 24 members on the 2011 team. They come from California to Berlin, Germany and places in between, like Wilmette, IL.

• Their races include 4K, 5K and 6K.

• There were 133 Academic All-Big Ten honorees in the years 1986–2010.

dips

Apple Dip

Mary & Coach Gary Barnett,
**Former NU Football Head Coach
(Rose Bowl 1996);
Mary is a founder of CatBackers**

YIELD: 1-1/2 CUPS

INGREDIENTS

8 ounces cream cheese

1/2 cup powdered sugar

1/2 jar Mrs. Richardson's Butterscotch Carmel Fudge Sauce

1/2 cup chopped nuts or nut topping, optional

Blend cream cheese and sugar together. Put in serving bowl and pour fudge sauce over the top. Sprinkle on nuts. Serve with sliced red and green apples. Granny Smith and Red Delicious are good.

COACHES QUOTES

Gary Barnett,
Former Football Head Coach:

"Expect Victory!"

Hot Apple Pie Dip

Julie Kent

INGREDIENTS

1 package (8 ounces) cream cheese, softened

2 tablespoons light brown sugar

1/2 teaspoon pumpkin pie spice

1 Granny Smith apple, peeled, cored and chopped, divided

1/4 cup shredded cheddar cheese

1 tablespoon finely chopped pecans

Mix cream cheese, sugar and spice until well blended. Stir in half of the apples. Spread into pie plate or small casserole dish. Top with remaining apples, cheddar cheese and nuts. Bake at 375 degrees for 10 to 12 minutes or until heated through. Serve with wheat crackers.

Artichoke Dip

Maureen Dowd,
Lacrosse Mom — Katrina 2010

YIELD: 1-1/2 CUPS

INGREDIENTS

fresh Parmesan cheese

8 ounces cream cheese

2 cloves garlic, chopped

1 jar marinated artichokes, drained

1/2 cup mayonnaise

paprika for color

Blend all the ingredients in a bowl. Let set overnight if you can. Warm in the oven and serve with crackers.

Crab and Artichoke Dip

Executive Chef Joe Decker,
Wildfire Restaurant, multiple locations

YIELD: 8 CUPS

INGREDIENTS

DIP:

8 ounces cream cheese

2 cups mayonnaise

1 pound lump crab meat

1 cup grated Asiago cheese

3/4 cup chopped canned artichoke
    hearts

1/2 cup sliced green onions

1/2 cup diced red bell peppers

1/2 cup diced celery

1/4 cup chopped fresh parsley

2 tablespoons sherry wine vinegar

2 teaspoons Tabasco sauce

2 teaspoons salt

1 teaspoon ground white pepper

TOPPING:

1 cup panko bread crumbs

1/4 cup chopped fresh parsley

1/2 cup grated Asiago cheese

Preheat oven to 400 degrees.

DIP: Whip cream cheese with mixer until smooth and light. Add mayonnaise; combine well with mixer. Fold in all remaining ingredients by hand with rubber spatula until combined well. Transfer to an oven proof casserole dish.

TOPPING: Combine bread crumbs, parsley and Asiago cheese; evenly sprinkle over the dip. Dust with paprika and bake for 18 to 20 minutes or until golden brown and hot in center. Serve with toast points, pita chips, crackers, or anything that you may desire.

Black Bean Salsa Dip

Mary & Coach Gary Barnett,
**Former NU Football Head Coach (Rose Bowl 1996);
Mary is a founder of CatBackers**

YIELD: 1-1/2 CUPS

From the menu of Gary Barnett's Restaurant in Evanston, which is now closed.

INGREDIENTS

1 can (15 ounces) black beans, rinsed
    and drained

1/4 cup thinly sliced green onions

1/4 cup chopped red bell pepper

2 tablespoons fresh chopped cilantro

1 cup Pace thick & chunky salsa

1-1/2 teaspoons freshly squeezed lime
    juice

1 clove garlic, minced

1/4 teaspoon ground cumin

1 small ripe avocado

Combine beans, onion, pepper and cilantro and set aside. Combine salsa, lime juice, garlic and cumin. Mix well and pour over bean mixture. Mix gently. Chill 2 hours or overnight. To serve, peel and chop avocado and add to dip. Serve with corn chips.

The Dip

Luke Sundheim, 2005,
Baseball

Y<small>IELD: 12 TO 16 APPETIZER SERVINGS</small>

I<small>NGREDIENTS</small>

- 1 bag El Ranchero Tortilla Chips or your favorite brand
- 1 can (15 ounces) Hormel No Bean Chili
- 8 ounces low fat cream cheese
- 6 ounces shredded Mexican blend cheese
- 1 jar (6 ounces) (or more) La Preferida jalapeño peppers, optional

Use a 9x9 square or 9 to 10 inch round baking dish

Preheat the oven to 375 degrees.

Coat the bottom of the baking dish using the entire container of cream cheese. Layer the chili over the cream cheese. Be sure that the chili is spread evenly over the dish. Spread the jalapeños over the chili.

Spread the shredded Mexican cheese liberally over the chili. Be sure to cover the entire dish with cheese.

Bake for approximately 20 minutes or until cheese is golden brown.

Remove and let cool for 10 to 15 minutes. Serve with El Ranchero Tortilla Chips (other chips may be used but these are best).

Baked Mexican Dip

Jane Haeger, 1957

Y<small>IELD: 10 TO 12 SERVINGS</small>

I<small>NGREDIENTS</small>

- 8 ounces cream cheese, softened
- 1 can (15 ounces) Hormel chili without beans
- 1 can (15 ounces) black beans, rinsed and drained
- 1 can (4-1/2 ounces) chopped green chilies
- 8 ounces shredded sharp cheddar cheese

For extra heat, use a similar amount of hotter chilies.

Heat oven to 350 degrees.

Spread cream cheese on bottom of 1-1/2 or 2 quart casserole. Mix Hormel chili, beans and green chilies in a bowl. Layer over cream cheese. Sprinkle shredded cheese evenly over top.

Bake in preheated oven for 20 minutes, or until cheese is just melted. Serve with tortilla chips of your choice.

This recipe can be doubled easily for a crowd (use a 3 quart casserole).

Baked Beef Dip

Mo Harty,
Associate Athletic Director

YIELD: 4 CUPS

INGREDIENTS

5 ounces dried/chipped beef or corned beef

16 ounces cream cheese

1 cup sour cream

1/4 cup milk

1 cup pecans

1 cup diced onions

1/2 teaspoon garlic salt

1 dash Worcestershire sauce

Mix all ingredients and place in a baking dish. Heat at 350 degrees for 20 minutes. Serve with crackers or bread.

Dried Beef (Budding) Dip

Sally Madden Hayward, 1961

YIELD: 2 CUPS

INGREDIENTS

1 package (about 2-1/2 ounces) dried or chipped beef chopped into small pieces

8 ounces cream cheese

8 ounces sour cream

1 tablespoon milk

1/4 cup finely chopped green, red or orange pepper

2 tablespoons finely chopped onion or scallions

freshly ground pepper, to taste

I usually double recipe, so I have leftovers, serving over toasted bread open-faced for lunch.

Blend cheese and sour cream with mixer. Stir in milk, chipped beef, onions and peppers. Top with pepper for flavor.

Serve with Triscut crackers.

Optional: Heat in 350 degree oven 10 to 15 minutes or in microwave 4 to 5 minutes. If refrigerated, it will keep up to one week.

Football Goop a.k.a. Goop and Scoop

Nancy Lee

YIELD: 10 TO 12 SERVINGS

INGREDIENTS

2 pounds lean ground beef

1 pound Velveeta (light is fine)

1 jar (16 ounces) of medium chunky salsa

Cook beef in large skillet, breaking into small pieces; drain fat. Cut Velveeta into chunks and let melt in skillet with beef. Add jar of salsa and stir.

Keep warm while serving: use a slow cooker, propane stove or chafing dish. Serve with scoop tortilla chips.

Beer Cheese Dip

Kelly Kowalski,
Wife of Ken Kowalski,
Director of Video Football

YIELD: 2 CUPS

INGREDIENTS

8 ounces cream cheese, diced and softened

8 ounces Velveeta, cubed

3/4 teaspoon garlic powder

1/2 cup beer, room temperature

To vary flavors, try different types of beer or replace Velveeta with 8 ounces of another smooth melting cheese.

In medium sauce pan, melt together the cream cheese, Velveeta, garlic powder and room temperature beer. Cook until heated through and smooth. Serve with pretzels or Beer Bread Rolls. *(see recipe)*

Serve warm or at room temperature.

Debbie's Dip

Debbie Vaughn,
Football Mom — Justan (#28) 2010

YIELD: 1-1/2 CUPS

INGREDIENTS

8 ounces cream cheese

8 ounces chipolte sauce

1 box water crackers

Pour chipolte sauce over cream cheese. Dip with crackers. Amazing taste!

Easy Blue Cheese Dip

Sue Bragiel

YIELD: 2-1/2 CUPS

INGREDIENTS

8 ounces cream cheese

4 ounces blue cheese

4 ounces butter

1/2 bunch (about 6) green onions, chopped

1 cup black olives, chopped

Soften cream cheese, blue cheese and butter. Mix with onion and olives. Serve with Wheat Thins and Triscuit crackers. May also be prepared and frozen.

Pepperoni Pizza Dip

Megan Anderson, 1976

YIELD: 1-1/2 CUPS

INGREDIENTS

8 ounces cream cheese, softened

1/2 cup sour cream

1 teaspoon oregano

1/8 teaspoon garlic powder

1/8 teaspoon crushed red pepper

1/2 cup pizza sauce

1/2 cup chopped pepperoni

1/4 cup sliced green onions

1/4 cup chopped green pepper

8 ounces shredded mozzarella

SERVE WITH:

pepper strips

broccoli flowerettes

crackers

Beat together first 5 ingredients. Spread evenly in a 9 or 10 inch quiche dish or pie pan. Spread pizza sauce over cream cheese mixture. Sprinkle with pepperoni, onions and pepper. Bake at 350 degrees for 10 minutes. Top with mozzarella cheese and bake 5 more minutes. Serve warm with veggies or crackers.

Slop — Salsa Layer Dip

Katheryn French, 2007

YIELD: 6 SERVINGS

INGREDIENTS

8 ounces cream cheese

1 can (16 ounces) Hormel chili — hot, no beans

2 cups Mexican shredded cheese

1 jar (16 ounces) Pace Picante Salsa — Hot

1 bag Tostitos Crispy Rounds tortilla chips

For a milder version, use mild chili and salsa.

Preheat oven to 350 degrees.

Spread cream cheese over the bottom of a 12 inch diameter x 1 inch deep oven safe bowl. Layer the Hormel chili over the top of the cream cheese. Layer the shredded cheese on top of the chili. Layer the salsa over the top.

Place bowl in oven for 30 to 35 minutes. Allow to cool for 5 minutes. Serve with tortilla chips.

Fino's Taco Dip

Linda Finocchiaro,
Lacrosse Mom — Lindsay 2007

INGREDIENTS

2 packages taco seasoning

8 ounces cream cheese

12 ounces sour cream

1 head iceberg lettuce, shredded

1 can (2 or 3 ounces) sliced
black olives, drained

5 tomatoes, cut and drained, seeded
if desired

1 large jar (16 ounces) of salsa,
drained

1 bunch scallions, chopped and
drained, about 1-1/2 cups

2 cups shredded cheddar cheese

Mix taco seasoning, sour cream and
cream cheese together. Place the smooth
mixture on a large serving tray. In order,
one at a time, place on top of taco mixture: salsa, lettuce, tomatoes, scallions,
olives, and finally cheddar cheese. Serve
with Tostitos Scoops.

Annie's Dip

Kathy Newcomb

YIELD: 1 CUP DIP

INGREDIENTS

4 ounces softened cream cheese

1/3 cup sour cream

2 tablespoons tomato juice

1 tablespoon dry Italian dressing

Mix all ingredients. Great with chips and
vegetables.

Blazing Buffalo Dip

Jayne Donohoe,
Lacrosse Mom — Casey 2009

INGREDIENTS

6 boneless chicken breasts

8 ounces cream cheese

2/3 cup Frank's Redhot sauce

1 jar (16 ounces) Marie's blue cheese
dressing

2 cups grated cheddar cheese

Poach chicken in water, chicken broth or
vegetable broth until done.

Cut chicken into little pieces or shred.
Mix chicken, cream cheese, hot sauce and
dressing together and put into a slow
cooker. Put cheese on top. Heat until
cheese melts and mixture is warm. Serve
with pita bread, celery or crackers. Players
love it!

Or, bake in a 350 degree oven for about
20 minutes.

Buffalo Blue Cheese Chicken Dip

Betsy Flanagan, 1996,
Field Hockey

INGREDIENTS

3 boneless breasts of chicken

1 cup chunky blue cheese dressing

1 cup Frank's Redhot Sauce (more or
less depending on your taste)

8 ounces cream cheese, softened

1-1/2 to 2 cups shredded cheddar
cheese, divided

Cook and shred chicken. Mix cream
cheese, hot sauce, blue cheese dressing
and 1 cup of shredded cheese together in
large bowl. Add chicken and mix well.
Spread into deep casserole or baking dish
and top with shredded cheese. Cook at
350 degrees for 25 to 30 minutes or until
bubbly and cheese is melted. Serve with
scoop style chips. **N**

Buffalo Ranch Chicken Dip

Jaime & Coach Adam Cushing,
Offensive Line Coach, Football

YIELD: 10 TO 12 SERVINGS

INGREDIENTS

1 cup ranch dressing

3/4 cup Frank's Redhot Sauce

1 can (10 ounces) chicken in water

16 ounces cream cheese

8 ounces shredded cheddar cheese

Preheat oven to 350 degrees. Drain
chicken.

Mix ranch dressing, Frank's Redhot
Sauce, chicken and cream cheese in a
9x13 inch glass pan. Mix with a fork and
mash ingredients together. Bake for 10 to
15 minutes.

Remove from oven and put cheese on top
of mixture. Bake an additional 10 to 12
minutes until cheese is melted on top.

Serve with chips. **N**

Buffalo Hot Wing Dip

Darren Drexler, 1996,
Football

INGREDIENTS

3 cups chopped cooked chicken
(rotisserie or poached)

8 ounces cream cheese

1/2 cup hot wing sauce

1/2 cup ranch dressing

2 cups shredded cheese, divided

Preheat oven to 350 degrees. In medium
bowl mix all ingredients but use only half
of the shredded cheese. Spread into an
8x12 inch baking pan. Bake for 25 to 30
minutes. Add remaining cheese.
Continue to bake until cheese on top is
melted (5 to 10 minutes). Serve with tortilla chips or celery. **N**

Frank's Redhot Chicken Dip

Juli Hanrahan,
Football Mom — Tim #28

INGREDIENTS

1 package (8 ounces) cream cheese, softened

2 cans (9-3/4 ounces each) chunk chicken breast, drained or 2 cups of cooked chicken

1/2 cup any flavor Frank's Redhot sauce

1/2 cup blue cheese salad dressing

1/2 cup crumbled blue cheese

assorted veggies, crackers or chips for dipping

Preheat oven to 350 degrees. Mix ingredients in deep baking dish until smooth. Bake for 20 minutes until hot and bubbling.

Cheese Fondue

Suzy Shurna,
Men's Basketball Mom—John #24

YIELD: 8 SERVINGS

Serving this fondue is a Christmas Eve tradition at our house.

INGREDIENTS

2 pounds Jarlsberg cheese

1/4 pound Gruyère cheese

2 tablespoons flour

2 cups dry white wine

1 clove garlic, cut

1/2 teaspoon salt

1/4 teaspoon black pepper

1/2 teaspoon nutmeg

1/4 cup kirsch (white cherry brandy)

2 loafs crusty French bread

Cut French bread into bite-sized chunks and place in serving dish.

Cut Jarlsberg and Gruyère cheese into chunks, place in food processor and shred. Add flour and pulse once to blend.

Heat dry white wine to simmering in a cooking dish or pan that has been rubbed with garlic. (The top pan of a double boiler type chafing dish is ideal). Add cheese and stir constantly for about 10 minutes until cheese is melted. Add salt, pepper and nutmeg.

Continue stirring constantly to prevent separation. Heat to boiling, add kirsch and serve at once in a chafing dish.

Quick Hot Mexican Dip

P J Sinopoli,
Cheerleading Mom — Jenny

YIELD: 2 CUPS

INGREDIENTS

1 can (15 ounces) Wolf brand chili
     with beans
8 ounces softened cream cheese (or
     more if you prefer)
1/2 to 1 cup shredded cheese (cheddar
     or Mexican mix)
sour cream
chopped green chilies or scallions,
     optional

Spread cream cheese evenly on bottom of a round casserole or pyrex pie plate. Spread can of chili evenly over top of cream cheese. Generously sprinkle shredded cheese on top of chili. Microwave for approximately 3 minutes. Dollop top of hot dip with sour cream. Serve with tortilla chips such as Tostitos Scoops.

Optional: Add green chilies or onions prior to sprinkling with cheese. If dip gets cold, can be reheated for 1 to 2 minutes.

Taco Dip

Courtney Magnuson,
Account Executive, Athletic Event Sales, Athletic Department

YIELD: 6 TO 8 SERVINGS

INGREDIENTS

1 tomato, chopped
1 green pepper, chopped
1 small white onion, chopped
1 jar (16 ounces) of salsa
1 can (15 ounces) light or dark red
     kidney beans, rinsed and
     drained
1 can (15 ounces) of Mexicali corn
2 cups shredded Mexican blend cheese

Mix all ingredients together in large bowl. Serve immediately or refrigerate until served. Pairs wonderfully with corn or flour tortilla chips.

Southwestern Corn Dip

Linda Grube Eisenhauer &
Ron Eisenhauer,
Linda 1959 SESP and Ron 1958 WCAS

INGREDIENTS

1 can (15 ounces) yellow corn kernels,
    drained

1 can (2-1/4 ounces) sliced black
    olives, drained

1 can (4 ounces) chopped green
    chilies, drained

1/2 jar or more roasted red peppers,
    chopped, to taste

1 cup shredded Monterey Jack/Colby
    cheese

1/2 cup grated Parmesan cheese

1 cup mayonnaise

Preheat oven to 350 degrees. Add all
ingredients to a bowl and mix. Spray
2-quart baking dish with oil and add
mixture. Bake until top is bubbly all over,
about 30 minutes.

Serve with Tostitos or similar chips.

COACHES QUOTES

Pat Fitzgerald, Football:

"Wildcat Character — Who you are
when no one is watching."

Hot Fiesta Dip

Marietta Paynter

YIELD: 2 CUPS

Marietta was married to
John Paynter, a Northwestern
alum who served as director
of the NU Marching Band
from 1953 to 1996.

INGREDIENTS

10 ounces frozen whole kernel corn

1-1/2 cups refrigerated fresh salsa

3/4 to 1 cup shredded Mexican-style
    cheese

2 to 3 tablespoons chopped green
    onions

Vary flavors with type of salsa or with
roasted corn

Microwave frozen corn per package directions. Drain corn and combine with salsa
on microwaveable plate or flat bowl.
Cover with plastic wrap and vent.
Microwave on high for 2 minutes or until
bubbly. Sprinkle cheese over corn mixture, cover and let stand 5 minutes or
until cheese melts. Top with chopped
onions. Serve with tortilla chips, pita
bread or crackers.

Cucumber Dip

Sue Littau

INGREDIENTS

8 ounces cream cheese, softened
1/4 teaspoon garlic powder
1/4 teaspoon salt
1/4 teaspoon ground black pepper
1 tablespoon Worcestershire sauce
3/4 cup chopped onions
1/4 cup mayonnaise
2 cups peeled, diced, seeded cucumber

Mix all the ingredients together and chill for 4 hours before serving. Serve with an assortment of crisp crackers.

Sweet Pea and Curry Dip

Joan Borg

YIELD: 1-1/2 CUPS

This dip is bright green, very healthy and a fun ice breaker because everyone loves it and no one can decide what is in it!

INGREDIENTS

16 ounces frozen green peas
2 scallions
1 teaspoon kosher salt
1-1/4 teaspoons curry powder
1/4 cup olive oil

Thaw peas. Chop scallions. In a food processor with metal blade, purée the peas, scallions, kosher salt and curry powder. Slowly drizzle in olive oil and blend until smooth. Serve with pita chips.

Olive Caviar

Mary Weed

YIELD: 2-1/2 CUPS

INGREDIENTS

1 cup chopped green olives with pimentos, rinsed and drained
1 cup chopped black olives, drained
1/2 cup chopped pecans
1/4 cup (or less) mayonnaise

Spread pecans on baking pan and bake at 375 degrees for about 3 to 5 minutes until evenly toasted. (Or toast in pan on stove, shaking pan constantly until done.) Mix with olives, adding enough mayonnaise to hold together. Serve on crackers.

Easy Baked Vidalia Onion Dip

Rick Taylor,
Former Athletic Director

YIELD: 2 CUPS

INGREDIENTS

1 cup chopped Vidalia onions
1 cup shredded Parmesan cheese
1 cup mayonnaise (regular)
1 clove garlic, chopped
3 to 5 drops Tabasco sauce

Make sure you use regular mayonnaise. Light and non-fat do not work!

Preheat oven to 375 degrees. In 1 quart casserole, combine all ingredients. Bake 25 minutes or until golden brown. Serve with your favorite crackers.

The Real Cowboy Caviar

Nichole Ellis,
Associate Coach, Women's Swim Team

Now, I have seen a lot of variations of Cowboy Caviar (or Texas Caviar, if you prefer) over the years. Some people add tomatoes, eggplant, tomatillos, corn, green peppers, bottled Italian dressing and avocados. As far as I am concerned, those people are just making salsa with beans. If I wanted salsa, I would make salsa.

INGREDIENTS

1 can (15 ounces) black eyed peas
1 can (15 ounces) black beans
2 to 3 roasted red peppers
1 to 2 habanero peppers
1 to 2 jalapeños
2 to 3 cloves of garlic
2 to 3 green onions
1/2 cup chopped cilantro
    (about 1/2 bunch)
1 tablespoon lime juice
1 tablespoon white wine vinegar
2 to 3 tablespoons vegetable oil
1/2 to 1 teaspoon liquid smoke
salt and pepper, to taste

Rinse and drain beans. Chop cilantro, peppers, onions and garlic. Mix with white wine vinegar, lime juice, oil and liquid smoke. Stir in beans. Add salt and pepper, to taste.

Marinate in refrigerator for 6 to 8 hours to let the flavors open up and permeate the beans.

Serve cold with corn chips.

Cowboy Caviar with Olives

Liz Kerr, 1981

YIELD: 2 CUPS

Great low calorie snack.

INGREDIENTS

1 can (15 ounces) black eyed peas,
    rinsed and drained
1/4 cup thinly sliced green onions
1/4 cup finely chopped red pepper
2 cloves garlic, minced
1/4 cup chopped olives
1 small avocado, chopped
2 tablespoons olive oil
2 tablespoons cider vinegar
cracked black pepper
dash salt

Mix all ingredients together and chill to blend flavors. Serve with tortilla chips.

Salmon Mousse

Executive Chef Jim Freeland,
**Lou Malnati's, Evanston and over
30 locations throughout Chicagoland**

Yield: about 10 cups

INGREDIENTS

12 ounces cooked salmon
6 cups whipping cream
2 envelopes unflavored gelatin
6 tablespoons water
1/2 cup chopped chives
4 tablespoons lemon juice
5 teaspoons minced onion
4 teaspoons salt
pinch white pepper
10 drops Tabasco

Oil one large or several individual molds; set aside. Combine salmon with 1 cup cream and process until smooth. Press through a sieve; set aside. Dissolve gelatin and water over low heat; combine with remaining whipping cream and whip until it peaks. Add chives, juice, onion, salt, pepper and Tabasco. Stir 1/4 mixture into puréed salmon, then fold in the rest. Spoon into mold. Chill 1-1/2 hours, then unmold.

Lime Shrimp Dip

Elizabeth Kurz

Yield: about 3-1/2 cups

Can also be served on lettuce as a salad.

INGREDIENTS

1-1/2 pounds shrimp
  (use precooked small shrimp or
  larger shrimp chopped)
Salt & pepper, to taste
1/2 cup ketchup
1/4 cup horseradish
  (add sparingly at first)
1/2 cup fresh lime juice
cilantro, chopped, to taste
hot sauce, to taste
1 small avocado, chopped

Mix all together and refrigerate. If making a day ahead, do not add the avocado until a few hours before serving. Serve with Lime Tostito Chips.

Crab Dip

Jayne Donohoe,
Lacrosse Mom — Casey 2009

YIELD: 3 CUPS

INGREDIENTS

1 pound crab meat
16 ounces cream cheese
1/2 pint sour cream
1 teaspoon lemon juice
4 tablespoons mayonnaise
1 teaspoon dry mustard
2 teaspoons Worcestershire sauce
Cheddar cheese, shredded, for topping

Combine all the ingredients except the crab and cheddar cheese. Mix using mixer. Stir in crab meat. Put into slow cooker to heat and top with cheddar cheese. Serve with crackers.

BLT Dip

Patrick Hunt

YIELD: 50 PIECES

INGREDIENTS

2 cups sour cream
2 cups mayonnaise
6 seeded, diced, plum tomatoes
1/2 cup diced green onions
1 container Hormel Real Bacon Bits
2 cups cheddar cheese

Mix sour cream, mayonnaise and bacon bits. Add tomatoes, green onions and cheddar cheese and stir well.

Refrigerate for at least one hour before serving.

Crab Meat Dip

Sandra Schultz Miner, 1958

YIELD: 2 CUPS

INGREDIENTS

8 ounces cream cheese, softened
1/2 cup Miracle Whip
2 tablespoons minced onion
2 tablespoons ketchup
2 to 4 tablespoons Kraft
    Creamy French Dressing
    (must be Kraft Creamy)
1 can (6 to 7-1/2 ounces) crab meat

Beat all ingredients except crab. Stir in crab. Serve with chips or crackers.

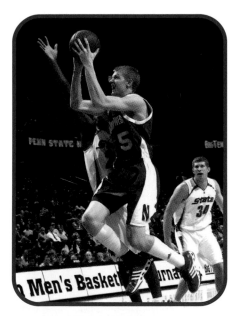

finger food

Bacon Wrapped Apricots with Sage

Debbie Hinchcliff Seward, 1974

YIELD: 24 PIECES

INGREDIENTS

24 fresh sage leaves

24 large dried apricots

8 slices bacon, cut crosswise into thirds

2 tablespoons pure maple syrup

toothpicks for serving

Heat oven to 375 degrees. Place a sage leaf on each apricot. Wrap with a piece of uncooked bacon. Place seam-side down on a baking sheet sprayed with non-stick cooking oil. Bake until the bacon is crisp, about 14 to 16 minutes, turning after 7 minutes. Remove from oven and brush with maple syrup. Serve with toothpicks.

Zliders — An East Lot Exclusive

Marilyn Zilka, 1975

YIELD: 12 PIECES

INGREDIENTS

3/4 pound ground round beef

1 packet Mrs. Grass's dry onion soup mix

8 ounces shredded cheddar cheese

1-1/2 tablespoons mayonnaise

1 dozen 2 inch square dinner rolls such as Hawaiian Rolls or Pepperidge Farm

1 disposable aluminum foil baking tray to fit rolls

Preheat oven to 350 degrees.

In a medium bowl, thoroughly mix ground beef, cheddar cheese, onion soup mix and mayonnaise.

Take package of rolls and make a horizontal cut of all the buns; keep as one top and one bottom piece. Place bottom half of the rolls into the aluminum baking tray.

Spread meat mixture over entire bottom layer of rolls; place top portion of rolls over mixture. Cut so you have 12 individual rolls, but it looks like one big roll. Cover and wrap with several pieces of aluminum foil.

Bake for 30 to 35 minutes until meat is cooked.

Alternate: Refrigerate wrapped tray of Zliders overnight and bake 40 to 45 minutes the next day (if placed in oven directly from refrigerator.)

Brie and Apricot Phyllo Bites

Elizabeth Kurz

YIELD: 30 PIECES

From Every Day Feast (Junior League of Tampa), with permission.

INGREDIENTS

8 ounces Brie, rind removed

30 frozen phyllo cup/shells

1/2 cup butter, melted

2/3 cup apricot preserves

2 cups finely chopped fresh or dried apricots

1/4 to 1/2 cup sliced almonds, to taste

Preheat oven to 350 degrees. Cut the Brie into thirty 1/2 inch cubes. Arrange the phyllo shells on a baking sheet; brush with melted butter. Bake 5 minutes. Remove from the oven and let cool on the baking sheet. Spoon 1 teaspoon of the apricot preserves into each shell; add a piece of the Brie into each. Top with a small amount of apricot preserves and a sprinkle of almonds. Bake for 5 to 10 minutes or until the Brie is melted and beginning to brown. Serve warm.

Cheese Wafers

Zoe T Barron

YIELD: 200 PIECES

INGREDIENTS

2 cups flour

1/4 teaspoon cayenne pepper

1/4 pound butter, softened

1/4 pound margarine, softened

2 cups shredded sharp cheddar cheese

salt, garlic salt or celery salt

Mix the cayenne into the flour, add shredded cheese and toss with your hands. Add butter and margarine, mix with your hands. Dough will be very stiff. Shape dough into 3 logs about 18 inches each. Wrap each log in waxed paper and refrigerate overnight on a tray or cookie sheet.

Preheat oven to 350 degrees. Slice rolls a shy 1/4 inch thick and place on baking sheet. Bake for 8 to 10 minutes or until beginning to brown a bit. Top wafers with salt as soon as they come out of the oven. Remove wafers from sheet and cool on a wire rack. Keep in a tightly covered tin or freeze up to 6 months.

COACHES QUOTES

Stephanie Foster, Women's Soccer:

"It's hard to beat someone who never gives up."
—Babe Ruth

Chili Willie Cups

Beth Trumpy,
Football Mom — Mike #29

YIELD: 10 PIECES

A crowd pleaser at the football parent tailgates.

INGREDIENTS

1 package wonton wrappers
1-1/2 pounds boneless chicken breast, poached and shredded
1/4 teaspoon salt
1/4 teaspoon pepper
2 teaspoons dry chili mix
2 cups shredded Mexican blend cheese
4 ounces canned green chilies
1 cup ranch dressing

Preheat oven to 350 degrees. Line mini muffin tin with wonton wrappers and bake 5 minutes. Mix together remaining ingredients and spoon into cups. Baked filled cups an additional 10 to 12 minutes.

Tailgate Buffalo Wings

Larry Villella, 2000

YIELD: 48+ PIECES

INGREDIENTS

24 to 30 whole chicken wings
3 jars (12 ounces each) Buffalo wing sauce

Any wing sauce will do: pick your favorite. If you search the internet for: Tailgate Northwestern University Medium Wing Sauce, you can even find a Wildcat branded one, and it's quite good!

Cut wings into 3 parts; discard tips. Empty bottles of wing sauce into a stockpot and heat over a camping stove or directly on the grill until it starts to boil. Add wings and heat for about 10 minutes at the lowest heat possible.

Transfer wings to the grill and grill for 5 to 10 minutes, or just until they start to burn. Transfer back to stockpot and heat for another 10 minutes. Transfer back to grill for 5, then back to stockpot for 5, then finally back to the grill for a third time for 5 minutes. Serve from the grill.

Classic Hot Wings with 4 Variations

Cease Giddings

YIELD: 6 TO 8 SERVINGS

INGREDIENTS

2 tablespoons all-purpose flour

1 teaspoon salt

2 pounds chicken wings

2-1/2 tablespoons Frank's Redhot sauce

2 tablespoons unsalted butter, melted

CLASSIC: Preheat oven to 500 degrees. Line a baking sheet with foil and spray with non-stick spray. In a bowl, mix the flour with the salt. Add the chicken and toss to coat. Spread the chicken on the baking sheet in a single layer and spray with vegetable oil. Roast the chicken for 45 minutes, turning once or twice until brown and crispy. In a bowl, toss the chicken with hot sauce and butter.

GINGER-HONEY: to the flour, add 1 teaspoon ground Szechuan peppercorns and 1/4 teaspoon five spice powder.

MANGO-CURRY: to the flour, add 2 teaspoons hot curry powder; to the hot sauce add 2 teaspoons Major Grey's chutney.

MAPLE-CHIPOTLE: to the flour, add 1 teaspoon dried sage; to the hot sauce add 1 minced can of chipotle and 2 tablespoons pure maple syrup.

SWEET-STICKY: to the flour, add 1/2 teaspoon each garlic powder and onion powder and 1 teaspoon smoked paprika. To the hot sauce add 2 tablespoons melted hot pepper jelly.

Mary DiNardo's Chicken Anisette

Larry DiNardo,
Football Dad — Jack #90

YIELD: 6 TO 8 SERVINGS

INGREDIENTS

4 pounds chicken legs, thighs, breasts

3 medium sized sweet onions sliced

1/4 cup finely chopped Italian (flat leaf) parsley

crushed red pepper, to taste

1 to 1-1/2 cups anisette liqueur

olive oil, about a cup

salt, to taste

Cut chicken into bite-sized pieces, leaving bones in place. Sauté in 1/4 inch of olive oil in pan, until well browned. Remove chicken from pan and set aside. In same pan, sauté onions until lightly browned and soft, adding oil if necessary. Return browned chicken pieces to pan, add anisette, freshly chopped parsley, red pepper, salt and simmer until liquid is largely evaporated and chicken has caramelized, about 45 minutes, turning a few times to coat all sides (Best if meat is in a single layer in the pan). Taste to correct for salt. Add crushed red pepper, to taste. Remove from heat and serve as appetizer.

Ling's Chicken Wings

Ling & Ed Albrecht,
Lacrosse Parents — Sarah 2006

INGREDIENTS

1/2 cup soy sauce
1/4 cup sesame oil
1/4 cup whiskey
1 thumb-sized piece of ginger,
    finely chopped
1 clove garlic, finely chopped
1 stalk green scallion, finely chopped
dash pepper, to taste
2 pounds chicken wings

Remove tip of each wing and separate the other 2 sections. Combine all ingredients except wings. Pour over wings and marinate for 2 to 3 days. The easiest way is to put everything in a zip lock bag and turn it over at the end of the day to evenly marinate the wings.

Drain wings and discard marinade. Grill wings on high.

Mini-Max Pizzas

Ellen & Ivan Zilka, 1941

YIELD: 16 PIECES

INGREDIENTS

8 English muffins, split in half
1 can (8 ounces) pizza sauce
1 cup shredded Mozzarella cheese
4 ounces sliced pepperoni or other
    meat topping

Toast muffin halves. Spread each with sauce and pepperoni, sprinkle with cheese. Broil 4 to 5 inches from flame for 4 to 6 minutes.

Wildcat Fudge

Joann Skiba

YIELD: 9X13 INCH PAN

INGREDIENTS

6 well-beaten medium eggs
1 pound shredded Monterey Jack
    cheese
1 pound shredded sharp cheddar
    cheese
2 cans (4 ounces each) chopped green
    chilies

Lightly grease a 9x13 inch pan. Preheat oven to 375 degrees.

Spread one cheese on bottom of pan, cover with chilies. Spread the second cheese over the chilies. Pour eggs over the top of the mixture. Bake for 30 minutes or until set.

Dill Crackers

Judy Kelley

INGREDIENTS

2 packages (10 to 12 ounces each)
    oyster crackers
1 cup salad oil
1 package Hidden Valley Ranch dry
    dressing
1/4 teaspoon garlic powder
1/2 teaspoon lemon pepper
1/2 teaspoon dill weed

Place crackers in a large double paper bag. Mix remaining ingredients with a whisk and pour over crackers. Close bag and shake well. Pour into baking dish and bake at 250 degrees for 20 minutes, stirring once during that time. Store in a sealed container.

Chinese Tea Eggs

Donna Su,
Assistant Director, Medill Graduate Admissions & Financial Aid

YIELD: 12 SERVINGS

INGREDIENTS

12 eggs
3 bags black tea
1 tablespoon soy sauce
2 whole star anise
1 tablespoon five spice powder
1/2 teaspoon salt

Boil eggs with salt until hard cooked. Remove eggs but save water.

After eggs are done, you have two options: you can either lightly crack each egg shell to get a pretty marbled look or you can peel each egg for an even brown look.

Add soy sauce, tea bags, star anise and five spice powder to the water; put the eggs back in. Bring to boil and let simmer and steep for an hour.

Ham and Cheese Sliders

Robin Studlien,
Football Mom — Will #56

YIELD: 24 PIECES

INGREDIENTS

2 dozen Hawaiian sweet rolls,
　　sliced open
1 pound honey baked ham, sliced thin
24 slices Swiss cheese
3/4 cup melted butter
1-1/2 tablespoons Dijon mustard
1-1/2 tablespoons poppy seeds
2 tablespoons dried onion flakes
1/2 teaspoon Worcestershire sauce

Spray bottom of 9x13 inch baking dish with cooking spray. Split rolls in half and place bottom half in dish. Combine the melted butter, mustard, poppy seeds, onion and Worcestershire sauce in a bowl. Brush half of the mixture on the bottom rolls. Top with ham and cheese. Add tops and brush them with remaining butter mixture. Bake uncovered for 15 to 20 minutes.

Ham-Cheese Delights

Ellen & Ivan Zilka, 1941

Yield: 8 to 10 servings

Ingredients

2 cups ground ham
1 cup shredded cheddar cheese
1/2 cup sweet pickle relish, drained
4 teaspoons chopped onions
1/2 cup mayonnaise
30 slices party size rye

Combine ham, cheese, relish, onions and mayonnaise and mix well. Spread 1 tablespoon of mixture on each bread slice.

Serve as is or broil at 450 degrees (4 to 5 inches from flame) for 4 to 6 minutes.

Palmiers with Honey Mustard and Prosciutto

Megan Anderson, 1976

Yield: 30 slices

Palmiers refers to the shape of the pieces.

Ingredients

1 box puff pastry (2 sheets)
honey mustard
4 to 6 ounces thinly sliced proscuitto
grated Parmesan cheese
1 egg

Preheat oven to 400 degrees. Unroll one sheet of pastry on work surface; cover with a thin layer of mustard. Arrange prosciutto evenly over mustard. Sprinkle with Parmesan cheese. Lightly press with rolling pin. Roll at long edge like jelly roll to middle, then roll up other side making 2 rolls that meet in the center. Using a serrated knife, cut across into 1/2 inch slices. Place on parchment paper lined baking sheet and press lightly with palm to flatten. Repeat with other sheet of pastry. Beat 1 egg and 2 teaspoons water in bowl and brush on top of pastry rolls. Bake at for approximately 10 minutes.

Sugar-spiced Nuts

Judy Kelley

Ingredients

1 egg white
2 tablespoons cold water
1 cup sugar
1 tablespoon cinnamon
1/4 teaspoon ginger
1/4 teaspoon nutmeg
7 cups nuts, whole or in large pieces
(use your favorites)

Beat egg white and water until frothy. Stir in nuts to coat. Drain in colander for 2 minutes if too wet. Mix together sugar and spices. Put in a plastic bag. Add the nuts and shake to coat. Spread wet nut mixture on a flat pan in a single layer. Bake at 200 degrees for 1 hour, stirring every 15 minutes. Cool. Store in sealed container.

Roasted Red Pepper Crostini

Zoe T Barron

YIELD: 2 LOAVES

INGREDIENTS

SPREAD:

1 jar (12 ounces) roasted red
    bell peppers, drained

1 tablespoon minced garlic

1 cup walnuts

1/3 cup panko bread crumbs

2 tablespoons olive oil

2 teaspoons fresh lemon juice

1/4 teaspoon cayenne pepper

8 ounces cream cheese

CROSTINI:

2 loaves French bread, cut into
    1/3 inch thick slices

2 to 3 tablespoons olive oil

salt and pepper, to taste

SPREAD: Mix all spread ingredients (except cream cheese) in a food processor. The spread may be refrigerated for up to one week.

CROSTINI: Preheat oven to 350 degrees. Brush both sides of bread slices with olive oil and place on a cookie sheet. Sprinkle tops with salt and pepper. Bake for 8 to 10 minutes. Cool completely.

ASSEMBLY: spread the crostini with cream cheese and top with the roasted red pepper spread. The spread may be used as a dip for vegetables or chips.

Mini Lemon Pork Sandwiches

Mary Pat Watt,
Football Mom — Kevin #42

YIELD: 24 APPETIZERS

INGREDIENTS

1 package 24 dinner rolls

2-1/2 pounds pork tenderloin

MARINADE:

1/2 cup vegetable oil

1/4 cup fresh lemon juice

1 tablespoon sugar

1/2 teaspoon salt

1/8 teaspoon ground red pepper

1 to 2 cloves garlic, minced

SAUCE:

1 cup mayonnaise

2 cloves garlic, minced

2 tablespoons lemon juice

2 teaspoons chopped fresh tarragon

1/8 teaspoon salt

Rinse tenderloin(s); pat dry. Combine marinade ingredients in resealable freezer bag or shallow dish; add tenderloins, seal and chill at least 4 hours.

Remove pork from marinade, discarding marinade. Preheat oven to 400 degrees. Place pork on rack of broiler pan that has been sprayed with nonstick cooking spray. Bake pork for 20 to 30 minutes or until meat thermometer registers 160 degrees. Let stand 15 minutes. Cut pork into 1/4 inch slices.

SAUCE: Combine mayonnaise, garlic, lemon juice, tarragon and salt. Chill.

Spread mayonnaise on insides of rolls. Place a slice or two of pork on each roll.

Rib-O-Rama

NU Past-president Henry Bienen and Professor Chad Mirkin

INGREDIENTS

4 pounds ribs (baby back pork or beef)

2 tablespoons bacon drippings

1 medium onion, finely chopped

1 clove garlic

1 bottle (14 ounces) ketchup

1 tablespoon tomato paste

6 tablespoons Worcestershire sauce

2 tablespoons cider vinegar

1/4 cup dry white wine

1 teaspoon dry mustard

2 tablespoons dark brown sugar

1-1/2 tablespoons crushed hot red chili pepper

1/4 teaspoon cayenne

3/4 teaspoon ground cumin

1/4 teaspoon ground coriander seed

1 teaspoon liquid smoke

Cook enough bacon to get two tablespoons of fat and set bacon aside (it can be minced and added to sauce also). Add onion to the bacon drippings and sauté until the onion is transparent. Add the remaining ingredients and let simmer for about 30 minutes. Set aside until ready to use. This makes about 3 cups of sauce, good for 4 pounds of ribs.

Make a pile of coals on one side of the barbecue and sear both sides of the ribs, about 2 minutes per side. Remove the ribs from the grill and spread the coals evenly on the bottom. Cover the grill with heavy aluminum foil, making plenty of ventilation holes. Place the ribs on the foil and generously cover with sauce. Put the cover on the barbecue and let cook for about 20 to 25 minutes. Turn the ribs over and generously cover with sauce. Cover the barbecue and for about 20 to 25 minutes until the meat is no longer pink. Transfer the ribs to a cutting board and cut the ribs apart. Grab as many as you can!

Wildcat's Stuffed Jalapeños

Lori Hooten,
Wife of Jay Hooten, Assistant Director, Football Strength and Conditioning

YIELD: 20 TO 25 PIECES

INGREDIENTS

2 links hot Italian sausage

1 package Béarnaise cheese sauce mix

2 pounds bacon

20 to 25 large jalapeños

Remove casing and brown the sausages (like hamburger). Add the Béarnaise cheese sauce and let simmer to a nice thick texture. Cut the tops off and hollow out jalapeños. Stuff with sausage and wrap in a slice of bacon. Grill until bacon is cooked.

Polish Burger Bites

Joe Slowik

YIELD: ABOUT 48 PIECES

INGREDIENTS

1 pound ground beef
1 pound Polish sausage
2 teaspoons Tabasco
1 pound Velveeta, cut into cubes
1/2 teaspoon dried oregano
1/2 teaspoon Worcestershire sauce
3/4 teaspoon garlic powder
1/2 teaspoon cayenne
1-1/2 pounds snack rye bread

Use smoked or fresh sausage; adjust seasonings, to taste, based on the spiciness of the sausage.

Remove casing from sausage. Grind both meats in food processor until well mixed and of uniform consistency. Add Tabasco and pulse once. Lightly brown mixture in frying pan, crumbling into small pieces; drain fat. Immediately transfer to a large bowl and mix in Velveeta, oregano, Worcestershire and garlic powder. Meat should be hot enough to melt the cheese; if not, heat bowl in microwave or over hot water. Taste and adjust seasonings. Spread mixture generously over the rye slices, covering the bread to the edges. Place on cookie sheet and freeze. When frozen, remove from sheet and place in storage bags.

When ready to serve, place on cookie sheet, and heat in 350 degree oven for about 15 minutes, until the mixture is hot and the bread just begins to toast. Note: best to cook from frozen even if making and serving on the same day to prevent soggy bread.

Sausage Rye Bread Canapes

Megan Anderson, 1976

YIELD: 25 PIECES

INGREDIENTS

1 pound ground beef
12 ounces Jimmy Dean sausage
1 pound Velveeta cheese, cubed
1 teaspoon Worcestershire sauce
1 teaspoon oregano
1/2 teaspoon salt
1/2 teaspoon garlic powder, optional
dash black pepper
1 package party rye bread

Brown hamburger and sausage together, drain excess fat. Add Velveeta to sausage mixture. Stir until cheese is melted and well blended. Add remaining ingredients except bread and mix together. Place a hearty spoonful on each slice of bread. Broil on high for 3 to 5 minutes until bubbly and brown (or bake at 350 degrees for 12 to 15 minutes). These may be prepared ahead and kept in the freezer until ready to broil and serve.

Panchetta-wrapped Prawns

Chef William King,
**McCormick & Schmick's,
multiple locations**

YIELD: 12 PIECES

INGREDIENTS

12 large prawns (U-12 or 12 per
    pound), peeled and deveined
12 thin slices panchetta
1/2 cup Asian BBQ Sauce (below)

PEANUT SALSA:

1/2 cup finely diced Roma tomatoes
4 tablespoons finely chopped red,
    green and yellow peppers
1 tablespoon chopped fresh cilantro
3 tablespoons chopped green onions
1/2 teaspoon minced garlic
1 tablespoon chunky peanut butter
1 tablespoon chili paste with garlic or
    sambal oelek
4 tablespoons chopped, salted
    cocktail peanuts
1 sprig fresh cilantro, for garnish

ASIAN BBQ SAUCE:

1 cup plum sauce
1/8 cup hoisin sauce
1/8 cup freshly squeezed orange juice
1 tablespoon chopped fresh cilantro
pinch crushed red chili flakes

SAUCE: Combine plum and hoisin
sauces, juice, cilantro and pepper flakes.
Blend thoroughly. Best if made a day in
advance.

PEANUT SALSA: Combine tomatoes,
peppers, cilantro, green onions, garlic,
peanut butter, chili paste and peanuts.

PRAWNS: Wrap each prawn with
panchetta and grill both sides until the
panchetta is browned.

SERVING: Coat the prawns with the
Asian barbecue sauce. Place salsa in the
center of plate and arrange the prawns
around the salsa. Garnish with a sprig of
cilantro.

BLT Bites

Mary Ellen Baker,
Football Mom — Hayden #68

YIELD: 8 SERVINGS

INGREDIENTS

20 cherry tomatoes
1 pound bacon, cooked and crumbled
1/2 cup mayonnaise
1/3 cup chopped green onions
3 tablespoons Parmesan cheese
2 tablespoons chopped fresh parsley

*Make sure the tomatoes are large enough
to stuff, at least 1 inch in diameter. Use
a grapefruit spoon or small serrated knife
to scoop out the tomatoes.*

Scoop out insides of tomatoes. Place
tomatoes, scoop side down, on paper
towels to drain. Combine other ingredients. Spoon into tomatoes and refrigerate
for at least 2 hours before serving.

Mary DiNardo's Italian Spinach Pie

Larry DiNardo,
Football Dad — Jack #90

YIELD: 10 TO 12 SERVINGS

INGREDIENTS

1 to 2 packages (10 ounces each) frozen chopped spinach

1/2 pound diced Genoa salami

1/2 pound diced provolone cheese

2/3 cup grated Parmesan Reggiano cheese

1-1/2 cups tomato sauce seasoned with Italian herbs

1/2 cup olive oil, divided

1 cup chopped black olives

2 pieces pizza dough (home made or prepared such as Rhodes) allowed to rise per instructions

1 tablespoon oregano

1 tablespoon garlic powder

salt and pepper

2 tablespoons butter

1 egg

1 tablespoon whole milk

Prepare mixture of one egg and one tablespoon whole milk to brush on top crust after baking.

Preheat oven to 350 degrees. Roll out first piece of dough with rolling pin and spread onto 12x16 inch heavy weight jelly roll pan. While preparing dough, cook spinach according to package instructions; cool and squeeze out water. Spread 2 tablespoons olive oil onto dough and rub in lightly with spoon. Cover dough with thin coat of tomato sauce. Spread spinach across dough, sprinkle on diced salami and provolone. Sprinkle olives on dough and then generous amount of Parmesan Reggiano cheese. Drizzle some olive oil, then season, to taste with oregano, garlic powder, salt and pepper. Roll out second dough and carefully cover pie, crimping the edges tightly to the first piece of dough. Bake for one hour or until golden brown. Remove from oven and brush top with butter and then egg/milk mixture. Allow to rest 10 minutes, then slice and serve.

The Other Team in a Blanket a.k.a. Pigs in a Blanket

Lori Hooten,
Wife of Jay Hooten, Assistant Director, Football Strength and Conditioning

YIELD: 16 PIECES

INGREDIENTS

1 package hot dogs

1 roll of refrigerated croissant dough

Cut all of the hot dogs in half. Set aside. Cut each croissant triangle into two or three smaller triangles, depending on how much dough you want on each piece of meat. Wrap each half dog in one croissant triangle. Follow the baking directions on the back of the croissant package. Serve with mustard.

Bruschetta

Debbie Smith

YIELD: 24 PIECES

INGREDIENTS

SPREAD:

3 large ripe tomatoes, seeded, diced
1/3 cup light olive oil
1/4 cup sherry or red wine vinegar
1/4 cup finely diced onion
2 tablespoons capers
2 tablespoons minced fresh parsley
2 tablespoons minced fresh cilantro
1 large clove of garlic, minced
1 teaspoon salt
1/4 teaspoon black pepper
1 teaspoon dried basil

TOAST:

1/2 cup butter
1 tablespoon or more extra-virgin
    olive oil
1 loaf French bread (baguette)

Preheat oven to 350 degrees.

TOAST: Melt butter with olive oil. Brush over slices of bread on a baking sheet. Bake for approximately 8 minutes until toasted, but watch so the bread does not burn.

SPREAD: Combine all the ingredients in a bowl and mix. Spoon on toasted French bread and serve.

Fiori Di Zucca Fritti

Mayor Elizabeth Tisdahl,
City of Evanston

YIELD: 16 PIECES

INGREDIENTS

16 zucchini flowers
150 grams (2/3 cup) flour
2 eggs, separated
white wine
2 teaspoons olive oil
nutmeg, to taste
salt and pepper
oil for deep frying
water

In a bowl, mix the flour, salt, pepper, nutmeg, olive oil and 2 egg yolks. Dilute this with a 50/50 mix of white wine and water until the batter reaches the right consistency, somewhat thick but still fluid. Let it rest for about half an hour and when you are ready to use, add stiffly beaten egg whites.

Prepare the flowers by removing the stalks and inside stamens. Dip them in the batter, draining off the excess batter and then fry in the hot oil. Serve them hot.

Chex Mix

Noah Weiss, 2014,
Graduate student

YIELD: 18 CUPS

INGREDIENTS

3 cups Wheat Chex

3 cups Rice Chex

3 cups Corn Chex

3 cups Quaker Oatmeal Squares

3 cups Cheetos

3 cups pretzel sticks

1/2 pound butter

4 tablespoons Worcestershire sauce

4 teaspoons seasoned salt

Preheat oven to 250 degrees.

Combine all dry ingredients and divide between two baking pans, 9x13 inch or larger. Melt the butter, add the Worcestershire sauce and seasoned salt. Pour the sauce over the dry ingredients, then stir to distribute.

Bake for 15 minutes. Stir and bake for another 15 minutes. Repeat for a total of 45 minutes.

Store in a container lined with newspaper. Leave it in open air lest it become soggy.

plated

Shrimp Ceviche

Karen & Dave Eanet,
Voice of the Cats! WGN-Radio

YIELD: 10 TO 12 SERVINGS

Great tailgate dish

INGREDIENTS

1 pound shrimp (41 to 50 count)

1/2 cup fresh lime juice (2 to 3 limes)

1/2 cup diced white onion

1 small ripe avocado, cubed

1/2 cup ketchup

1/2 cup peeled, seeded, diced cucumber

1/2 cup peeled and diced jicama

1/3 cup fresh chopped cilantro

2 tablespoons olive oil

1 tablespoon Tabasco or Mexican Hot Sauce, to taste

1/2 teaspoon kosher salt

Toss shrimp and lime juice together in a glass bowl. Chill one hour. Rinse onion under cold water in a strainer. Add to marinated shrimp and lime juice. Add avocado, ketchup, cucumber, jicama, cilantro, olive oil and toss. Season with salt. Refrigerate if not serving immediately. Serve with tortilla chips.

Day Boat Sea Scallops with Yuzu Marmalade

Chef Mark Grosz,
Oceanique — Evanston

YIELD: 4 SERVINGS

INGREDIENTS

12 ounces day boat sea scallops, dried
6 tablespoons virgin olive oil, divided
Pink Himalayan sea salt
freshly ground black pepper
4 ounces sauvignon blanc
2 teaspoons shallots, minced, divided
pinch saffron or turmeric
2 ounces unsalted butter, cold
2 tablespoons yuzu or
        orange marmalade
12 kumquats, sliced thin
2 blood oranges, segmented
1 bunch red or green watercress

Prepare sauce by reducing wine with saffron and 1 teaspoon shallots until a syrup. Slowly whisk in butter over low heat; add yuzu marmalade and season with salt and pepper; keep warm.

Combine blood orange segments and kumquats with 1 teaspoon shallots, 2 teaspoons olive oil, salt and pepper.

Season scallops with salt and pepper. Sauté in hot non-aluminum pan with 4 tablespoons olive oil until golden brown on each side, about one minute per side. Don't overcook, serve rare.

To serve: arrange scallops on 4 plates. Place orange-kumquat salad over scallops. Spoon sauce around plate and garnish with watercress. Serve immediately. Serve with a white Beaujolais wine.

skewer/pick

Meatballs Appetizers

Scott Hiller & Coach Kelly Amonte Hiller,
Head Coach, Lacrosse

YIELD: APPROXIMATELY 55 MEATBALLS

INGREDIENTS

1/2 onion, chopped very fine
1/2 cup Parmesan cheese
1 clove garlic
3 tablespoons parsley
3 packages ground meat (hamburger)
1 loaf Italian bread (let it sit out so it
        gets hard)
3 large eggs
1 teaspoon pepper
2 teaspoons salt

Preheat oven to 350 degrees. Soak the bread in water and ring out the water; then break it up into fine pieces. Chop onions, parsley and garlic. Add bread, onions, garlic, parsley, salt, pepper and Parmesan cheese to the meat and mix them together. Add eggs and mix again. Roll into meatballs. Place the meatballs on a rack and bake for 25 minutes at 350 degrees.

Cranberried Meatballs

Kelly Kowalski,
Wife of Ken Kowalski,
Director of Video Football

YIELD: 10 TO 12 SERVINGS

You can cook these either in a slow cooker or on the stove.

INGREDIENTS

1 bag precooked meatballs
1 can (16 ounces) jellied cranberry sauce
1 bottle (16 ounces) chili sauce
2 tablespoons brown sugar

In a medium sauce pan, mix together cranberry sauce, chili sauce and brown sugar.

Heat sauce until cranberry sauce and brown sugar liquefies. Add meatballs and cook until heated through.

Brown Sugar Smokies

Mary Ellen Baker,
Football Mom — Hayden #68

YIELD: 8 TO 12 SERVINGS

INGREDIENTS

1 pound Little Smokey sausages
1 pound bacon
1 cup brown sugar

Preheat oven to 350 degrees. Cut bacon slices in half. Roll each smokey link in bacon; secure with toothpick. Place in glass 9x13 inch pan, sprinkle with sugar and bake until bacon is done. Drain on paper towel if desired. Cool slightly before serving.

Grape Jelly and Chili Sauce Meatballs

Bruce Paynter, 1973, 1976,
NUMB

INGREDIENTS

32 ounces grape jelly
24 ounces Heinz chili sauce
3 to 5 pounds frozen, cooked, small meatballs, thawed
1/8 teaspoon cayenne, optional
1/4 cup vinegar base BBQ sauce (Carolina style), to taste

You can substitute Little Smokies or cocktail wieners for meatballs.

Prepare in a large pot, but slow cooker works best of all. Combine grape jelly and chili sauce; simmer until sauce has thickened. Add meatballs and cook uncovered for 45 minutes, stirring to coat meatballs with sauce.

Taste sauce to make sure it is not overly sweet. I add vinegar base (Carolina style) BBQ sauce to give the sauce a little more tang.

COACHES QUOTES

Tracey Fuchs,
Women's Field Hockey:

"It's the hard that makes it great."
–League of Their Own

Coquille St. Jacques

Colleen Siemian,
Football Mom — Trevor #13

YIELD: 8 SERVINGS

INGREDIENTS

olive oil for sautéing

2 teaspoons chopped garlic

1/2 teaspoon tarragon

1/2 teaspoon thyme

12 ounces white button mushrooms, washed and sliced

salt and pepper, to taste

1/3 cup dry white wine

48 medium fresh sea scallops

2 cups heavy cream

1/4 pound butter

thinly shaved Parmesan cheese

seasoned breadcrumbs

4 to 6 ounces olive oil

2 to 3 sprigs of thyme, rosemary, basil or other favorite herb

INFUSED OIL: Put herb in oil in a jar, cover and shake well. Allow to sit for at least an hour or overnight.

SCALLOPS: Put oil in a sauté pan, then add chopped garlic, thyme and tarragon. Add mushrooms; salt and pepper, to taste. Deglaze pan with white wine, add scallops and cook until white (opaque). With a colander positioned over a metal bowl, drain the scallop mixture. Next divide the scallop mixture evenly among eight shell-shaped, oven-proof serving dishes. Set aside.

Pour the drained pan juices back into the sauté pan. Add cream and butter; cook, stirring until the mixture thickens. Pour mixture over scallops in serving dishes.

Drizzle with herb-infused oil. Sprinkle with bread crumbs and shaved Parmesan. Broil until tops are golden. Serve immediately.

Kelsey's Flank Steak

Diane Keuth

YIELD: FEEDS MANY FRIENDS

A re-sealable bag (gallon size) and 24 to 48 hours of marinating time is key! This is a great recipe to prepare ahead of time. I have frozen the meat with the marinade. As it thaws it marinates the meat. Thanks to the white tent guys for their help with this recipe.

INGREDIENTS

2 to 3 pounds flank steak

1-1/2 cups teriyaki sauce

1 cup A-1 Steak Sauce

1/4 cup hot sauce

1/4 cup tequila

2 to 3 cloves garlic, minced

1/4 cup lemon or lime juice

Assemble all the ingredients in a pitcher. Cut the flank steak with the grain in 1/2 inch strips. Place all the meat in the bag. Pour the marinade in the bag, seal and refrigerate. After marinating for hours, the meat is ready to grill.

spreads

Marinated Cheese

Ann Marie Bernardi,
Field Hockey Mom

YIELD: 1 DISH

INGREDIENTS

1/2 cup olive oil
1/2 cup white wine vinegar
3 tablespoons chopped fresh parsley
3 tablespoons minced green onion
1 teaspoon sugar
3/4 teaspoons dried basil
1/2 teaspoon salt
1/2 teaspoon ground pepper
3 cloves garlic, minced
1 jar (2 ounces) diced pimiento, drained
1 block (5x2x1 inch) of sharp cheddar cheese, chilled (8 ounces)
8 ounces chilled cream cheese
fresh parsley for garnish

Combine first 10 ingredients in a jar; cover tightly, and shake vigorously. Set marinade aside.

Cut block of cheddar cheese in half lengthwise. Then cut crosswise into 1/4 inch slices; set aside. Repeat procedure with cream cheese. Arrange slices, alternating cheddar cheese and cream cheese, in a shallow baking dish, standing slices on edges. Pour marinade over slices. Cover and marinate in refrigerator at least 8 hours. Before serving, spoon marinade over cheese slices and serve with crackers.

Boursin

Jean Yale, 1957,
Athletic Development/Special Events

YIELD: 6 TO 8 SERVINGS

INGREDIENTS

8 ounces cream cheese
1 teaspoon Beau Monde Seasoning
1 garlic clove, minced
1 teaspoon red wine vinegar
1 teaspoon Worcestershire sauce
1/2 teaspoon lemon pepper, or to taste

Mix all ingredients and form into a ball. Top with lemon pepper and serve with crackers.

Olive Nut Spread

Nancy Lee

YIELD: 2 CUPS

INGREDIENTS

8 ounces cream cheese (light OK)
1/4 cup mayonnaise (light OK)
1 cup chopped green olives, any type
1/2 cup chopped toasted pecans
2 tablespoons olive juice
1 to 2 tablespoons milk if needed

Great with Ritz Crackers. Olives with pimento add color.

Add all ingredients to softened cream cheese and stir. Add milk, if necessary, to reach your desired consistency.

Baked Goat Cheese and Caramelized Onion

Cyndy Abbott

YIELD: 1-1/2 CUPS

INGREDIENTS

12 large garlic cloves

2 tablespoons butter

1 medium red onion, thinly sliced

1 tablespoon brown sugar, packed

1 tablespoon balsamic vinegar

1/4 cup sliced fresh basil

10 ounces soft goat cheese, crumbled such as Montrachet

baguette slices

Preheat oven to 350 degrees. Roast garlic until tender, about 30 minutes. Melt butter in skillet. Add onion and sauté until almost brown. Add brown sugar; stir until melted. Let cool.

Arrange onion mixture on bottom of 8x8 inch glass baking dish. Sprinkle cheese and arrange garlic on cheese. (Can be prepared 1 day ahead, cover and chill.) Bake 25 minutes until cheese melts. Add balsamic vinegar. Sprinkle with basil. Serve warm or at room temperature. Serve with baguettes.

Cowboy Caviar with Shoepeg Corn

P J Sinopoli,
Cheerleading Mom — Jenny

Also good as a burger topping.

INGREDIENTS

1 can (15 ounces) black eyed peas, rinsed and drained

1 can (11 ounces) white shoepeg corn, rinsed and drained

2/3 cup chopped cilantro

2 diced avocados

1 cup chopped Roma tomatoes

1/4 cup chopped green onions

1/4 cup red wine vinegar

1/4 cup oil

1 teaspoon cumin

1 teaspoon salt

1/4 teaspoon black pepper

1 teaspoon minced garlic

Mix cilantro, avocado, tomatoes and onions; add black eyed peas and white shoepeg corn. In measuring cup, add red wine vinegar, oil, cumin, salt, black pepper and garlic. Mix and pour over veggies. Chill and serve with tortilla chips.

Lemon Hummus

Cynthia Wuellner

YIELD: 3 CUPS

Wonderful lemony flavor.

INGREDIENTS

2 cups canned chickpeas

2/3 cup tahini

3/4 cup fresh lemon juice

2 cloves garlic, minced

1 teaspoon salt

3 tablespoons chopped parsley, optional

Drain and rinse the chick peas. Chop the peas in a food processor. Add all of the remaining ingredients to the processor and mix until smooth. Mixture will keep at least a week in the refrigerator.

Roasted Red Pepper and Garlic Spread

Jeff Bowen,
Lacrosse Dad — Hilary 2009

YIELD: 20 TO 25 PIECES

INGREDIENTS

6 sweet red peppers

2 cloves garlic

4 tablespoons olive oil

1/2 cup fresh grated Parmesan cheese

salt and pepper, to taste

2 large loaves ciabatta bread (or 1 large loaf of French bread)

Halve red peppers, remove core and seeds; place on a cookie sheet, cut side down. Squash with palm of your hand. Broil until charred. Put peppers in paper bag, tied securely, and let steam 10 to 15 minutes, until cool enough to handle. Remove skins. Preheat oven to 375 degrees. With motor running, drop garlic down feed tube of food processor. Add peppers, olive oil, Parmesan cheese, salt and pepper; purée. Heat bread 5 to 10 minutes. Slice bread and serve with spread.

Smoked Salmon Mousse

Susan Izard

Susan is the mother and first cooking teacher of Stephanie Izard.

INGREDIENTS

1 package (8 ounces) cream cheese, softened

1 can (7 ounces) salmon, drained

few drop Wright's liquid smoke

chopped parsley

chopped nuts, optional

Combine cream cheese with salmon. Add liquid smoke. Spread on a platter. Cover with chopped parsley. Add chopped nuts, if desired. Serve with your favorite crackers.

Corn Salsa

Jacqueline Mafuli,
Football Mom — Niko #93

YIELD: 8 TO 10 SERVINGS

INGREDIENTS

2 cans (15 ounces each) corn, drained
1 can (15 ounces) black beans, rinsed
  and drained
3 green onions, chopped
1 red bell pepper, chopped
1/3 cup olive oil
1/4 cup balsamic vinegar
1 clove garlic, minced
4 to 8 drops hot pepper sauce
1 tablespoon ground cumin
1 teaspoon chili powder
juice of a lime
1 avocado, diced
salt and pepper, to taste

Mix all ingredients and serve with tortilla chips. The flavor improves if allowed to sit overnight.

Great for tailgating!

Salsa

Joann Skiba

YIELD: ABOUT 2 CUPS

Great with purple margaritas!

INGREDIENTS

8 medium tomatoes, seeded and
  chopped
3 tablespoons chopped fresh cilantro
1 medium red onion, chopped
2 tablespoons fresh lemon or lime
  juice (1 lemon or lime)
1 large jalapeño pepper, seeded and
  chopped
1 clove garlic, chopped
1 shallot, chopped
1 pinch granulated sugar
salt and pepper, to taste

Mix all ingredients together and chill in the refrigerator for 2 hours. Serve with tortilla chips.

Roasted Poblano Salsa Verde

Sara Pecherek, 2007

YIELD: 1 CUP

INGREDIENTS

4 tomatillos, husks removed, rough chopped

2 poblano peppers

1 jalapeño pepper

1/2 yellow onion, rough chopped

1/3 cup chopped fresh cilantro

1 lime (juice only)

1 teaspoon salt

2 cloves garlic

1-1/2 tablespoons honey

Broil the whole poblano peppers and jalapeño on high; cook until skin starts to burn, then flip so other sides are exposed. Broil until all sides are burned, roughly 15 minutes.

Once all the pepper skins are blackened, use tongs to place them into a paper bag. Fold the bag so it is closed, set aside. Let cool, about 10 to 15 minutes.

Once cool, run the peppers under cold water from the faucet and remove charred outer skin, stem and seeds. Chop the peppers roughly, then put them in the food processor with the remaining ingredients. Pulse until smooth and serve with chips.

Roasted Corn Salsa/Relish

Ellen Watkins,
Football Mom — Evan #18

YIELD: 8 TO 10 CUPS

Good with chips or as a side dish.

INGREDIENTS

SALSA:

1 pound frozen corn

1/2 cup chopped red onion

2 jalapeño peppers, seeded, chopped

2 cans (15 ounces each) black beans, rinsed and drained

2 to 3 tablespoons oil

1 chopped red bell pepper

6 fresh Italian plum tomatoes

2 teaspoons minced garlic

1 cup fresh chopped cilantro

DRESSING:

1 tablespoon salt

3/4 teaspoon ground cumin

5 tablespoons vegetable oil

6 tablespoons lime juice

2 tablespoons cider vinegar

Preheat oven to 450 degrees. Combine corn and oil, toss and place on cookie sheet. Bake 18 to 22 minutes, until golden brown. Stir a few times while it bakes. Remove from oven and cool. Mix with other ingredients except cilantro.

Combine the dressing ingredients; pour over corn mixture and toss. Refrigerate if not ready to serve. Add the cilantro just before serving and toss.

Ahi Tuna Tartar with Meyer Lemon Relish

Connie & Rob Walker,
Coach Randy Walker's sister-in-law and brother

YIELD: 8 TO 12 SERVINGS

INGREDIENTS

6 Meyer lemons
2 jalapeños, roasted, seeded, skinned and diced
3 scallions
1/2 red bell pepper, diced very small
1/2 red onion, diced very small
1/2 bunch Italian parsley, roughly chopped
1/2 to 1 cup extra virgin olive oil
1 bunch (15) breakfast radishes
12 ounces Ahi tuna, diced
salt and pepper, to taste
caviar, optional

Meyer lemons are sweeter and less acidic than regular lemons, but regular lemons can be used. A breakfast radish is milder than the round red radish.

Combine all the ingredients except the tuna and radish; check seasoning to your taste. Mix the tuna with some of the relish, using mostly the oil, and season with salt and pepper. Present the tuna in a ring and pour the relish around the tuna. Add the radishes around the plate. You can also add some caviar to the top of the tuna for added flavor and color.

COACHES QUOTES

Randy Walker,
Former Football Head Coach:

"I've made my commitment clear to Northwestern. I'm not a 1-800 guy, calling everybody. Does everyone have a price? Sure. But there's a value in the kind of kids I get to coach, the institution I represent, where I live. I don't know if there's a better job."

Cat Nips

SWIMMING/ DIVING

Men's:

Head Coach Jarod Schroeder (2009–present)

• First swim meet was in 1924.

• There were 144 Academic All-Big Ten honorees in the years 1987–2011.

Women's:

Head Coach Jimmy Tierney (1994–present)

• First swim meet was in 1984.

• There have been hundreds of All-Americans and Academic All-Big Ten student athletes on the women's swim team. Thirteen women also received the honor of Big Ten Distinguished Scholar, the most in any conference.

Diving:

Head Coach Alik Sarkisian (2006–present)

• Coach Sarkisian was the head diving coach for the USSR National Team from 1980–1990.

alcoholic

Tom's Famous Bloody Marys

Tom Rucks,
Football Dad — Alex 2008

YIELD: 8 SERVINGS

Served from 2004 thru 2008 at the Players' Family Tailgates!

INGREDIENTS

2 bottles Longbranch Bloody Mary
    Zinger
2 bottles Mr & Mrs T's Bold and
    Spicy Bloody Mary Mix
1 bottle vodka
8 stalks celery
8 green onions
8 large olives
1 lime, cut into 8 pieces
1 jar horseradish sauce
Morton's Natures Season Seasoning
    Blend

use cheap vodka — with all the other tasty ingredients, no one will be able to tell the difference.

Combine equal parts of Longbranch and Mr & Mrs T in a large pitcher. Fill 24-ounce cups with ice. Fill 1/4 full with vodka. Fill remainder with the Bloody Mary mixes. Throw in a dollop of horseradish sauce. Squeeze in a lime. Sprinkle on the Seasoning Blend. Add the celery, onion and olive. Pop in a straw and enjoy!

Now here's the fun part. Depending on the Big Ten opponent, add a little something extra to the glass:

ILLINOIS: Illini crush (slice of orange, smashed)

INDIANA: Hoosier candy pants (small candy cane) — Many of their students wear red and white striped overalls.

IOWA: Hawk wings (baked chicken wing)

MICHIGAN: Eye of Wolverine (thin strip of roast beef wrapped around an olive stuck with a toothpick)

MICHIGAN STATE: Spartan spare ribs (a pork spare rib)

MINNESOTA: Gopher balls (two meatballs on a stick)

NEBRASKA: Baby corn (a small baby corn)

OHIO STATE: Worthless nuts (couple of stale peanuts leftover from baseball season)

PENN STATE: Lion meat (hunk of Italian beef — Paterno style)

PURDUE: Bloody boiler (shot of beer)

WISCONSIN: What else! (chuck of cheddar and a piece of sausage on a toothpick — because there is a cheese and sausage shop on every corner in Wisconsin)

Bloody Marys Tom Style

Zach Strief, 2005,
Football/NO Saints

Yield: 1 serving

This recipe is homage to the best darn Bloody Mary in the world created by Tom Rucks. We never did get his recipe, but the presentation is all Tom.
[Ed. note: see Tom's official recipe]

Ingredients

4 parts tomato juice
1 part Kettle One Vodka
2 to 4 shakes Frank's Redhot Chili n Lime Hot Sauce, to taste

Pour contents over ice and garnish.

Garnish: mini meatballs, cocktail shrimp, celery, carrot strips, chicken wings, mini corns, mini pickles, strips of marinated cooked beef, olives, pearl onions.

Mix and match and skewer together. You can really create a meal in a drink and make it a great way to start your game day!

Bloody Mary

The Spice House,
Evanston — Owners Patty and Tom Erd

Yield: 4 servings

Provided to The Spice House by Charlotte Henning from Baltimore

Ingredients

4 shots of vodka (6 ounces)
10 dashes Tabasco sauce
1 teaspoon Worcestershire sauce
1/2 to 1 teaspoon English Prime Rib Rub
2 teaspoons Chesapeake Bay Seasoning
1/2 teaspoon celery salt
1/2 teaspoon dill weed
3 cups tomato juice
freshly ground black pepper, to taste
2 dill pickle spears
Sprinkle of Red and Black spice, optional
splash of lemon or juice, optional

Fill a large shaker or plastic jar with lid with ice cubes. Add all ingredients except pickle, cover and shake vigorously for 10 seconds. Pour liquid into 2 ice-filled highball glasses and garnish with pickle. Top with juice and spice.

Apple Pie Drink

Daniel R Barron, KSM

YIELD: 10 SERVINGS

INGREDIENTS

1/2 gallon apple cider
1 gallon apple juice
3 cups sugar
8 sticks cinnamon
1 fifth of Everclear (grain alcohol)

Mix cider, juice, sugar and cinnamon in a large pot. Bring to a boil, turn off burner and let sit overnight, uncovered. The next day, add the bottle of Everclear and mix well. Refrigerate. Serve over ice or straight. Be careful — it's strong! Tastes just like apple pie.

Lemon Whiskey Slush

Julie Kent

INGREDIENTS

3 cans (12 ounces each) frozen
    lemonade concentrate,
    thawed slightly
2 cups water
2 cups whiskey
6 cups ginger ale

Mix the ingredients in large freezer container. Cover and freeze until slushy, at least 8 hours. Spoon into cocktail glasses; serve topped with a splash of ginger ale or club soda.

Game Day Whiskey Sours

Joann Skiba

YIELD: 4 TO 6 SERVINGS

Can be made ahead of time, frozen and taken to the stadium the day of the game. We always win when these are served.

INGREDIENTS

4-1/2 ounces lemon juice
5 tablespoons sugar (heaping)
10-1/2 ounces whiskey
1/4 cup club soda
ice
maraschino cherries and orange slices
    for garnish

Fill the blender 3/4 full of ice. Mix all ingredients in blender. Serve over ice. Garnish with a slice of orange and a maraschino cherry.

COACHES QUOTES

Jimmy Tierney,
Women's Swimming & Diving:

"Dreams are like stars … you may never touch them, but if you follow them they will lead you to your destiny."
–Anonymous

Windy City Mojo Punch

Angie Jackson, **Certified Master Mixologist, adjunct professor at Kendall College**

YIELD: 16 SERVINGS

INGREDIENTS

16 fluid ounces Indian Summer Apple juice

16 fluid ounces Ocean Spray white cranberry juice

8 fluid ounces organic pear juice

4 to 6 fluid ounces freshly squeezed lemon juice

14 fluid ounces Voodoo spiced rum

6 fluid ounces Domain de Canton ginger liqueur

orange wheels

freshly grated cinnamon

freshly grated nutmeg

cinnamon sticks

Use fruit juice, not fruit drinks.

This punch can be served hot or cold, for two different drink flavors.

COLD: Add ingredients to punch bowl. Add ice and orange wheels. When serving, dust each cup with cinnamon and/or nutmeg.

HOT: Add ingredients to large pot. Add a few cinnamon sticks. Heat to almost boiling. When serving, include a cinnamon stick or dust with cinnamon and/or nutmeg.

Game Day Sangria

Jackie & Joe Kent

YIELD: 12 TO 14 SERVINGS

INGREDIENTS

1 bottle (750 milliliters) dry white wine

1 cup sugar

1 cup vodka

1 cup orange juice

1 cup 7Up

1 orange, sliced

1 lemon, sliced

1 lime, sliced

1 apple, cored, diced

1 nectarine or plum, diced

Easily doubled. Prepare overnight so the fruit ferments.

Alternatives: Substitute dry red wine for the white wine or 1 cup of brandy or peach liquor instead of vodka.

Mix, chill and serve!

Fox and Hounds Hot Buttered Rum

Dean & Arlene Scane, 1960

YIELD: ROUGHLY 2 DOZEN MUGS

INGREDIENTS

1 pound brown sugar
1/4 pound butter
1 pinch salt
1/4 to 1/2 teaspoon ground nutmeg
1/4 to 1/2 teaspoon ground cinnamon
1/4 to 1/2 teaspoon ground cloves
1 bottle Puerto Rican rum
kettle of boiling water

Cream butter and sugar until smooth. Add nutmeg, cinnamon, cloves; mix until blended.

Preheat 6 ounce mugs with boiling water, then empty. Drop one heaping table-spoon of batter into mug. Add 1-1/2 ounces (or more, to taste) rum. Fill remainder of mug with boiling water.

Note: unused batter keeps in the refrigerator.

White Sangria

Frank

YIELD: 6 TO 8 SERVINGS

Frank is from H-E-B in San Antonio

INGREDIENTS

1 bottle (750 milliliters) non-oaky chardonnay
1 bottle (64 ounce) CranPeach or CranStrawberry juice
3 to 4 peaches diced
1 pint sliced strawberries

Mix all ingredients. Chill and serve over ice.

Beer Margaritas

Liz Kerr, 1981

YIELD: 6 TO 8 SERVINGS

So simple and people really don't know you made it with beer, unless you tell them.

INGREDIENTS

1 can (12 ounces) frozen limeade, slightly defrosted
24 ounces beer, any kind
6 ounces or more tequila, any kind

Pour the limeade into a pitcher. Add beer slowly so it doesn't bubble too much. Add tequila. Stir. Fill glasses with ice before pouring.

French 75

Liz Kerr, 1981

Yield: 4 servings

Ingredients

ice cubes

2 ounces fresh lemon juice

2 ounces simple syrup

1 bottle champagne

4 ounces gin

Substitute brandy for the gin and the drink is a French 76

Fill 4 tall glasses 3/4 full with ice. Add 1/2 ounce lemon juice, 1/2 ounce simple syrup, 1 ounce gin, in that order. Fill with champagne. Add orange slices and maraschino cherry as garnish.

Touchdown Juice

Liz Kerr, 1981

Yield: 12 to 14 servings

This tastes a lot like a long island ice tea and is also known by the name of Stumplifter

Ingredients

6 tablespoons instant tea (any kind)

3 cups water

1 can (6 ounces) pineapple juice concentrate

1 can (6 ounces) lemonade concentrate

12 ounces water

2 cups rum

In a large bowl, mix instant tea with 3 cups water to dissolve. Add the pineapple juice and lemonade concentrate and 2 cans of water. Add 2 cups (more or less) of rum. Stir and refrigerate. Best over lots of ice.

Tucson Joe's Magic Margarita

Pam Kerr, KSM

Yield: 6 servings

Ingredients

1 can (12 fluid ounces) of frozen limeade concentrate

12 fluid ounces good tequila

12 fluid ounces can of ice

12 ounces beer

juice of 1/2 orange

slice of lime per drink

1/4 slice of orange per drink

Combine limeade, tequila, ice and orange juice in a blender with ice. Blend until smooth. Pour over ice into a salted glass and garnish with a slice of fresh lime and 1/4 slice of fresh orange.

Mai Tais

Joann Skiba

YIELD: 10 SERVINGS

INGREDIENTS

6 cups pineapple juice, chilled

1-1/2 cups dark rum

1-1/2 cups light rum

1 can (12 ounces) frozen orange juice
concentrate, thawed

1 cup lemon juice, freshly squeezed

2 tablespoons orgeat

*Orgeat (or-zat) is an almond and
orange-based syrup.*

Combine all ingredients in a pitcher.
Stir well. Chill and serve over ice.

Tailgate Punch

Joann Skiba

YIELD: 30 TO 35 SERVINGS

INGREDIENTS

48 ounces Hawaiian Punch

48 ounces apple juice

48 ounces cranberry juice

2 liters ginger ale

4 cups vodka, optional

1/2 cup orange liquor, optional

Combine all ingredients into a large
punch bowl or 5-gallon insulated
beverage container. Add ice and serve.

Pumpkin Martinis

Liz Kerr, 1981

YIELD: 8 SERVINGS

*This is a seasonal recipe. Pumpkin liquour
is found in liquor stores in the fall.
Pumpkin spice coffee creamer is available in
grocery stores late September to December.*

INGREDIENTS

2 cups pumpkin liqueur

2 cups vodka

3/4 cup pumpkin spice liquid coffee
creamer

Mix ingredients together in a pitcher and
stir. Taste to adjust for the amount of
pumpkin spice you like. You can add
orange food coloring (or equal parts red
and yellow food coloring) to enhance the
color. Serve over lots of ice.

non-alcoholic

Hot Mulled Cider

Joann Skiba

YIELD: 24 SERVINGS

INGREDIENTS

64 ounces cranberry juice
128 ounces apple juice
1/2 cup brown sugar
1 teaspoon cloves
2 teaspoons cinnamon
peel from 1 orange
peel from 1 lemon

Pour juices into a percolator. Put brown sugar, cloves, cinnamon and citrus peels into the brewing basket. Brew until hot. Or, put all ingredients in a large pot, heat until warm and strain.

Homemade Hot Chocolate

Ruth Anne Velaer-Wheeler, 1988

YIELD: 8 SERVINGS

INGREDIENTS

1/2 cup cocoa powder
3/4 cup raw sugar
3 cups dried milk powder
dash kosher salt

Sift all ingredients together and store in an airtight container in a cool, dry location.

Add 4 tablespoons of hot chocolate mix to 8 ounces of boiling water. Top with whipped cream, cinnamon, nutmeg, or vanilla powder, to taste.

COACHES QUOTES

April Likhite, Cross Country:

"It's not the easy or convenient life for which I search, but rather life lived to the edge of all my possibility."
—Unknown

Starting Lineup

Breakfast

FOOTBALL

Head Coach Pat Fitzgerald (2006–present)
– *29th head coach*

- The first varsity football games took place in 1882 with two games against Lake Forest. Each team won one.

- In 1924, Wallace Abbey wrote in the Chicago Tribune about an NU/Chicago game that "Stagg's boys" were "stopped dead by a Purple Wall of Wildcats." From that time on, all NU athletic teams were known as Wildcats!

- 19 NU student-athletes have been drafted by the NFL since 1999.

- 51 NU students-athletes from 14 of our varsity teams have been named Big Ten Distinguished Scholars for 2010–2011, including seven members of the football team This new award encompasses only student-athletes with a minimum GPA of 3.7 or higher for the previous academic year.

casserole

Green Chili Quiche

Julie Wood, 1982

YIELD: 10 TO 12 SERVINGS

INGREDIENTS

1 unbaked 9 inch pie crust

4 eggs

1-1/2 cups Monterey Jack cheese, shredded

1 cup shredded cheddar cheese

1 can (4 ounces) green chilies, drained

1 cup half-and-half or milk

2 green onions, chopped

1 teaspoon ground cumin

6 to 10 dashes hot sauce

Preheat oven to 400 degrees. Bake pie crust for approximately 12 minutes, until it begins to brown. Remove pie crust from oven and reduce temperature to 325 degrees. Sprinkle cheeses over partially baked pie crust, reserving 1/4 cup cheddar cheese. Evenly distribute green chilies and green onions over cheese. In a medium bowl, add eggs, half-and-half or milk, cumin and hot sauce. Whisk until well-blended. Pour egg mixture over cheese, chilies and onions. Sprinkle reserved 1/4 cup cheddar cheese over the top.

Bake for 45 to 50 minutes, or until the center of the pie appears set when gently shaken. Let stand for at least 5 minutes before serving.

Green Chili Egg Casserole

Julie Kent

YIELD: 8 TO 10 SERVINGS

INGREDIENTS

10 large eggs

1/4 cup flour

1 teaspoon baking powder

1/2 cup butter, melted

1 pint regular or low-fat cottage cheese

1 pound shredded Monterey Jack cheese

1 can (6 ounces) diced green chilies

Heat oven to 350 degrees. Whisk eggs, flour, baking powder and butter together in large bowl. Stir in cheeses and chilies. Pour into a lightly greased 9x13 inch baking pan. (Casserole may be refrigerated up to 24 hours before baking; remove from refrigerator 15 minutes before placing in the oven.) Cover; bake until set, cheese is melted and beginning to brown, about 35 minutes.

Apple Breakfast Lasagna

Julie Kent

YIELD: 12 TO 15 SERVINGS

INGREDIENTS

1 cup sour cream

1/3 cup packed brown sugar

12 slices frozen French toast

1/2 to 1 pound boiled ham, sliced

2 to 3 cups shredded cheddar cheese

1 can (20 ounces) apple pie filling

1 cup granola

Preheat oven to 350 degrees. Mix sour cream and brown sugar; set aside.

Place 6 French toast slices in bottom of greased 9x13 inch pan. Layer ham, 3/4 of the cheese and remaining 6 slices of French toast. Spread apple pie filling over top; sprinkle with granola. Bake for 25 minutes. Top with remaining 1/4 of cheese and bake 5 minutes more or until cheese is melted.

Serve with sour cream mixture.

Bacon and Egg Casserole

Marilyn Zilka, 1975

YIELD: 4 TO 6 SERVINGS

INGREDIENTS

1/4 pound store bought puffed pastry, thawed

12 slices bacon, cut into 1/2 inch strips

1 medium onion, halved and thinly sliced

3 large eggs

1/2 cup cream

1/4 teaspoon salt

1/8 teaspoon pepper

1-1/2 cups grated Gruyère (about 4 ounces)

Preheat oven to 400 degrees.

On a lightly floured surface, roll pastry into a 10-inch square. Place in 8 inch square baking pan, folding corners to fit. Prick bottom of dough with a fork in several places.

Heat a large skillet over medium heat, add bacon, cook and stir occasionally until pieces start to brown, 4 to 5 minutes. Add onions and cook until bacon is crisp and onions are lightly brown, 5 to 7 minutes. With a slotted spoon, transfer mix to a plate and let cool.

Scatter onion and bacon mixture over pastry. In a small bowl, whisk eggs, salt and pepper. Pour egg mixture into pastry shell. Sprinkle Gruyère over top. Bake until top is golden brown, about 40 minutes.

Yummy Egg Brunch

Marlene Moffet, 1981

YIELD: 8 TO 10 SERVINGS

Everyone needs a good egg dish.

INGREDIENTS

2-1/2 cups herb flavored croutons

2 cups shredded cheddar cheese

2 pounds breakfast sausage, crumbled,
    browned, drained

8 eggs

1 cup milk

3/4 teaspoon dry mustard

Grease a 9x13 inch glass dish. Spread the croutons on the bottom of the dish. Sprinkle cheese on top, put sausage on top of cheese. Beat the eggs with milk, add the dry mustard and mix well. Pour over top of other ingredients. Cover and refrigerate overnight. Bake in preheated 300 degree oven for 1 hour.

Deviled Sausage

Julie Kent

YIELD: 6 TO 8 SERVINGS

INGREDIENTS

2 pounds regular breakfast sausage

1 cup chopped green pepper

1 cup sliced mushrooms

2 tablespoons butter

2 tablespoons flour

1 teaspoon curry powder

1-1/2 cups milk

2 tablespoons soft bread crumbs

2 tablespoons grated Parmesan cheese

salt and pepper, to taste

Sauté mushrooms if desired. Preheat oven to 350 degrees.

Fry sausage until brown, separating into small pieces with a fork. Drain fat. Add green pepper and mushrooms, mix well. In a separate pot, melt butter, then blend in flour and curry powder. Gradually add milk and cook, stirring until thickened.

Add salt and pepper and cook 1 minute. Mix with the sausage combination and spoon into a 1-1/2 quart casserole. Sprinkle with bread crumbs and Parmesan cheese.

Bake uncovered for 30 minutes.

Cheese Sausage Strata

Ginny Gillis

YIELD: 12 TO 14 SERVINGS

INGREDIENTS

1-1/2 pounds pork sausage (bulk)

9 whole eggs, slightly beaten

3 cups 2% milk

9 slices white bread, cubed

1-1/2 cups shredded cheddar cheese

1/2 pound bacon, cooked and crumbled

1-1/2 teaspoons ground mustard

In a large skillet cook pork sausage over medium heat until no longer pink and then drain.

Add eggs, milk, bread, cheese, bacon and mustard. Transfer all ingredients to greased 9x13 inch baking dish. Cover and chill overnight in the refrigerator.

Remove from the refrigerator 30 minutes before baking. Preheat oven to 350 degrees. Cover and bake for 55 to 65 minutes or until a knife inserted near the center comes out clean.

Breakfast Sausage Casserole

Mark McDonnell

YIELD: 8 TO 10 SERVINGS

INGREDIENTS

3 English muffins

1 tablespoon margarine, softened

1 pound bulk pork sausage

4 ounces canned chopped green chilies, drained

3 cups shredded cheddar cheese

1-1/2 cups sour cream

12 eggs, beaten

Spread cut side of each English muffin with 1 teaspoon butter and place buttered side down in a lightly greased 9x13 inch baking dish. Cook sausage in a skillet until browned, stirring to crumble then drain. Layer half of each sausage, chilies and cheese over English muffins. Combine sour cream and eggs, pour over casserole. Repeat layers with remaining sausage, chilies and cheese. Cover and refrigerate for eight hours.

Preheat oven to 350 degrees. Remove from refrigerator and let stand at room temperature for 30 minutes. Bake, uncovered for 35 to 40 minutes.

Purple Passion

cereal

Granola

Teri Jensen,
Football Mom — Mike #80, 2013

YIELD: 7 CUPS

Use for topping yogurt, ice cream or eating as a cereal with milk.

INGREDIENTS

2-1/2 cups nuts, such as almonds, walnuts, pecans, cashews, hazelnuts
3 cups rolled oats
1/2 cup sunflower seeds (shelled)
1/2 cup pumpkin seeds (shelled)
1/2 cup unsweetened shredded coconut
3/4 cup honey
1/4 cup unrefined sesame oil (not Oriental sesame oil)
1/2 teaspoon sea salt
1 teaspoon vanilla extract
1/2 teaspoon ground cinnamon
1/2 teaspoon ground cardamom
1 cup chopped dried fruit, such as prunes, raisins, dates, peaches, apples, banana chips or cranberries

Preheat the oven to 325 degrees.

Break the nuts into halves. Combine the nuts, oats, seeds and coconut in a bowl. Mix together the honey, oil, sea salt, vanilla, cinnamon and cardamom. Pour this mixture over the grain mixture stirring to combine. Spread the mixture out on an 11x17 inch pan and bake for 7 minutes. Stir and spread the mixture out again in an even layer. Return to oven for another 7 minutes. Stir, then check every 5 minutes, or until the oats are crisp and brown but not burned. Remove from the oven and pour into a large wooden bowl or onto another pan to stop the cooking.

Add the dried fruits. Let cool thoroughly. Store in an airtight container in a cool dry place.

Crunchy Granola

Marian Kurz, MSJ

INGREDIENTS

4 cups coarsely chopped nuts (walnuts, almonds, pecans, hazelnuts, cashews)*
8 cups rolled oats
1 cup oat bran
1 cup sunflower seeds*
1 tablespoon cinnamon*
1 cup canola oil
1 cup honey
1 cup dried fruit (raisins, currants or cranberries)*

* *more or less, to taste.*

Toast nuts on a cookie sheet 5 to 10 minutes. Mix oats, bran, seeds, cinnamon and nuts in a large pan or roaster. Add oil and then honey. Stir until the ingredients are thoroughly coated. Bake in a 350 degree oven, stirring the ingredients thoroughly every 20 minutes, until the granola is a deep golden brown, at least 1 hour. Make sure that the ingredients at the bottom and corners of the pan are turned. Add the dried fruit, stirring well to incorporate. Return to oven. Turn off oven. The dried fruit is added at the end because it will turn to carbon if added at the beginning of the baking process. Let granola sit in oven for about 30 minutes. Let granola cool. Pack in airtight containers or Ziploc bags.

Golden Granola

Steve Schnur, 1996,
Football, Rose Bowl (1996)

YIELD: ABOUT 14 CUPS

INGREDIENTS

6 cups old fashioned oatmeal
  (one canister)

12 ounces unsalted butter

1/2 cup honey

1-1/2 cups shredded coconut
  (sweetened or unsweetened)

1-1/2 cups chopped pecans

1-1/2 teaspoons cinnamon

3/4 cup light brown sugar

1/2 teaspoon salt

1 cup cranberries and/or raisins

Preheat oven to 350 degrees. Melt butter
and honey. Mix oatmeal, nuts, coconut,
cinnamon, sugar, salt and cranberries in
extra large bowl. Pour butter/honey mixture over all other ingredients and stir
well. Place in a 9x13 inch baking dish.
Bake for 30 minutes. Stirring every 8 to
10 minutes. Do not stir when you take
out of the oven. Cool completely before
storing in an airtight container.

coffee cake

Apple Cake

Matt Grevers, 2007,
Men's Swimming

YIELD: 8 TO 10 SERVINGS

INGREDIENTS

2/3 cup butter

2 cups sugar

2 eggs

2 teaspoons vanilla extract

3 cups sifted cake flour

2-1/2 teaspoons baking powder

1 teaspoon salt

1 cup milk

5 Granny Smith apples

2 tablespoons sugar

2 to 3 tablespoons cinnamon

2-1/2 tablespoons butter, thinly sliced

Preheat oven to 350 degrees.

Cream the butter and add sugar
gradually, beating until light, about
10 minutes. Add eggs and vanilla, beat
until fluffy. Sift dry ingredients together
and add gradually to mixture, alternating

with milk, adding about 1/3 at a time. Beat after every addition and 1 more minute when done.

Grease and lightly flour a 9x12 inch casserole dish. Put mixture in dish. Core, peel and slice the apples. Mix sugar and cinnamon through the slices. Put the slices on top of the batter and push them into the batter. Sprinkle more sugar and cinnamon on top and add thinly sliced butter.

Bake between 50 minutes and 1 hour.

Blueberry Sausage Breakfast Cake

Mary Pat Watt,
Football Mom — Kevin #42

YIELD: 9X13 INCH PAN

INGREDIENTS

CAKE:

2 cups all-purpose flour

1 teaspoon baking powder

1/2 teaspoon baking soda

1/2 cup margarine or butter

3/4 cup sugar

1/4 cup packed brown sugar

2 large eggs

8 ounces dairy sour cream

1 pound bulk pork sausage

1 cup blueberries

1/2 cup chopped pecans

SAUCE:

1/2 cup sugar

2 tablespoons cornstarch

1/2 cup water

2 cups fresh or frozen blueberries

1/2 teaspoon lemon juice

CAKE: Cook and drain sausage; set aside.

In medium mixing bowl stir together flour, baking powder and baking soda; set aside.

In a large mixer bowl, beat margarine or butter with an electric mixer on medium to high speed until fluffy. Add sugars and beat until combined. Add eggs, one at a time, beating 1 minute after each addition. Add flour mixture and sour cream to egg mixture, alternately, adding about 1/3 each time, beating after each addition just until combined.

Fold in sausage and berries. Pour batter in an ungreased 9x13 inch baking pan. Spread batter evenly in pan; sprinkle pecans on top. (At this point, you can cover and chill overnight. In the morning, bake as directed.) Bake in 350 degree oven for 35 to 40 minutes or until a toothpick comes out clean. Cool on a wire rack. Serve warm with blueberry sauce.

SAUCE: In a medium saucepan, combine sugar and cornstarch. Add water and blueberries. Cook and stir over medium heat until thickened and bubbly. Cook and stir 2 minutes more. Stir in lemon juice.

COACHES QUOTES

Laurie Schiller, Women's Fencing:

"Focus on what you can control and the outcomes will generally be good. If you focus on the outcome, it will generally not be what you want."

Blueberry Coffee Cake

Lisa Rosenblate

YIELD: 9x9 INCH PAN

INGREDIENTS

TOPPING:
1/4 cup butter
1/4 cup flour
1 cup brown sugar

CAKE:
1/2 cup butter
1 cup sugar
3 large eggs
1 teaspoon baking powder
1/2 teaspoon salt
1 teaspoon baking soda
1 teaspoon vanilla extract
2 cups flour
1 cup sour cream (light, if desired)
2 cup blueberries, raspberries or
  blackberries

When berries are in season, I add more.

Preheat oven to 350 degrees. Cream butter and sugar. Add eggs, baking powder, salt, baking soda and vanilla. Alternate mixing in flour and sour cream, beginning with the flour. Fold in berries. Spread in 9x9 inch greased, floured pan. Spread on topping. Bake for 30 to 35 minutes until toothpick comes out clean.

Mildred's Melt-In-Your-Mouth Blueberry Cake

John Christy, Law

YIELD: 9x9 INCH PAN

Serve warm as a main course or side dish for breakfast.

INGREDIENTS

1-1/2 cups sifted flour
1 teaspoon baking powder
1/2 teaspoon salt
2 large eggs, at room temperature,
  separated
1/2 cup butter, at room temperature
1 cup sugar
1/3 cup milk
1 teaspoon vanilla extract
1-1/2 cups blueberries
flour for dusting blueberries
sugar for topping, optional

Preheat oven to 350 degrees. Sprinkle blueberries with flour to coat, shake off excess. Sift flour, baking powder and salt together. Set aside.

Cream butter and sugar until light and fluffy. Beat in egg yolks until well beaten. Add vanilla and the milk with the dry ingredients and beat well.

In a separate bowl, beat egg whites until stiff. Fold beaten egg whites into batter. Fold in blueberries. Bake in a greased 9 inch square pan for 45 minutes. Sprinkle with sugar before baking for a nice topping.

Dot's Coffee Cake

Jenni Glick,
Assistant Director, Clubs — NAA

Yield: 1 cake

Ingredients

1 package yellow cake mix
1 package (3-3/4 ounces)
    vanilla instant pudding
1 envelope Dream Whip topping
4 eggs
3/4 cup vegetable or canola oil
3/4 cup water
1 teaspoon vanilla extract
1/2 cup sugar
2 teaspoons cinnamon
2 teaspoons chopped pecans or
    walnuts, optional

Preheat oven to 350 degrees.

TOPPING: Mix together sugar, cinnamon and nuts.

CAKE: In a large bowl, mix together the cake mix, pudding, Dream Whip, eggs, oil, water and vanilla. Beat on medium speed for 6 minutes. Pour half the batter into a greased Bundt pan or long 4x16 inch loaf pan. Sprinkle half of the topping over the batter. Pour the remaining batter into the pan and cover with the rest of the cinnamon topping. Bake for 45 to 50 minutes or until toothpick comes out clean.

Pumpkin Apple Bundt Ring

Jean Yale, 1957,
Athletic Development/Special Events

Yield: 12 servings

Ingredients

1-1/2 cups sugar
2 large eggs
1/2 cup butter or margarine, softened
1 cup canned pumpkin
1-1/2 cups shredded apples,
    peeled if desired
2 cups flour
1 teaspoon baking powder
1/4 teaspoon salt
1/4 teaspoon baking soda
1/2 teaspoon cinnamon
1/2 teaspoon nutmeg
1/4 teaspoon ginger
1/4 teaspoon cloves

Preheat oven to 350 degrees. In food processor, combine sugar, eggs and butter for one minute. Add shredded apples and pumpkin. Combine all dry ingredients. Fold into the butter mixture.

Turn into greased and floured Bundt pan and bake for 55 minutes. Cool in pan for 10 minutes, remove and top with sifted powdered sugar.

Do Ahead Coffee Cake

Joann Skiba

YIELD: 9x13 INCH PAN

INGREDIENTS

2/3 cup softened butter
3/4 cup granulated sugar
1/2 cup firmly packed brown sugar
2 large eggs
1 teaspoon vanilla extract
2 cups sifted flour
1 teaspoon baking powder
1/2 teaspoon salt
1 teaspoon baking soda
1 teaspoon cinnamon
1 cup buttermilk

TOPPING:

1/2 cup brown sugar
1 teaspoon cinnamon
1/2 cup chopped pecans

Combine topping ingredients; set aside.

Cream butter. Add granulated and brown sugars. Beat in eggs; mix well. Add vanilla. Combine dry ingredients. Add dry ingredients alternately with buttermilk. Pour into a greased 9x13 inch pan. Sprinkle topping over batter. Cover and refrigerate overnight.

Preheat oven to 350 degrees. Bake for 40 to 45 minutes until toothpick comes out clean. Serve warm.

Sour Cream Coffee Cake

Clara Littau

YIELD: 1 BUNDT CAKE

INGREDIENTS

1/2 pound butter or margarine
2 cups sugar
2 large eggs
1 cup sour cream
2 cups flour
1 teaspoon baking powder
1 teaspoon vanilla extract

TOPPING:

2 tablespoons brown sugar
1 teaspoon cinnamon
1/2 cup chopped pecans

Preheat oven to 350 degrees.

TOPPING: Mix together brown sugar, cinnamon and chopped pecans; set aside.

CAKE: Cream butter and sugar. Mix in eggs then fold in sour cream. Mix in flour and baking powder. Add vanilla. Pour half the batter in a buttered and floured 10 inch tube or Bundt pan. Sprinkle on half of the topping mixture. Add rest of the batter then add topping mixture, gently mixing the topping into the batter. Bake for 65 to 70 minutes.

Allow to cool completely before removing cake from the pan.

Sour Cream Coffee Cake

Gordon Newton &
Ramune Kubiliunas, 1990

YIELD: 10 INCH CAKE

INGREDIENTS

1 cup butter, softened

2 cups sugar

2 eggs

1 cup sour cream

1 teaspoon vanilla extract

2 cups flour

1 teaspoon salt

1 teaspoon baking powder

TOPPING:

1/2 cup chopped pecans

2 teaspoons cinnamon

4 tablespoons brown sugar

CAKE: In large bowl, cream butter and sugar. Add eggs one at a time. Fold in vanilla and sour cream. Sift flour, salt and baking powder and add to batter.

Put half the batter in 10 inch greased tube pan.

TOPPING: Mix pecans, cinnamon and brown sugar.

ASSEMBLY: Sprinkle half of brown sugar mixture over batter. Add remaining batter. Add remaining topping. Bake at 350 degrees for 50 to 60 minutes, until toothpick inserted in center comes out clean.

Sour Cream Coffee Cake

Jan Forsman, 1981

YIELD: 9X13 INCH PAN

A family favorite

INGREDIENTS

1/2 cup butter or margarine

1 cup granulated sugar

2 eggs

1 cup sour cream

1/4 teaspoon salt

2 cups flour

1 teaspoon baking soda

1 teaspoon baking powder

1 teaspoon vanilla extract

TOPPING:

1/3 cup white sugar

1/3 cup brown sugar

1 cup chopped nuts, optional

1 teaspoon cinnamon

Drizzle with white frosting or glaze if desired.

Preheat oven to 350 degrees. Cream butter and sugar. Add eggs and sour cream. Add dry ingredients and then vanilla. Mix topping in separate bowl. In a 9x13 greased pan, alternate 1/2 cake mixture, 1/2 topping mixture, 1/2 cake, 1/2 topping. Bake for 30 minutes or until toothpick comes out clean. When cool, drizzle thinned white frosting over the top.

eggs

Tailgate Sausage Bread

Beth Trumpy,
Football Mom — Mike #29

YIELD: 8 TO 12 SERVINGS

INGREDIENTS

2 pounds pork sausage

3 eggs, beaten

8 ounces shredded cheddar cheese

8 ounces shredded mozzarella cheese

2 tablespoons Parmesan cheese

1 teaspoon garlic salt

1 teaspoon oregano

1 teaspoon parsley

1 teaspoon salt

4 packages (8 ounces each)
    crescent rolls

Brown and drain sausage. Add eggs, cheddar cheese, mozzarella cheese, Parmesan cheese and spices. Stir well. Unroll each dough roll on parchment paper and flatten into four rectangles. Divide sausage mixture among the rectangles. Roll up long sides of dough, sealing edges. Place seam side down, two rolls to a baking sheet. Do not crowd or rolls will not brown on the sides. Brush tops with reserved egg. Bake at 375 degrees for 20 minutes or until brown. Slice and serve.

Legendary Studdard Good Luck Burritos

Peggy Heinz,
Football Mom — Brian 2006

YIELD: 24 TO 30 SERVINGS

INGREDIENTS

24 to 30 large flour tortillas

1 package (30 ounces) southern-style
    hash browns (cooked)

2 pounds bulk breakfast sausage,
    browned

30 large eggs, scrambled

3 cups grated cheddar cheese

2 cans (4 ounces each) diced chilies

Mix together the hashbrowns, sausage, eggs, cheese and chilies. Scoop about 1 cup of the ingredients into the burrito. Wrap in foil individually. Re-warm on the grill. (Can be frozen and heated up when needed.)

Matzoh Brei

Cathleen & Coach Laurie Schiller,
Head Coach, Women's Fencing

YIELD: 1 SERVING

This recipe was handed down from my Jewish grandmother and modified by me. Matzoh Brei is Yiddish.

INGREDIENTS

2 full size matzoh crackers
2 medium eggs
1 tablespoon milk
1 tablespoon butter

In a bowl, break up the matzoh into pieces but don't reduce the crackers to crumbs. Fill the bowl with cool water to cover the matzoh and soak for about 2 minutes until soft — middling between crisp and soggy. Drain and put aside. Mix eggs with milk with a wire whisk in a second bowl. Heat butter in a frying pan. Add matzoh and fry for a couple of minutes until butter is absorbed. Add egg mixture and stir until eggs cover the matzoh. Fry until eggs look cooked but be careful not to cook until dry. Salt and pepper, to taste.

pancakes

Big Pancakes

Amylou Dueck, 1999,
Women's Golf

YIELD: ABOUT 10 PANCAKES

These crepe-like flapjacks are German in origin. While a bit less refined than their French counterparts, these are far more fun. These pancakes were a specialty of my grandma but now have become the basis for a holiday tradition in which friends and family congregate for an evening of Big Pancakes and merriment.

INGREDIENTS

1-1/2 cups flour
1/2 teaspoon salt
3 eggs
1-3/4 cups milk, divided
6 ounces light beer
butter blended with canola for frying

Mix flour, salt, eggs and 1 cup milk in a bowl with a mixer or by hand until smooth. Add beer and up to 3/4 cup milk until the batter is very thin. Heat a fry pan on medium-high heat on the stove top. Add a healthy spoonful of butter blend to the hot fry pan and swirl pan to coat the bottom. Next, add a ladle (about 1/4 cup) of batter to the hot fry pan and swirl to cover the entire bottom with a thin layer. Bake on medium-high heat until batter is set. Flip and bake the other side until golden brown. Serve immediately. Repeat butter blend and batter application for the next pancake.

Popular toppings include sliced strawberries and whipped cream; bacon or sausage rolled inside a pancake and then covered with maple syrup.

Blueberry Pancakes with Lemon and Ricotta

Chef Kerry Hieber,
Executive Chef,
Hilton Orrington/Evanston

YIELD: 4 TO 5 SERVINGS

INGREDIENTS

1-1/2 cups all-purpose flour

1 teaspoon salt

1/2 cup sugar

1/2 tablespoon baking soda

1 tablespoon baking powder

2 cups milk

1 cup ricotta cheese, drained

3 large eggs

3 tablespoons unsalted butter, melted

2 lemons, zested and juiced

1 cup blueberries, washed and dried

 GLAZE:

juice of 2 lemons

2 cups confectioners' sugar

GLAZE: Combine lemon juice with sugar, stirring until smooth.

PANCAKES: Stir together flour, salt, baking powder, baking soda and sugar in a large mixing bowl. In a separate bowl whisk together milk, eggs, some of the melted butter, lemon zest and juice. Add wet ingredients to the dry ingredients and stir until just combined. Add remaining butter and stir. Gently fold in blueberries and ricotta.

Heat a griddle to medium-high heat. Spray with non-stick spray or brush lightly with oil. Drop batter onto griddle using a 2 ounce ladle. Cook pancakes for approximately 3 to 5 minutes on first side until bubbles appear through surface of batter, edges of pancakes begin to look dry and undersides are brown. Flip the pancakes and cook until the second side is browned.

Serve pancakes immediately with butter and lemon glaze.

Lemon Cottage Cheese Pancakes

Elizabeth Kurz

YIELD: 3 SERVINGS

From Greyfield Inn, Cumberland Island with permission.

INGREDIENTS

3 eggs, separated

2 tablespoons sugar

1/4 cup all-purpose flour

1/4 teaspoon salt

3/4 cup cottage cheese

1 tablespoon grated lemon zest

1/4 cup butter

Beat the egg whites until they hold stiff peaks. Set aside. In another bowl, stir together sugar, salt, yolks, cottage cheese, zest and butter; add the flour and mix. Right before cooking, gently fold the whites into the mixture with a spatula. Pour onto flat grill, forming 3 inch pancakes and cook as you would regular pancakes. These are fluffier than regular pancakes.

Serve with choice of syrup and top with berries if desired.

Debbi's Outstanding Potato Pancakes (Latkes)

Debbi Miller-Rosenstein

YIELD: 10 TO 12 PANCAKES

INGREDIENTS

4 large peeled Idaho potatoes
4 extra large eggs
1 large peeled white onion
1-1/2 teaspoons salt
1 teaspoon white pepper
3 tablespoons matzo meal
canola oil

Cut potatoes and onions into one inch chunks. Break 1 egg into blender, add some of the potatoes and onions. Blend using grate speed then pour mixture into bowl. Continue with eggs, potatoes and onions until all grated. Add salt, pepper and matzo meal. Stir well.

Heat frying pan with canola oil until hot. Drop potato mixture by large spoonful into hot oil. Cook until brown. Turn and cook other side. When pancake is done, remove and place on paper towel to remove excess oil. Continue until mixture is used up. Place pancakes on a foil lined pan and keep warm in 225 degree oven. Do not overheat.

Serve immediately with sour cream and applesauce. Can be used as main entree or side dish.

Zucchini Pancakes

Executive Chef Jim Freeland,
Lou Malnati's, Evanston and over 30 locations throughout Chicagoland

YIELD: 6 SERVINGS

INGREDIENTS

6 cups shredded zucchini
2 eggs, slightly beaten
pinch nutmeg
pinch salt
pinch black pepper
1 cup flour
2 teaspoons baking powder
3 ounces grated Parmesan cheese

Shred zucchini in food processor. Pour into a bowl, add egg, nutmeg, salt and pepper, mix well. Sift flour and baking powder over mixture and blend thoroughly. Stir in cheese. Pour mixture over hot griddle to form pancakes. Cook until lightly browned, then flip and cook other side.

Palacinke (Croatian Crêpes)

Ivan Vujic,
Assistant Coach, Men's Basketball

YIELD: 20 TO 24 CRÊPES

INGREDIENTS

2 eggs
salt
1 quart milk
1 pound flour
sparkling mineral water
vegetable oil
Nutella or jam
powdered sugar

Mix eggs and a bit of salt in a bowl. While mixing, add milk and flour slowly until the batter is of the texture of a milkshake. Add a bit of sparkling mineral water. Heat a frying pan or a crepe pan with a teaspoon of oil until hot. The hotter the pan, the easier the pancakes come off. Use a soup ladle to fill the pan to about half from center, then slowly rotate the pan while slightly tilted until the batter is uniformly spread in the pan. Fry on both sides until lightly brown. When done, remove from pan and spread jam or Nutella over the pancake and roll into a long cylinder. Sprinkle on top with powdered sugar.

Sunday Morning Pancakes

Marian Kurz, MSJ

YIELD: 4 SERVINGS

We love Sunday morning breakfasts and often prepare something special. These are quick and tasty! Pancakes should be eaten immediately before they lose their puffiness.

INGREDIENTS

4 eggs
2 cups sour cream
1/4 cup cake flour
3 tablespoons sugar
2 tablespoons cornstarch
1/2 teaspoon baking soda
1/2 teaspoon salt

Beat the eggs in bowl (or use blender, whisk, or food processor) and then beat in the sour cream.

Mix together the dry ingredients in another bowl; add to the egg mixture and beat until smooth.

Pour large spoonfuls of batter into a warmed, lightly greased skillet. Pancakes should be about 3 inches wide. Cook until the bubbles appear on top, then turn over for another couple minutes at most.

Top with syrup and butter, powdered sugar, sweetened fruit or jam.

Holiday Pancakes

Natasha Brown Moss, 1992

YIELD: 3 TO 4 SERVINGS

My husband, William also an alum (we met new student week of freshman year), is a huge fan of breads and sweets. We first tasted these pancakes at a local restaurant many years ago. Unfortunately they only served them around Thanksgiving and wouldn't share the recipe. It's taken me years to perfect this recipe but after much trial and error I finally mastered a mix worthy to be called Holiday Pancakes!

INGREDIENTS

1-1/2 cups flour

1 teaspoon baking powder

1/4 teaspoon baking soda

1/4 teaspoon salt

1-3/4 teaspoons ground ginger

2-1/2 teaspoons ground cinnamon

1/2 teaspoon ground allspice

1/4 teaspoon ground nutmeg

1 egg

1/2 teaspoon vanilla extract

3 tablespoons firmly packed
    brown sugar

1-1/2 cups water

granola, optional

macadamia nuts, optional

Preheat oven to 425 degrees; place cast-iron skillet or griddle in oven. Mix ginger, cinnamon, allspice and nutmeg in a small bowl and set aside. Whisk together egg, water and vanilla in a different bowl and set aside.

In a large mixing bowl, sift (or whisk) flour, baking powder, baking soda, salt and brown sugar. Whisk spice mix into flour mixture. Add egg mixture to dry ingredients, whisking together until just combined (small lumps are okay). Allow batter to rest for 2 to 3 minutes. Remove skillet from oven and place on stove over medium flame. Add teaspoon of butter or oil to skillet. Use spatula to move oil around pan.

Pour batter into skillet. Add granola or nuts. Cook until bubbles appear throughout (about 2 to 3 minutes) then flip. Cook for 1 to 2 minutes longer. Pancakes should be golden brown in color. Top with butter and syrup. Note: If pancakes are too dark or too light, adjust skillet temperature accordingly.

Finnish Pancakes

Sandy & Wally White,
Fencing Parents — Whitney 2010

YIELD: 6 TO 8 SERVINGS

This recipe is very easy and yet it brings compliments from all who taste it. Not many people have ever had something so good but so easy to make. The trick is to use the proper size pan.

INGREDIENTS

8 eggs
1 quart milk
4 tablespoons sugar
1 teaspoon salt
1 cup flour
1/4 pound butter

Can also serve with fresh fruit and powdered sugar.

Preheat oven to 450 degrees. Spray 12x16 inch roasting pan with cooking spray (if you use smaller pan, plan to bake longer). Melt all butter in pan. Mix remaining ingredients thoroughly with beater. Pour into pan. Bake 15 to 20 minutes until very puffy and golden. Serve immediately with maple syrup. Pancake will deflate as steam escapes.

toast

Apple Cinnamon Baked French Toast

P J Sinopoli,
Cheerleading Mom — Jenny

YIELD: 8 TO 10 SERVINGS

INGREDIENTS

1 large loaf French bread
8 extra large eggs
3-1/2 cups milk
1 cup sugar, divided
1 teaspoon vanilla extract
3 teaspoons cinnamon, divided
1 teaspoon nutmeg
5 or 6 medium cooking apples, peeled, cored, sliced
1 to 2 tablespoons butter

Slice bread into 1-1/2 inch slices. Spray 9x13 inch pan with cooking spray. Place bread in dish, packing tightly. In a separate bowl, beat eggs, 1/2 cup sugar, milk, 1 teaspoon of cinnamon and vanilla with whisk for 30 seconds. Pour half of the egg mixture over bread.

Toss apples with remaining sugar, remaining cinnamon and nutmeg; spoon over bread. Slowly pour remaining egg mixture over everything. Dot with butter. Cover and refrigerate overnight.

Preheat over to 350 degrees. Uncover dish. Bake in water bath for 1 hour. Let rest for 5 to 10 minutes before serving. Slice in squares and serve with hot syrup.

Blueberry Stuffed French Toast

Nancy Lee

YIELD: 8 TO 10 SERVINGS

Perfect for a brunch or tailgate breakfast.

INGREDIENTS

12 slices French bread, including crust

16 ounces cream cheese (light OK)

2 cups fresh blueberries, rinsed and drained

1 dozen large eggs

1/2 cup real maple syrup

2 cups milk (whole or 2%)

blueberry or maple syrup

Cut bread into 1 inch cubes. Cut chilled cream cheese into 1 inch cubes. Spray 9x13 inch baking pan with nonstick cooking spray. Place half of the bread cubes evenly in prepared pan. Scatter cream cheese cubes over bread and sprinkle with all of the blueberries. Arrange remaining bread cubes over blueberries.

In large bowl combine eggs, syrup and milk; whisk to blend. Pour evenly over reserved bread mixture. Cover with foil and chill overnight.

Preheat oven to 350 degrees. Bake, covered with foil, on middle rack for 30 minutes. Remove foil and continue baking 30 more minutes, or until puffed and golden brown.

Serve with blueberry syrup and maple syrup.

Stuffed French Toast

Julie Kent

YIELD: 6 TO 8 SERVINGS

INGREDIENTS

18 slices cinnamon bread, quartered

8 ounces cream cheese, cut into cubes

1 dozen large eggs

2 cups milk

1/3 cup maple syrup

Put half of bread in 9x13 inch baking pan. Top with cream cheese and remaining bread. Whisk together eggs, milk and syrup. Pour mixture over bread. Cover pan with foil; refrigerate overnight.

Heat oven to 375 degrees (350 degrees if using a glass pan). Remove foil; bake until golden brown, approximately 35 minutes. If still mushy in the middle and the top is getting too brown, cover with foil and bake another 5 to 10 minutes until done.

Serve warm with more syrup.

Purple Haze

Baked French Toast

Betsy Cromer

YIELD: 4 TO 6 SERVINGS

Great at tailgates!

INGREDIENTS

1 cup maple syrup

1/2 cup melted butter

6 to 8 slices sour dough bread (3/4 to 1 inch thick)

5 to 6 eggs

1-1/2 cups whole milk

1 teaspoon real vanilla extract

Pour the butter and syrup in the bottom of a 7x14 inch pan. Place sliced bread in pan so that the bottom of the pan is completely covered. Combine eggs, milk and vanilla; pour the mixture over the bread. Cover with foil and store in the refrigerator overnight. Bring to room temperature the next morning while the oven heats to 350 degrees. Bake for 30 minutes or until bubbling and turning slightly brown on top.

Fran's French Toast a la Alpha Kappa Alpha

Adrianne Hayward, 1971

YIELD: 6 TO 8 SERVINGS

INGREDIENTS

1/2 cup milk

3/4 cup orange juice

5 eggs, beaten

1/4 cup Grand Marnier

6 tablespoons sugar

1/2 teaspoon vanilla extract

1 orange rind, grated

1 pinch cinnamon

2 loaves French bread (16 inch loaves)

Cut bread on an angle into 1 to 1-1/2 inch slices. Coat a 9x13 inch casserole dish with cooking oil spray.

Mix all ingredients (except bread) in a bowl and beat well. Dunk sliced bread in mixture and arrange slices in casserole dish.

Pour remaining mixture over bread, cover with plastic wrap and refrigerate at least one hour but as long as overnight. Flip bread slices once during refrigeration for maximum absorption.

Preheat oven to 400 degrees. Bake, turning after about 20 minutes, until both sides are golden brown.

Crunch Time

Salads

LACROSSE

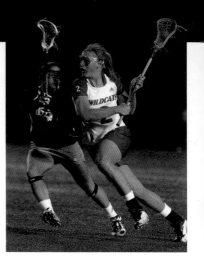

Head Coach Kelly Amonte Hiller (2001–present) – *4th head coach*

- They are a member of the American Lacrosse Conference (ALC).

- They have been NCAA National Champions six out of the last seven years.

- Had 36 consecutive victories from 2/25/07 to 4/20/08.

- There were 103 Academic All-Big Ten honorees in the years 2002–2011.

beans/rice

Cold Wild Rice and Dried Cranberry Salad

Christy Weiss,
Former director of admissions and associate dean of student affairs at NUDS

YIELD: 8 TO 10 SERVINGS

INGREDIENTS

1/2 cup diced red pepper
1/2 diced yellow pepper
1/2 cup chopped pecans, toasted
3/4 cup dried cranberries
1/2 cup olive oil
1/2 cup vegetable oil
6 tablespoons balsamic vinegar
2 tablespoons brown sugar
1 teaspoon Dijon mustard
1/2 teaspoon salt
4 cups salted water
1 cup uncooked wild rice
salt and pepper

To cook rice, bring salted water to a boil, add the rice and stir. Bring back to a boil and lower heat to medium. Cover and simmer for about 25 to 30 minutes or until rice is tender. Drain and cool.

Combine wild rice with celery, peppers, pecans and cranberries.

Whisk the vinegar, salt, brown sugar and mustard in a small bowl. Slowly whisk in the oils until well emulsified.

Dress the salad with enough dressing to coat and flavor well (may not require all the dressing). Season with salt and pepper.

Bean and Rice Salad with Cilantro

Mary Pat Watt,
Football Mom — Kevin #42

YIELD: 8 TO 10 SERVINGS

INGREDIENTS

2 cups cooked, long grain white rice, chilled
1 cup canned black beans, drained
1-1/4 cups halved cherry tomatoes
1 cup shredded Queso Blanco (white Mexican cheese)
1 fresh lime
2 cloves garlic, minced
1/2 teaspoon kosher salt
1/2 cup virgin olive oil
2 tablespoons red wine vinegar
1 teaspoon Dijon mustard
1-1/2 tablespoons chopped fresh cilantro

Combine rice, beans, tomatoes and cheese in a large bowl. Squeeze fresh lime juice over mixture.

Whisk ingredients for the cilantro vinaigrette: minced garlic, salt, mustard, olive oil, vinegar and cilantro. Pour over rice salad. Toss and serve.

Confetti Rice Salad

Phyllis Funkenbusch

YIELD: 8 TO 10 SERVINGS

INGREDIENTS

2 boxes Uncle Ben's Quick Cooking
 Long Grain and Wild Rice

1/2 cup chopped red onion

1/2 cup chopped green pepper

1/2 cup chopped red pepper

1 can (15 ounces) black beans, rinsed
 and drained

1 can (11 ounces) corn, drained

1/4 cup vegetable oil

2 tablespoons white vinegar

2 tablespoons sugar

1/4 teaspoon salt

1/8 teaspoon black pepper

*This is my favorite combination of
vegetables, but you can change them to
fit your preferences. Some suggestions:
green onions, garbanzo beans, diced
carrots, peas, slivered almonds, light or
dark raisins, dried cherries or dried
cranberries.*

Cook rice according to package directions, omitting the butter. Set aside to
cool. Combine oil, vinegar, sugar, salt and
pepper in a clean jar with a tight lid;
shake vigorously to combine. Set aside.
When the rice has cooled, transfer to a
large bowl. Combine the rice and
vegetables. Toss with the dressing, using
2/3 or more, to taste. Refrigerate until
ready to serve.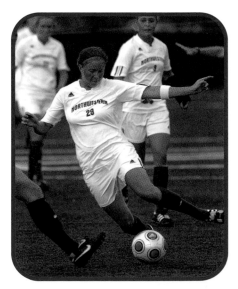

Cold Rice Salad

Janie Varley

YIELD: 6 TO 8 SERVINGS

INGREDIENTS

1 package (regular size)
 Chicken Rice-a-Roni

1 jar (8 ounces) chopped
 marinated artichokes

15 black olives (or more)

15 green olives (or more)

1 tablespoon curry

1/2 cup mayonnaise

Cook Rice-a-Roni and cool. Add artichokes, olives and curry. Refrigerate.
Before serving, add mayonnaise.

entrée

Guacamole Salad

Amanda Sloan,
Director of Clubs, Northwestern Alumni Association

YIELD: 6 TO 8 SERVINGS

INGREDIENTS

1 can (15 ounces) black beans, rinsed and drained

1 can (12 ounces) sweet yellow corn, rinsed and drained

1 pint grape tomatoes, halved

1/2 cup diced red onion

1 jalapeño pepper, seeded and minced

1/2 teaspoon grated lime zest

2 limes, juice squeezed

1/4 cup olive oil

1 teaspoon salt

1/2 teaspoon black pepper

1/2 teaspoon garlic, minced

2 ripe avocados, half inch diced

1/4 cayenne, optional

Whisk lime juice, olive, salt, pepper, garlic and cayenne pepper in a small bowl. Mix tomatoes, black beans, corn, red onion, jalapeño peppers and lime zest in a large bowl. Add whisked sauce to the veggies, stir, and let sit for 30 minutes before serving.

Serve at room temperature.

Corn and Black Bean Salad

Arvid Swan,
Head Coach, Men's Tennis

YIELD: 4 TO 6 SERVINGS

INGREDIENTS

1 jar (8 ounces) corn relish

1 can (15 ounces) black beans, rinsed and drained

1 whole avocado, peeled, cored and cut into 1/2 inch cubes

1 cup halved cherry tomatoes

Combine all ingredients, toss and serve.

COACHES QUOTES

Arvid Swan, Men's Tennis:

"Each Day give 100 percent effort 100 percent of the time in every part of your life."

Easy & Delish Chinese Chicken Salad

Jenn Shull, 2000,
Softball

Yield: 8 to 10 servings

This tried-and-true recipe, passed down a few generations in my family, is that of the classic Chinese Chicken Salad. Trust me, people love it!

Ingredients

2 tablespoons sliced almonds

1/2 cup sesame seeds

1 head green cabbage, chopped

4 green onions, chopped

1 package ramen (chicken flavor)

4 cooked chicken breasts halves

DRESSING:

2 tablespoons sugar

1/2 cup sesame oil

3 tablespoons rice vinegar

1 teaspoon sea salt

1/2 teaspoon pepper

SALAD: Lightly toast the almonds and seeds in the oven about 5 minutes. Mix cabbage, onions and chicken together.

Crumble ramen noodles into the salad.

DRESSING: combine sugar, oil, vinegar, salt, pepper and the flavor packet. Whisk together until the sugar is dissolved and it tastes perfect!

Add dressing to salad and toss.

Chicken Salad

Jayne Donohoe,
Lacrosse Mom — Casey 2009

Yield: 16 to 20 servings

Ingredients

5 pounds boneless chicken breast

10 chicken bouillon cubes

1 cup or more chopped onion

1 cup or more chopped celery

1 cup or more halved grapes

1 to 2 cups Hellmann's mayonnaise

2 tablespoons apple cider vinegar

1/8 cup vegetable oil

pepper, to taste

paprika for color

Use the larger amount of mayonnaise for a very moist salad; adjust oil and vinegar, to taste.

The day before serving, dissolve bouillon cubes in 10 cups of water. Cook chicken breasts in bouillon until tender and the meat falls apart. Cool. Let chicken sit in bouillon overnight.

Chop chicken. In a large bowl mix chicken with onion, celery and grapes. In a separate bowl, mix mayonnaise, oil and vinegar, then add to chicken mixture. Add pepper, to taste and sprinkle paprika on top.

Hot Chicken Salad

Jeannette Lindenman

YIELD: 8 SERVINGS

INGREDIENTS

4 cups cooked chicken, cut in bite-
    sized cubes
2 tablespoons lemon juice
3/4 cup mayonnaise
1 tablespoon salt
2 cups chopped celery
4 eggs, hard boiled
3/4 cup condensed cream of chicken
    soup
1 tablespoon finely chopped onion
2 pimentos, finely chopped
1 cup grated cheddar cheese
1/2 cup crushed potato chips
2/3 cup finely chopped almonds

Preheat oven to 400 degrees.

TOPPING: In small mixing bowl, combine cheese, potato chips and almonds.
Set aside.

SALAD: In 9x13 inch casserole, combine
remaining ingredients; cover salad with
topping. Bake 20 minutes or until heated
through.

Broiled Salmon and Spinach Salad

April Bertin,
Assistant Coach, Field Hockey

YIELD: 4 SERVINGS

INGREDIENTS

4 salmon fillets, 6 ounces each
3/4 teaspoon salt, divided
1/2 teaspoon black pepper, divided
4 teaspoons balsamic vinegar
2 tablespoons extra-virgin olive oil
2 teaspoons minced shallots
1 pint grape tomatoes, halved
5 cups loosely packed spinach
2 tablespoons pine nuts, toasted
1 lemon
crumbled goat cheese

Turn the broiler on high. Cover broiling
pan with aluminum foil. Place each
salmon fillet on foil; season with salt,
pepper, lemon and a drizzle of olive oil.
Cook 10 to 12 minutes.

While fish cooks, place vinegar in a
medium bowl. Gradually add oil, stirring
with a whisk. Stir in shallots.

Heat a medium size skillet over medium-
high heat. Add tomatoes, season with salt
and pepper; sauté for 3 minutes or until
tomatoes soften. Add tomatoes to vinaigrette; toss to combine.

Arrange 1-1/4 cups spinach on each of
4 plates; top each serving with 1 fillet.
Spoon about 1/2 cup tomato mixture
over each salad. Sprinkle with goat cheese
and 1-1/2 teaspoons pine nuts.

Crab, Mango & Avocado Salad

Chef William King,
**McCormick & Schmick's,
multiple locations**

Yield: 4 servings

Ingredients

- 3/4 cup diced mango
- 3/4 cup diced avocado
- 10 ounces Dungeness crab
- 4 tablespoons pomegranate reduction
- 4 tablespoons citrus-flavored vinaigrette
- 4 tablespoons chive oil (see below)
- 1/2 cup micro greens or spicy sprouts tossed in a small amount of citrus vinaigrette for garnish

CHIVE OIL:

- 1/2 cup vegetable oil
- 2 bunches coarsely chopped chives

If you can not find the pomegrante reduction at a specialty store or Asian-foods store, use a light syrup or pomegrante molasses.

CHIVE OIL: Blend chives and oil in a blender for five minutes. Place finished oil in a squirt bottle and set aside. Oil may be made a day ahead of time.

SALAD: To create a tower, place a 2-inch ring mold on a serving plate. Spoon 2 heaping tablespoons of diced mango into the mold. Layer 2 heaping tablespoons of avocado on top of the mango. Finish with 1-1/2 ounces of crab meat to fill the mold. Press down lightly to set the ingredients. Keeping your fingers or a spoon on the top of the tower, apply pressure, and gently slide the ring mold up and off the salad. Rinse and dry the mold and repeat for each plate. Garnish the top of each salad with the micro greens. Drizzle pomegranate reduction, citrus vinaigrette and chive oil on the plate and around the tower.

Shrimp Salad

Marietta Paynter

Marietta was married to John Paynter, a Northwestern alum who served as director of the NU Marching Band from 1953 to 1996.

Ingredients

- 1 loaf (1 pound) Pepperidge Farm white bread
- 1/2 to 3/4 pound butter, softened for easy spreading
- 4 hard boiled eggs, chopped fine
- 1-1/2 cups finely chopped green onions
- 1 cup mayonnaise or as needed
- 1 pound large shrimp, cooked, cut into thirds

Remove crust from bread, then butter and cube. Mix bread, chopped eggs and onions, then refrigerate overnight.

About 1 hour before desired serving time, add shrimp to the bread mixture and add sufficient mayonnaise to hold together. Return to refrigerator until serving time.

fruit

Avocado and Grapefruit Salad

Megan Anderson, 1976

YIELD: 6 SERVINGS

INGREDIENTS

4 grapefruits, segmented, saving juice

3 avocados, peeled and sliced

poppy seeds

1 chopped shallot

1 tablespoon runny honey

1 teaspoon minced fresh ginger or 1/4 teaspoon ground ginger

3 tablespoons red wine or champagne vinegar

1/2 teaspoon Dijon or honey Dijon mustard

5 ounces sunflower oil

salt or sea salt, to taste

pepper, to taste

Serve on butter or bibb lettuce.

Place all the dressing ingredients in a bowl. Gradually whisk in the oil until the dressing emulsifies and thickens. Arrange alternating avocado slices and grapefruit segments on a serving platter. Brush the avocado with grapefruit juice to stop discoloration. Spoon the dressing over the salad and sprinkle with poppy seeds prior to serving.

Purple Grape Salad

Chris & Coach Stephanie Foster, 1998, Head Coach, Women's Soccer

YIELD: 12 TO 14 SERVINGS

INGREDIENTS

1 to 2 pounds purple grapes

8 ounces cream cheese

8 ounces sour cream

1 cup powdered sugar

1 teaspoon vanilla extract

1/2 cup brown sugar, to taste

1 bag (6 to 8 ounces) chopped walnuts, optional

You can add green grapes, but I use red (purple) exclusively for NU functions. You can substitute almond extract for vanilla or do both using 1/2 teaspoon of each. This can also be a dessert, served over pound cake or angle food cake.

Wash grapes and pick them off of the stems. In a mixing bowl, mix cream cheese, sour cream, vanilla and powdered sugar until creamy. Stir in grapes. Transfer to serving bowl and top with walnuts and brown sugar. Serve chilled.

Summer Fruit Salad with Mint Sugar

Elizabeth Kurz

YIELD: 6 TO 8 SERVINGS

INGREDIENTS

- 1/4 cup loosely-packed fresh mint
- 3 tablespoons sugar
- 1-1/4 pounds blackberries, left whole
- 1-1/2 pounds sweet cherries, pitted and halved, OR
- 1-1/2 pounds honeydew melon, cut into bite-sized pieces (squeeze fresh lime juice on melon)
- 1-1/2 cups halved seedless green grapes

Pulse mint and sugar in food processor or blender until finely chopped. Sprinkle mint sugar over fruit in a large bowl and toss gently to combine. Let stand at least five minutes before serving.

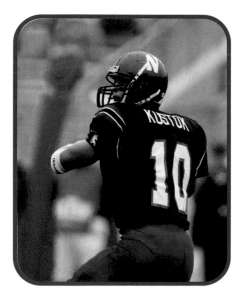

Peterman's Speedy Strawberry Salad

Britta Helwig & Eric Peterman, Britta 2010 Cross Country and Eric 2008, Football, Chicago Bears

INGREDIENTS

- 1/3 cup cider vinegar
- 3/4 cup sugar
- 2 tablespoons lemon juice
- 1 teaspoon salt
- 1 cup vegetable oil
- 1/2 small red onion, grated or chopped fine
- 1-1/2 tablespoons poppy seeds
- 1 teaspoon dry mustard
- 1/2 teaspoon paprika
- 1-1/2 pounds fresh spinach, torn
- 1 can (14 ounces) hearts of palm, drained and chopped
- 2 cups sliced strawberries
- 1 cup cashews

Combine cider vinegar, sugar, lemon juice and salt, heat until sugar is dissolved. Remove and let cool. Then whisk in the vegetable oil, red onion, poppy seeds, dry mustard and paprika.

Combine the spinach, hearts of palm, strawberries and cashews; serve with dressing.

greens

Springtime Spinach Salad

Nancy Tierney,
Director, Fitness/Wellness, NUDAR

YIELD: 10 SERVINGS

INGREDIENTS

1 pound fresh asparagus, trimmed and cut into 1-inch pieces
1 tablespoon olive oil
1 package (10 ounces) fresh spinach, torn
2 cups sliced fresh strawberries
1/2 cup chopped walnuts, toasted
1/3 cup vegetable oil
3 tablespoons raspberry vinegar
1 teaspoon sugar
1/2 teaspoon salt

Place asparagus in a foil-lined 10x15 inch baking pan; sprinkle with olive oil and toss to coat. Bake, uncovered, at 400 degrees for 15 minutes or until crisp-tender, turning occasionally. Cool.

In a large bowl, combine the spinach, strawberries, walnuts and asparagus. In a jar with a tight-fitting lid, combine the vegetable oil, vinegar, sugar and salt; shake well. Drizzle over salad and toss to coat. Serve immediately.

Spinach Salad

Mary Pat Watt,
Football Mom — Kevin #42

YIELD: 6 TO 8 SERVINGS

INGREDIENTS

1 pound fresh spinach
1 can (14 ounces) bean sprouts or use fresh
8 slices bacon, cooked and crumbled
4 large eggs, boiled and chopped
1 cup croutons
1/2 cup vegetable oil
1/4 cup ketchup
1/4 cup red wine vinegar
1/4 cup honey
1 medium onion, grated
1 tablespoon Worcestershire sauce
1/2 teaspoon salt

To make dressing, mix vegetable oil, ketchup, vinegar, honey, grated onion, Worcestershire sauce and salt. Mix well.

Toss spinach, sprouts, bacon and hard boiled eggs with dressing. Top with croutons.

Chopped Endive Salad

Emily Fletcher,
Head Coach, Women's Golf

Yield: 4 servings

INGREDIENTS

6 cups chopped endive lettuce
1/2 cup chopped walnuts
1/2 red onion, thinly sliced
1 pint fresh raspberries
4 ounces blue cheese, crumbled
    (feta or goat cheese if desired)
1 bottle raspberry balsamic vinaigrette

Divide the lettuce among four salad plates. Arrange the walnuts, onions and raspberries in the lettuce. Add the blue cheese. Pour raspberry dressing over the salad right before serving.

Serve with crostini or French bread.

Crunch Salad

Julie Kent

Yield: 6 to 8 servings

INGREDIENTS

GREENS:
1 head lettuce, chopped
1 can rice noodles
4 ounces sunflower seeds
4 green onions, sliced
1/2 cup butter
1/4 cup sugar
2 ounces almonds
DRESSING:
6 tablespoons rice vinegar
4 tablespoons brown sugar
1/2 cup oil

Mix lettuce, rice noodles, sunflower seeds and onions in a large bowl. Melt together butter and sugar; sauté almonds in mixture until slightly brown. Pour almond mixture onto aluminum foil; let harden. Break up and add to lettuce mixture.

DRESSING: Mix together vinegar, oil and brown sugar.

Bok Choy-Chinese Lettuce Salad

Courtney Combe, 2009

YIELD: 8 TO 10 SERVINGS

INGREDIENTS

SALAD:

4 to 5 small heads of baby bok choy, washed and cut into bite-sized pieces

1 small package of slivered almonds

2 packages of ramen noodles without the seasoning

1/2 cup sesame seeds

1/2 cup margarine

5 green onions, diced

1 small head Chinese lettuce or cabbage, washed and chopped into bite-sized pieces

1/2 to 1 cup cranberries, optional

DRESSING:

1/2 cup or more sugar, to taste

1/4 cup or more vinegar, to taste

1/8 to 1/4 cup oil

3 tablespoons soy sauce

Break ramen noodles into small pieces. In a pan, brown the silvered almonds, ramen noodles and sesame seeds in margarine. Let cool.

Mix the diced bok choy and Chinese lettuce together with green onions. Pour the room temperature ramen noodle mixture into the bok choy mixture. Add dressing before serving. Add cranberries, if desired.

Tastes great the second day.

Snow Pea and Endive Salad

Robert Prischman, 1971

YIELD: 8 SERVINGS

A tasty vegetable/salad combo with a very attractive presentation.

INGREDIENTS

1 pound snow peas

6 whole Belgian endive

3 tablespoons red wine or balsamic vinegar

4 teaspoons Dijon mustard

1/2 teaspoon salt

1/2 cup olive oil

3 tablespoons shopped shallots

6 ounces goat cheese

pepper, to taste

DRESSING: Whisk vinegar, mustard and salt in a small bowl. Whisk in olive oil then mix in shallots. Allow to stand at room temperature for 2 hours.

SALAD: Blanch snow peas for 30 seconds in a large pot of boiling water. Drain and run under cool water. Spread onto towel and pat dry. Chill.

Trim endive and peel off outer leaves. Arrange endive leaves onto the outer edges of a platter and spoon a dab of goat cheese onto each leaf. Chop any remaining endive into strips and toss with snow peas and dressing. Mound snow peas into the center of the platter.

Bok Choy Salad

Jeanne Lindwall, 1971

YIELD: 4 TO 6 SERVINGS

This is a tailgate favorite I adapted from a recipe of one of the growers at the Evanston Farmers Market.

INGREDIENTS

1 to 2 bunches baby bok choy

1 to 2 sliced green onions, including green tops

1/3 cup vegetable oil

2 tablespoons red wine vinegar

3 tablespoons sugar, divided

1 tablespoon soy sauce

3 tablespoons butter

1 package ramen noodles

3 ounces slivered almonds

1 to 2 tablespoons toasted sesame seeds, optional

Wash and chop bok choy into bite-sized pieces. Combine with green onions.

Make dressing by combining vegetable oil, vinegar, soy sauce and 2 tablespoons of sugar. Mix well and set aside.

Crush the noodles; discard the flavor packet. Melt butter with the remaining one tablespoon of sugar in a wide frying pan over medium heat. Add noodles and almonds to the pan. Stir fry 4 minutes or until lightly browned. Add sesame seeds and stir fry for another 30 seconds. Let mixture cool.

Combine bok choy, green onions and noodle topping. Add dressing and mix well.

Costello's Awesome Feta and Cashew Green Salad

Katie Costello, 2011, Feinberg School of Medicine Content Specialist

YIELD: 8 TO 10 SERVINGS

INGREDIENTS

1/2 cup sugar

1/4 cup red wine vinegar

3/4 cup vegetable oil

3 tablespoons soy sauce

1 teaspoon dry mustard

2 tablespoons sesame seeds

1 teaspoon minced onion

2 bags mixed lettuce, about 11 ounces

4 ounces CranRaisins

4 ounces feta cheese crumbles

1 cup cashews

3 apples, cored and chopped

To make dressing, mix sugar, mustard, soy sauce, onion, red wine vinegar, vegetable oil and poppy seeds.

In a large bowl, combine the lettuce, CranRaisins, feta cheese, cashews and cut apples. Toss with dressing.

Byron's Salad Surprise

Byron Wilson

YIELD: 4 TO 6 SERVINGS

Rediscover the crunch of iceberg lettuce.

INGREDIENTS

1 head iceberg lettuce, outer leaves
    removed
3 to 4 tomatoes, blanched, skin
    removed
2 stalks celery, chopped
3 green onions, chopped
1 green or red pepper, chopped
sea salt and pepper, to taste
sliced black olives, to taste
sliced green olives with pimento,
    to taste
prepared chunky blue cheese dressing,
    to taste

Also good with raspberry vinaigrette.

*Mixing dressings gives your salad some
great and unexpected combinations.*

Break head of lettuce into smaller pieces,
tearing not slicing.

Toss all ingredients, add blue cheese
chunky dressing, to taste.

Company Salad with Sweet & Sour Dressing

Debbie Hinchcliff Seward, 1974

YIELD: 4 SERVINGS

INGREDIENTS

1/2 cup sugar
1/4 cup red wine vinegar
1/4 cup canola oil
1/2 teaspoon salt
1/2 tablespoon dried minced onion
8 cups mixed lettuces with Romaine
1 to 2 chopped tomatoes (or 1 cup
    grape tomato halves)
4 slices crisp cooked bacon, crumbled
feta cheese pieces
1 red onion, halved, sliced thin

Boil the sugar and red wine vinegar in
microwave 1-1/2 to 2 minutes, until
sugar dissolves.

Add the canola oil, salt and minced
onion. Stir together, then cover with plastic wrap and refrigerate for several hours.

Wash mixed lettuces, add the tomatoes,
bacon pieces, feta cheese and red onion
slices.

Stir dressing before pouring on salad.
Dressing will have thickened in
refrigerator.

Caeser Salad

Zoe T Barron

YIELD: 8 TO 10 SERVINGS

INGREDIENTS

DRESSING:
1/4 cup fresh lemon juice
1 teaspoon dry mustard
1 teaspoon freshly ground black
pepper
1/2 teaspoon salt
1 clove garlic, minced
1 tablespoon Worcestershire sauce
1 can (2 ounces) anchovies,
drained and rinsed
1/2 cup canola oil

SALAD:
2 heads Romaine lettuce, washed,
dried, torn
1/2 cup grated Parmesan cheese
prepared croutons

*Variation: 1 head Romaine and 1 head
green leaf lettuce*

DRESSING: Mix all the dressing ingredients except oil in a food processor or blender. Add canola oil with motor running and mix well. Set aside or refrigerate up to 4 days.

SALAD: Place lettuce in a large bowl and toss with Parmesan cheese and croutons. Add dressing, toss again and serve immediately.

jellied

Pretzel Salad

Allison McCormick, 1999

YIELD: 12 SERVINGS

INGREDIENTS

CRUST:
1-3/4 cups roughly crushed pretzels
1/2 cup melted butter
3 tablespoons sugar

MIDDLE LAYER:
8 ounces Cool Whip
8 ounces cream cheese
3/4 cup sugar

TOPPING:
2 cups boiling water
1 package strawberry Jell-O (6 ounces)
20 ounces frozen strawberries
(sweetened)

CRUST: Preheat oven to 350 degrees. Mix crushed pretzels, melted butter and sugar together and pat into a 9x13 inch pan. Bake for 8 minutes (no longer or they'll burn). Cool completely.

MIDDLE LAYER: Combine Cool Whip, cream cheese and sugar; mix well and spread on cooled pretzel crust. Make sure there are no holes in the cheese or the Jell-O will find its way to the pretzels.

TOPPING: Dissolve Jell-O in boiling water. Stir in frozen strawberries and let sit for 10 minutes until thickened. Carefully spread on top of cream cheese (use a cup to ladle it on so it doesn't go through the white layer). Refrigerate several hours or overnight. Best if served within 24 hours.

Pineapple Lime Jell-O Salad

Cathy & Coach Mike Hankwitz,
Defensive Coordinator, Football

YIELD: 8 SERVINGS

This is a very old family recipe. One of our favorites.

INGREDIENTS

1 package (6 ounces) lime Jell-O
1 can (20 ounces) crushed pineapple, drained, save juice
3 large bananas, sliced
3 cups mini marshmallows
4 cups boiling water
1/2 cup sugar
3 tablespoons flour
2 eggs, beaten
2 tablespoons butter
1 cup heavy cream, whipped

Add water to reserved pineapple juice to make 1 cup; set aside for topping.

FIRST LAYER: Pour lime Jell-O in 9x12 inch glass pan and add hot water. Stir 2 minutes until completely dissolved.

Pour in pineapple, bananas and marshmallows. Refrigerate until firm (about 4 hours).

TOPPING: In a saucepan, add reserved juice/water mixture, sugar, flour, eggs and butter. Cook until thick. Cool then fold in whipped cream. Pour over set Jell-O, cut in squares and serve.

Cran-raspberry Jell-O

Bonita Paynter, 1972, 1974

YIELD: 8 TO 12 SERVINGS

Make the Jell-O in a crystal bowl for a holiday dinner.

INGREDIENTS

3 ounces Raspberry Jell-O
3 ounces Lemon Jell-O
2 cups boiling water
10 ounces frozen raspberries
14 ounces cranberry-orange relish
7 ounces lemon-lime carbonated beverage

Dissolve raspberry and lemon Jell-O in the two cups boiling water. Make sure the water is boiling or the Jell-O will not set. Stir in frozen raspberries, breaking up large pieces with a fork. Add the cranberry-orange relish. Pour into mold. Carefully pour in the lemon-lime carbonated beverage. Chill until very firm.

COACHES QUOTES

Bill Carmody, Men's Basketball:
"Make Shots!"

Strawberry Pretzel Jell-O

Linda Nagel,
Football Mom —
Brett #40 and Aaron #45

YIELD: 12 TO 14 SERVINGS

INGREDIENTS

PRETZEL LAYER:

2 cups crushed pretzels

1/4 cup sugar

3/4 pound butter

MIDDLE LAYER:

8 ounces softened cream cheese

1 cup sugar

2 cups Cool Whip

JELL-O LAYER:

6 ounces strawberry Jell-O

20 ounces frozen strawberries
(with juice), defrosted

2 cups boiling water

PRETZEL BASE: Mix crushed pretzels with sugar and melted butter. Press into a 9x13 inch baking pan. Bake at 350 degrees for 10 minutes. Cool completely.

JELL-O LAYER: Dissolve Jell-O in boiling water. Add strawberries and juice. Put in freezer until partially gelled (about 20 minutes).

MIDDLE LAYER: Beat cream cheese, sugar and cool whip until smooth.

ASSEMBLY: Spread cream cheese mixture over cooled crust. Spread partially gelled strawberry topping over the cheese layer. Chill.

Seafoam Salad

Sandra Schultz Miner, 1958

YIELD: 8 SERVINGS

INGREDIENTS

1 cup pear juice

8 ounces cream cheese

1 can (15 ounces) pears in syrup

1 cup whipping cream or 2 cups
Cool Whip

1 package (3 ounces) lime gelatin

Dissolve gelatin in hot pear juice. Cut cream cheese into small chunks and stir into the gelatin until softened. Put pears and cheese into blender and blend on medium speed until smooth. Put blender in refrigerator and chill until partially set. Whip cream. Blend in whipped cream and pour in mold. Chill until firm. Serve.

pasta

Oriental Noodle Salad

Joann Skiba

YIELD: 8 TO 10 SERVINGS

INGREDIENTS

2 tablespoons sesame seeds, toasted

8 ounces linguine, broken in half

3 green onions, sliced

3/4 cup carrots, julienned

1/2 cup soy sauce

7 tablespoons vegetable oil

2 tablespoons creamy peanut butter

1 tablespoon cider or white vinegar

1 tablespoon granulated sugar

1-1/2 teaspoons ground ginger

1/4 teaspoon crushed red pepper
flakes

Cook linguine according to package directions. Reserve 1 cup of hot liquid.

Spread sesame seeds on a baking sheet. Bake 6 to 8 minutes until they begin to change color.

Combine linquine, sesame seeds, green onion and carrots in a large mixing bowl.

In another bowl, combine soy sauce, vegetable oil, peanut butter, vinegar, sugar, ginger and pepper flakes, stirring until smooth. Add to noodle mixture and mix lightly. Add hot liquid to thin the dressing, as needed. Chill well before serving.

Italian Pasta Salad

Mary & Coach Gary Barnett, **Former NU Football Head Coach (Rose Bowl 1996); Mary is a founder of CatBackers**

YIELD: 4 TO 6 SERVINGS

INGREDIENTS

1 pound medium shell pasta, cooked
al dente

1 cup fresh spinach, cut in strips

1-1/2 cups halved cherry tomatoes

string cheese, strung, to taste

1 cup chopped fresh basil

black olives, sliced

Toss ingredients with bottled Italian oil and vinegar dressing. Add salt and pepper, to taste. Refrigerate. Best the following day.

Spaghetti Pasta Salad

Jayne Donohoe,
Lacrosse Mom — Casey 2009

Yield: 6 to 8 servings

Ingredients

1 pound spaghetti (or any pasta)
3 tomatoes
1 bunch spring onions
2 cucumbers, seeded
1 small can sliced black olives
1 large bottle Kraft Zesty Italian
 dressing
1 jar Salad Supreme seasoning
Parmesan cheese

Cook the pasta, drain and rinse with cold water. Chop all the vegetables. Combine the dressing and Salad Supreme in a separate bowl. Place the pasta in a large bowl. Pour 1/2 of the dressing mixture over pasta. Place all the chopped vegetables on top. Add remainder of dressing mixture over vegetables. Sprinkle top with Parmesan cheese. Cover with lid overnight. Mix together before serving.

Fresh Pasta Salad

Kathy Quinlan,
Director, Operations & Strategy, NAA

Yield: 10 servings

Ingredients

1 pound penne, cooked according to
 package instructions
4 tablespoons extra-virgin olive oil
1 tablespoon balsamic vinegar
2 cloves garlic, minced
pinch salt
pinch freshly ground pepper
8 Roma tomatoes, diced
1/2 cup whole, pitted black olives
1/2 cup feta cheese

While pasta cooks, whisk together oil, vinegar, garlic, salt and pepper in a large bowl. Add tomatoes and olives; toss well.

When pasta is cooked, drain and add to dressing. Let cool for 5 minutes, add the feta cheese and serve.

This can also be made ahead and can sit in the refrigerator for 1 to 2 hours.

Cardiac Cats

potato

Peruvian Style Potato Salad

Suzanne Calder

YIELD: 8 SERVINGS

INGREDIENTS

2 pounds waxy potatoes such as new or fingerling

2 hard-boiled eggs

1 medium white onion, chopped

sprig parsley

1/2 cup olive oil

3 tablespoons vinegar

2 cans (6 ounces each) shredded tuna packed in water

1 can (7 ounces) pitted black olives, chopped

Wash but do not peel potatoes. Place in saucepan of water and bring to boil for 5 minutes. Add salt and simmer until cooked. Strain and remove skin while still hot.

Shell hard-boiled eggs, add to potatoes and refrigerate for one hour. When cool, cut eggs and potatoes in large slices and place on plate. In a bowl, mix chopped onion and parsley. Add olive oil, vinegar and a pinch of salt. Mix well and then pour over potatoes and eggs. Add tuna and black olives and mix well. Serve chilled.

Grandma Eunice's German Potato Salad

Kerri Schmidt,
Football Mom — Jacob #39

YIELD: 10 TO 15 SERVINGS

INGREDIENTS

4 pounds red potatoes

2 teaspoons salt

4 hard-boiled eggs

1/2 pound bacon

1 medium onion, chopped

1-1/2 cups water

1/2 cup vinegar

1/2 cup sugar

4 teaspoons salt

1/2 teaspoon pepper

1 teaspoon dry mustard

1/2 teaspoon crushed parsley

1/2 teaspoon rosemary leaves, crumbled

1/2 teaspoon celery seed

1/2 cup water

3 tablespoons flour

Boil potatoes with salt. Cook until done. Remove skins and dice; add to baking dish. Brown bacon; remove to a bowl and sauté onion, add to bacon. Pour off the fat. Add water, vinegar and sugar to the bacon mixture. Add salt, pepper, dry mustard, parsley, rosemary leaves and celery seed.

Mix together water and flour in shaker; shake until blended. Add this to bacon mixture, slowly stirring until thickened. Add salt or sugar, to taste.

Pour over diced potatoes and eggs; stir. Bake at 350 degrees until heated through, about 30 minutes.

Ella's German Potato Salad

Marge & Tom Kennedy,
**Football Grandparents —
Kevin Watt #42**

YIELD: 6 TO 8 SERVINGS

*This potato salad was Kevin's grandparents'
contribution to Football Family Tailgates.
It was gobbled up.*

INGREDIENTS

2-1/2 pounds potatoes
6 slices bacon
1 medium onion
1 tablespoon flour
1/2 cup sugar
1/2 cup vinegar
1 cup water

Boil potatoes in their jackets in water
until tender when pierced with a fork.
Remove skin and slice. Fry bacon, reserving fat. Crumble bacon. Sauté onion in
reserved fat. Add flour and stir well.
Cook for 3 to 4 minutes. Add sugar,
vinegar and water. Boil for 5 minutes.
Pour dressing over potatoes and stir. Add
crumbled bacon. Serve warm.

Tangy Mustard Potato Salad

Megan Anderson, 1976

YIELD: 12 SERVINGS

INGREDIENTS

3 pounds red new potatoes
1/4 cup Dijon mustard
1/4 cup grainy mustard
1/4 cup olive oil
1 tablespoon balsamic or sherry
    vinegar
3 tablespoons chopped fresh basil
1/8 teaspoon salt
1/8 teaspoon black pepper

Bring a medium size pot of water to a
boil and add salt. Scrub potatoes and cut
them into bite-sized pieces. Cook in
water until tender but still firm, 12 to 15
minutes. Drain.

Mix together the mustards, oil, vinegar
and basil; toss with potatoes. Season with
salt and pepper. Serve warm or at room
temperature.

This can be refrigerated for up to a day.
Return to room temperature before
serving.

slaw

Red, White and Blue Salad

Clare Jorgensen,
Football Mom — Paul #78

YIELD: 8 TO 10 SERVINGS

INGREDIENTS

1 head cabbage, chopped (or 16 ounce bag coleslaw mix)
1 jar (16 ounces) Marzetti's slaw dressing
8 ounces crumbled blue cheese
1 cup bacon bits
1 pint grape tomatoes, halved

Put cabbage in large bowl. Mix in crumbled blue cheese, bacon bits and slaw dressing. Top with grape tomatoes.

Broccoli Slaw

Megan Anderson, 1976

YIELD: 6 TO 8 SERVINGS

INGREDIENTS

1 package broccoli slaw (about 12 ounces)
3 chopped celery ribs
4 to 5 chopped green onions
2 tablespoons soy sauce
1/4 cup white wine vinegar
1/3 cup sugar
3/4 cup slivered almonds
1/2 cup raw sunflower seeds
1 can (3 ounces) Chinese noodles

Combine soy sauce, vinegar and sugar; mix well. Add other ingredients to a bowl, top with sauce and toss.

Chinese Slaw Salad

Joann Skiba

YIELD: 8 TO 10 SERVINGS

INGREDIENTS

3 ounces ramen noodles, toasted and crumbled
1 package coleslaw mix or shredded cabbage (about 4 cups)
1/2 cup slivered almonds, toasted
4 green onions, sliced
2 tablespoons sesame seeds, toasted
1/3 cup vegetable oil
3 tablespoons red wine vinegar
2 tablespoons sugar
1 packet ramen noodle seasoning
salt
pepper

Toast almonds, noodles and sesame seeds at 350 degrees for 8 to 10 minutes. Combine noodles, coleslaw (or cabbage), green onions, almonds and sesame seeds in a salad bowl. In a mixing jar, combine vegetable oil, vinegar, sugar, seasoning packet, salt and pepper, to taste; shake well. Pour dressing over salad mixture.

vegetables

Corn and Blueberry Salad

Helene Bak Slowik, 1973

YIELD: 10 SERVINGS

Great for a bar-b-que. Overnight refrigeration is important to develop flavors.

INGREDIENTS

4-1/2 cups fresh corn from about 6 ears
1 cup fresh blueberries
1 cup peeled, quartered, sliced cucumber
1/4 cup finely chopped red onion
1/4 cup chopped fresh cilantro
1/2 teaspoon salt
1 large jalapeño, seeded, finely chopped
2 tablespoons freshly squeezed lime juice
1 tablespoon honey
1 teaspoon ground cumin
2 tablespoons olive oil

Cook corn until tender, cool and cut from cobs. Combine corn, blueberries, cucumber, onion, cilantro and jalapeño. In a jar, combine lime juice, oil, honey, cumin and salt. Close jar and shake well. Add to salad and toss well. Refrigerate overnight. ℕ

Broccoli-Tortellini Salad

Ann Marie Bernardi,
Field Hockey Mom

YIELD: 8 TO 10 SERVINGS

INGREDIENTS

1 package (about 9 ounces) cheese tortellini
1 cup fresh broccoli florets
1/3 to 1/2 cup finely chopped fresh parsley, to taste
1 tablespoon chopped pimento
1 jar (6 ounces) marinated artichoke hearts, chopped
2 green onions, chopped
1/4 teaspoon dried basil
1/2 teaspoon garlic powder
1/2 cup chopped black olives
6 to 8 cherry tomatoes, halved
Italian dressing, to taste
Romano grated cheese, to taste

Cook tortellini and cool.

Combine tortellini with broccoli florets, fresh parsley, pimento, artichoke hearts, green onion, basil, garlic powder, black olives and cherry tomatoes. Add Italian dressing, to taste. Sprinkle with Romano cheese, to taste. Cover and refrigerate 4 to 6 hours. Mix before serving. ℕ

Broccoli Primavera

Denise Munday,
Lacrosse Mom — Lindsey 2006

YIELD: 6 TO 8 SERVINGS

INGREDIENTS

1 bunch broccoli (2 pounds)

3 carrots, peeled and cut into
    1/4 inch dice

1 yellow summer squash halved
    lengthwise and cut into
    1/4 inch slices

1 red bell pepper, cored, seeded and
    cut into 1/4 inch dice

1 cup frozen peas, thawed

zest of 1 lemon

2 tablespoons chopped fresh Italian
    flat leaf parsley

3/4 cup mustard vinaigrette *(below)*

VINAIGRETTE:

1 tablespoon Dijon mustard

3 tablespoons white wine or tarragon
    vinegar

1 tablespoon fresh chopped tarragon
    or 1 teaspoon dried

1/2 teaspoon salt

1/2 teaspoon freshly ground black
    pepper

3/4 cup extra-virgin olive oil

Trim the stems off broccoli and reserve them for another use. Cut the top into small florets and set aside. Bring a large saucepan of water to a boil. Add carrots and cook for 1 minute. Remove with a slotted spoon, rinse under cold water and drain. Set aside. Add the squash to the same saucepan and cook for 30 seconds. Remove with slotted spoon, rinse under cold water and drain. Set aside. Add the broccoli to the same saucepan and cook for 30 seconds. Drain, rinse under cold

water and drain again. Pat all vegetables dry with paper towels. (Make sure to dry off veggies to avoid watering down the dressing.) Combine the broccoli, carrots, squash, bell pepper, peas, lemon zest and parsley in a salad bowl. Add the vinaigrette, toss gently and serve.

VINAIGRETTE: Place mustard in a small bowl. Add vinegar, tarragon, salt and pepper; whisk well. Slowly drizzle in the olive oil, whisking constantly until the dressing is creamy. Makes 1 cup. 🅽

Refrigerator Cucumbers

Ellen & Ivan Zilka, 1941

YIELD: 8 TO 10 SERVINGS

INGREDIENTS

8 cups cucumbers, peeled and thinly
    sliced

1 large onion, sliced

2 teaspoons salt

1 cup sugar

1 cup white vinegar

Mix cucumber, onion and salt; let stand 3 hours. Drain liquid; taste and if too salty, rinse slightly in cold water. Add sugar and vinegar. Refrigerate for 3 days to blend. Will keep several months. 🅽

Scandinavian Cucumber Salad

Carol Carlsen

YIELD: 6 TO 8 SERVINGS

INGREDIENTS

1 teaspoon sugar substitute

6 tablespoons hot water

2 tablespoons distilled white vinegar

2 tablespoons chopped fresh dill or
1 teaspoon dried

1 teaspoon black pepper

3 cups peeled and sliced cucumber

Dissolve sugar in hot water. Add vinegar, dill and pepper. Pour mixture over cucumbers and marinate 10 minutes. N

Cucumber Salad with a Kick!

Top Chef Stephanie Izard,
Top Chef (Season 4) and chef/owner of the Girl and the Goat Restaurant, Chicago

YIELD: 4 SERVINGS

INGREDIENTS

1-1/2 to 2 teaspoons wasabi powder

1 tablespoon mirin (sweet sake)

1 tablespoon rice wine vinegar

1 teaspoon sugar

1/2 cup canola oil

salt and pepper, to taste

2 large English cucumbers, julienned
or just thinly sliced

English cucumbers are not waxed, so do not need to be peeled. You may want to seed them. In the store, English cucumbers are usually wrapped in plastic. If using regular cucumbers, peel and remove seeds.

Combine wasabi and mirin in bowl and mix to a paste. Whisk in vinegar and sugar. Whisk in oil and season with salt and pepper. Let stand to allow flavors to blend. Mix dressing with cucumbers about 10 minutes before serving. N

Creamy Cucumber Salad

Ellen Braun, 1965

YIELD: 6 SERVINGS

INGREDIENTS

1/2 cup dairy sour cream

1 tablespoon sugar

2 tablespoons snipped fresh parsley

2 tablespoons cider vinegar

1 tablespoon finely chopped onion

1/2 teaspoon dried tarragon

1 teaspoon dried dill weed

1 teaspoon salt

3 small cucumbers, pared and
thinly sliced

Place cucumbers in bowl and sprinkle with salt; allow to sit for an hour. Rinse and drain cucumbers, squeezing out excess water.

Stir together the sour cream, sugar, parsley, tarragon, vinegar, onions and dillweed. Gently fold in cucumbers. Cover and chill for two hours.

COACHES QUOTES

Arvid Swan, Men's Tennis:

"Care more about the team than yourself."

Panzanella with Marinated Mozzarella

Clare Jorgensen,
Football Mom — Paul #78

YIELD: 15 TO 20 SERVINGS

INGREDIENTS

1 large loaf crusty Italian bread,
cut into 3/4 to 1 inch cubes

2 cucumbers, quartered lengthwise,
peeled, seeded and diced

1 to 2 pounds marinated mozzarella,
drained, reserving marinade

12 medium tomatoes, diced
or 1 to 2 pints cherry tomatoes,
halved

1/4 medium red onion, thinly sliced

1 cup coarsely chopped basil,
about 1 bunch

3/4 cup reserved mozzarella marinade

1/2 cup red wine vinegar

kosher salt and pepper, to taste

Cut bread into cubes and let sit out overnight to dry. Or, bake in a very low oven (200 degrees), but take care not to dry to the point where it looks/feels like croutons. Combine with mozzarella, cucumbers, onions, tomatoes and basil; set aside. Mix oil, vinegar, salt and pepper. Test for flavor and add to salad. Mix well and serve.

Corn Salad

Mary Ellen Baker,
Football Mom — Hayden #68

Yield: 8 to 10 servings

Ingredients

4 cups cooked corn kernels
1/2 cup diced red bell pepper
1/2 cup diced red onion
2 teaspoons minced jalapeño pepper
with seeds
6 tablespoons vegetable oil
2 tablespoons Dijon mustard
2 tablespoons white wine vinegar
2 tablespoons sugar
2 tablespoons freshly chopped dill
1/2 teaspoon kosher salt

Combine the corn, bell pepper, onion and jalapeño pepper in a large bowl. In a saucepan, whisk together the oil, mustard, vinegar, sugar, dill and salt. Bring to a simmer. Pour the warm vinaigrette over the corn mixture and mix well. Let stand at room temperature until ready to serve.

Prepare

Tomato Bread Salad

Julie Kent

Yield: 8 servings

Ingredients

4 medium Roma tomatoes,
cut into 1-inch chunks
1/2 medium red onion, cut into
wedges
1 medium yellow pepper,
cut into 1-inch pieces
1/4 cup olive oil
1/4 cup red wine vinegar
1 tablespoon Dijon-style mustard
1/2 teaspoon Italian seasoning,
crushed
1/2 teaspoon salt
1/4 teaspoon pepper
8 ounces loaf ciabatta or focaccia
bread, cut into 1-inch pieces
1 tablespoon olive oil
1 cup small fresh basil leaves

In large bowl, combine the tomatoes, onion and pepper. In screw-top jar combine olive oil, red wine vinegar, mustard, Italian seasoning, salt and pepper; cover and shake well to blend. Add to tomato mixture and stir to coat. Cover and refrigerate overnight (up to 24 hours).

Preheat oven to 400 degrees. In a shallow pan, toss bread cubes with olive oil to coat. Bake about 10 minutes or until toasted, stirring once. Remove and cool. Add bread cubes and basil to tomato mixture, toss to coat.

Game Day

Main Dishes

SOCCER

FACTS

Men's:

Head Coach Tim Lenahan (2001–present)
– *3rd head coach*

- They have been a varsity sport since 1980 and have been a Big Ten sponsored sport since 1991.

- There were 108 Academic All-Big Ten honorees in the years 1986–2010.

- Coach Bob Krohn was the first coach and Coach Michael Kunert coached the team from 1983 to 2000.

Women's:

Head Coach Stephanie Foster (2006–present)
– *3rd head coach*

- They have been a varsity sport since 1994.

- Coached by Marcia McDermott (1994–2000) and Jenny Haigh (2001–2005)

- There were 153 Academic All-Big Ten honorees in the years 1994–2010.

baked

Breaded Chicken Roll ups

Denise Baker, 2011,
Softball

Yield: 4 servings

Ingredients

4 boneless chicken breast halves

Toothpicks

3/4 cups Italian seasoned bread crumbs

1 pound asparagus

3 tablespoons olive oil

1 teaspoon garlic powder

salt and pepper, to taste

1 pound sliced Swiss cheese

Preheat oven to 350 degrees. Wash and pat dry chicken breasts. Pound between sheets of plastic or parchment paper to 1/4 inch. Wash and break off ends of asparagus. Use only tops of asparagus.

On one chicken breast, place a few asparagus pieces and one piece of Swiss cheese. Roll up and secure with a toothpick. Repeat for all chicken pieces.

Mix bread crumbs with garlic, salt and pepper in one bowl, and pour olive oil in another bowl. Dip chicken breasts in olive oil, coat with a basting brush, then coat in the bread crumbs. Repeat with all chicken breasts.

Place all in a baking dish, and bake 15 to 20 minutes or until chicken is done.

Beer Chicken

Mike Deneen, 1990
Two great tastes that taste great together!

Ingredients

2 pounds chicken thighs
    or pieces of choice

1/4 pound bacon, cut to pieces

2 heads garlic, broken into cloves
    and peeled

1 sprig rosemary

6 bay leaves

1 tablespoon juniper berries

2 cups beer, preferably double malt

salt and pepper, to taste

Preheat oven to 475 degrees.

Put chicken in a single layer in an oven safe dish. Season with salt and pepper. Place garlic cloves, herbs and bacon pieces evenly over the chicken. Pour in beer. Bake 15 minutes. Turn chicken.

Bake another 20 minutes or until chicken is cooked through.

If sauce is too thin at this point, remove chicken to serving bowl, and boil the sauce on top of the stove until you get the desired consistency. Pour sauce over chicken and serve, preferably with mashed potatoes or other starch.

Chicken Fajita Pizza

Rev. Leigh VanderMeer,
Campus Minister,
University Christian Ministry

YIELD: 6 TO 8 SERVINGS

INGREDIENTS

2 cups cooked chicken breasts cut into 2x1/2 inch strips

1+ cup onion, thinly sliced

1+ cup mixed green and red bell pepper

1 package (10 ounces) refrigerated pizza crust

1+ cup mild salsa or picante sauce, preferably thick and chunky

2 cups (8 ounces) shredded Mexican blend cheese (or cheese mix, to taste)

2+ tablespoons oil

1 package fajita seasoning mix (1.12 ounce)

TIP: use package of precooked pulled chicken from your grocery store.

Heat stir-fry skillet over medium-high heat until hot. Mix oil and fajita seasoning together in skillet. Add onions and bell peppers; stir-fry 1 minute or until the vegetables are crisp-tender. Add cooked chicken. Mix thoroughly.

Heat oven to 425 degrees. Spray 15 inch baking stone with vegetable oil spray. Unroll dough and place on stone. Starting at center, roll dough into 14 inch circle using a rolling pin. Partially bake dough 8-10 minutes. Spoon chicken mixture over crust. Spoon salsa over the whole pizza; sprinkle with cheese. Bake 12-18 minutes or until crust is golden brown.

Mary's Cheesey Chicken

Jan Forsman, 1981

INGREDIENTS

6 boneless chicken breasts

Accent seasoning

cracked black pepper

1 can (10-3/4 ounces) condensed cream of chicken soup

1/2 cup low-fat mayonnaise

1 tablespoon lemon juice

1 cup grated sharp cheddar cheese

Preheat oven to 350 degrees. Sprinkle chicken breasts with Accent and cracked black pepper (to taste). Sauté chicken in oil for 4 minutes each side. Place chicken in casserole dish. Mix soup, mayonnaise and lemon juice; pour over chicken. Sprinkle with cheddar cheese. Cover with foil and bake for 30 minutes. Remove foil and bake another 10 minutes.

Aunt Cathy's Chicken Balls

Kyle Schack,
Assistant Coach, Swimming and Diving

YIELD: 6 TO 8 SERVINGS

This is an Armenian dish.

INGREDIENTS

1 tablespoon butter melted plus 1/4 cup, divided

1 small onion, chopped

2 stalks celery, chopped

2 cups shredded, cooked chicken, poached or rotisserie

24 ounces cream cheese, softened

1/4 teaspoon salt

1/4 teaspoon pepper

1/4 teaspoon paprika

Italian bread crumbs

2 packages (8 ounces each) crescent roll dough

GRAVY:

1 can (10-3/4 ounces) condensed cream of chicken soup

1 jar (12 ounces) chicken gravy

Preheat oven to 375 degrees. Melt 1 tablespoon butter and sauté onions and celery until softened. Add chicken, cream cheese and spices to onion mixture. Open one package of crescent rolls, seal seam perforations and make 4 squares. Cut each square of dough in half so 8 pieces result. Repeat with second package. Divide chicken mixture evenly into each of the 16 pieces and form a ball around the chicken. Dip in 1/4 cup melted butter and roll in bread crumbs. Place on sheet pan, seam side down. Bake for 20 to 25 minutes, until golden brown and heated through. Serve with gravy.

GRAVY: Combine soup and prepared gravy, heat and serve over chicken balls.

Unbaked chicken balls may be frozen, then baked directly from the freezer.

Jonny's Chicken

Kathy Newcomb

YIELD: 6 SERVINGS

INGREDIENTS

6 boneless, skinless chicken breast halves

4 cans (14.5 ounces each) diced tomatoes

4 cups shredded mozzarella cheese

1 cup shredded Parmesan cheese

1 pound angel hair pasta

Place chicken breasts in a baking dish. Cover with diced tomatoes and cheeses. Bake uncovered at 350 degrees for 1 hour, or until cheese is just starting to brown.

While chicken is cooking, cook pasta as directed on package. Serve chicken on pasta.

Chicken Breasts Poached in Herb Butter

Executive Chef Jim Freeland,
**Lou Malnati's, Evanston and over
30 locations throughout Chicagoland**

YIELD: 8 SERVINGS

INGREDIENTS

8 skinless, boneless chicken breasts

6 ounces butter, melted

1 tablespoon minced shallots

pinch tarragon

pinch salt

pinch pepper

1 teaspoon paprika

1 tablespoon (4 ounces) chopped
    fresh parsley

1 lemon, juiced

1 ounce white wine

1 ounce sherry

Preheat oven to 350 degrees. Pound out breasts for even cooking. Heat butter in a small pan. Add all ingredients (except chicken) and let simmer until flavors have blended. (Butter can be saved for later use.) Place breasts in greased baking dish and pour butter over them. Cover with greased baking paper and bake with lid for 12 to 15 minutes.

Chicken Roulades Stuffed with Goat Cheese and Sundried Tomatoes

Mary Pat Watt,
Football Mom — Kevin #42

YIELD: 4 TO 6 SERVINGS

INGREDIENTS

4 boneless, skinless chicken breast
    halves (2 pounds)

salt & pepper, to taste

4 ounces goat cheese, crumbled

8 oil packed sun-dried tomato halves,
    drained

8 fresh basil leaves

2 large eggs, beaten

1 cup dry breadcrumbs

1/4 finely chopped almonds or
    walnuts, optional

1/4 cup finely chopped fresh herbs, to
    taste, optional

1 lemon, cut into wedges

olive oil for drizzling

Try polenta with herbs instead of bread crumbs.

Preheat oven to 425 degrees. Julienne tomatoes if desired. Cut each breast in half lengthwise so you can have eight thin cutlets. Cover with plastic wrap and pound to flatten. Season chicken with salt and pepper and top each with goat cheese, tomatoes and basil. Roll up each piece starting with the narrow end, keeping filling centered. Secure with toothpicks. Dip each roulade in egg, then roll in breadcrumbs to coat. Transfer to baking sheet. Roast until chicken is firm to the touch (165 degrees) 25 to 30 minutes. Set broiler on high. Drizzel with olive oil. Broil until chicken browns (1 minute). Let roulades rest for few minutes, remove toothpicks. To serve, slice roulades in half on the diagonal.

Swiss Chicken

Rev. Leigh VanderMeer,
Campus Minister,
University Christian Ministry

YIELD: 6 SERVINGS

INGREDIENTS

1/2 cup white wine or chicken broth

1 cup crushed herb stuffing mix or croutons

6 boneless skinless chicken breast halves (1-1/2 pounds)

6 slices Swiss cheese

1 can (10.75 ounces) condensed cream of chicken or cream of mushroom soup

1 cup sliced mushrooms, optional

Preheat oven to 350 degrees. Place chicken in a greased 9x13 inch baking dish with a slice of cheese on each breast. Add mushrooms, if using. In a bowl, combine the soup and wine or broth; pour over chicken. Sprinkle with stuffing. Bake, uncovered, for 35 to 40 minutes or until chicken juices run clear.

Barron Meat Loaf

Daniel R Barron, KSM

YIELD: 8 SERVINGS

INGREDIENTS

LOAF:

1-1/2 pounds ground beef

1/2 cup bread crumbs

1 onion, finely chopped

1 egg

1-1/2 teaspoons salt

1/4 teaspoon pepper

2 cans (8 ounces each) tomato sauce, divided

SAUCE:

1/2 cup water

3 tablespoons white vinegar

3 tablespoons light brown sugar

2 tablespoons prepared mustard

2 teaspoons Worcestershire sauce

Preheat oven to 350 degrees.

LOAF: Mix beef, bread crumbs, onion, egg, salt, pepper and 1/2 can tomato sauce. Use your hands to mix and form into a loaf and place in a 9x13 inch baking pan.

SAUCE: Combine all other ingredients in a small bowl and pour over the meatloaf. Bake for 40 to 50 minutes, basting at least twice while cooking. Let loaf set 10 minutes then slice and serve.

Spiral Meatloaf

Connie & Rob Walker,
Coach Randy Walker's sister-in-law and brother

INGREDIENTS

1 pound extra lean ground beef

1-1/2 cups fresh bread crumbs

2 large egg whites

1/3 cup chopped onions

1/3 cup chopped celery

1/3 cup chopped parsley

1/2 teaspoon salt

1/4 teaspoon freshly ground pepper

1 can (5-1/2 ounces) V8 juice

1 tablespoon Worcestershire sauce

1 tablespoon Dijon style mustard

1 package (10 ounces) frozen chopped spinach, thawed, squeezed dry

1 teaspoon salt free herb seasoning

4 ounces very thinly sliced mozzarella cheese

4 red bell peppers, roasted, cored, seeded, peeled

1 teaspoon salt-free garlic-herb seasoning

I use canned roasted peppers.

Preheat oven to 350 degrees. In a large bowl combine beef, bread crumbs, egg whites, onion, celery, parsley, salt, pepper, juice, Worcestershire sauce and mustard. On sheet of foil or waxed paper, shape meat into 14x10 inch rectangle. Cover surface with thawed spinach. Sprinkle with herb seasoning. Layer mozzarella slices over top. Cover with roasted peppers. Sprinkle with garlic-herb seasoning. Start at a short side, roll up meatloaf to enclose filling, using foil or paper as a guide. Place loaf, seam side down, in rectangular nonstick baking pan. Tent loosely with aluminum foil. Bake meatloaf for 35 minutes. Remove foil. Bake, uncovered, 20 minutes more or until juices run clear. Let meatloaf stand 5 to 10 minutes before slicing.

Marjorie's Meat Loaf

Marjorie Rallins

YIELD: 6 TO 8 SERVINGS

INGREDIENTS

1 tablespoon good olive oil

1 cup chopped yellow onion

1 whole green pepper, chopped

1 teaspoon chopped fresh thyme

2 teaspoons kosher salt

1 teaspoon freshly ground black pepper

3 tablespoons Worcestershire sauce

1/3 cup chicken stock or broth

1 tablespoon tomato paste

2 pounds ground chicken

1/2 cup plain dry bread crumbs

2 large eggs, beaten

zest of 1 lemon

1/2 cup Parmesan cheese

1/2 cup ketchup

Preheat oven to 325 degrees.

Heat the olive oil in a medium sauté pan. Add the onions, green peppers, thyme, salt and pepper and cook over medium-low heat, stirring occasionally, for 8 to 10 minutes, until the onions are translucent but not brown. Off the heat add the Worcestershire, chicken stock and tomato paste. Allow to cool slightly.

In a large bowl, combine the ground chicken, onion mixture, bread crumbs, cheese, lemon zest and eggs and mix lightly with a fork. Don't mash or the

meat loaf will be dense. Shape the mixture into a rectangular loaf on a sheet pan covered with parchment paper. Spread the ketchup evenly on top. Bake for 1 to 1-1/4 hours until the internal temperature is 160 degrees and the meat loaf is cooked through. (A pan of hot water in the oven, under the meat loaf, will keep the top from cracking.) Serve hot.

Panko Baked Fish

Zoe T Barron

YIELD: 6 SERVINGS

INGREDIENTS

12 pollack fillets, thawed if frozen

1/2 cup mayonnaise

1/2 cup Grey Poupon mustard

pinch cayenne pepper

2 to 3 cups panko crumbs

Preheat oven to 350 degrees. Pat the fillets dry with paper towels. Mix the mayonnaise, mustard and cayenne. Spread this mixture on both sides of the fillets then coat with the panko crumbs.

Spray a rimmed baking dish with non-stick spray and arrange fillets in a single layer. Bake for 30 to 35 minutes.

Cod with Tomatoes and Thyme

Suzanne Calder

YIELD: 4 SERVINGS

INGREDIENTS

4 cod fillets, 3/4 inch thick

salt & fresh white pepper, to taste

2 tablespoons olive oil

1 fresh thyme sprig

1 cup canned plum tomatoes, chopped and well drained

Heat oven to 425 degrees. Season fillets with salt and pepper. Drizzle with 1 tablespoon olive oil. Place flat side down in baking pan. Pick up thyme sprig and run thumb and finger over stem to release leaves; chop leaves (about 3/4 tablespoon). Scatter over top of fish. Spread a little chopped tomatoes over the fish and distribute rest in pan. Season tomatoes with a little salt and pepper. Drizzle remaining 1 tablespoon of oil over all.

Bake until cooked through and very juicy, 12 to 16 minutes. Remove fish to warm platter. Heat juices in pan, adding any from platter. Boil 3 to 5 minutes. Spoon over fish.

COACHES QUOTES

Randy Walker,
Former Football Head Coach:

"Nothing great was ever accomplished without enthusiasm."

Oven Baked Sea Bass

Jeannette Lindenma

YIELD: 2 SERVINGS

INGREDIENTS

3 cloves garlic, minced

1 tablespoon extra virgin olive oil

1 teaspoon kosher salt

2 teaspoons coarsely ground
black pepper

12 ounces sea bass fillets,
cleaned & scaled

1/3 cup white wine

1/2 cup loosely packed fresh parsley
leaves

lemon wedges for garnish

Preheat oven to 450 degrees. In a small bowl, mix garlic, oil, salt and pepper. Place fish in a shallow 1 quart glass or ceramic baking dish. Rub fish with oil mixture. Pour wine over fish. Bake fish, uncovered, 15 minutes; sprinkle with parsley and bake 3 minutes longer or until opaque throughout and thickest part of fish flakes easily when tested with a fork. Drizzle any pan juices over fish and serve with lemon wedges.

Compete

Noodle Kugel

Phyllis Sex

YIELD: 8 TO 10 SERVINGS

INGREDIENTS

1 pound no-yolk wide noodles

1/4 pound margarine or butter,
melted

1 cup cinnamon sugar

4 eggs, beaten

light brown sugar

pecans or raisins, dried cranberries,
etc.

1 pound petite peas, thawed

Preheat oven to 350 degrees.

Cook the noodles in salted water per package instructions. Rinse in cold water and thoroughly drain.

Thoroughly spray a 10 cup ring mold with non-stick spray and then spray with butter. At the bottom of the mold where there is a small indentation, fill with light brown sugar. You may put pecans (upside down) on top of the sugar — or use raisins, dried cranberries, etc., for color and added flavor. Put the cooked noodles back in the pan you cooked them, stir in the melted margarine, add the beaten eggs and then the cinnamon sugar. Mix thoroughly, then put in the ring mold. This can be made the day before and kept refrigerated. Bake uncovered for 1 hour. Unmold on a plate and serve with a petite peas in the center of the ring — or use any vegetable you like.

Grandma Nev's Lemon Barbeque Ribs

Liz Luxem

YIELD: 3 TO 4 SERVINGS

INGREDIENTS

3 pounds baby back ribs

2/3 cup lemon juice

1 cup orange juice

2/3 cup ketchup

2 teaspoons salt

4 teaspoons paprika

1/2 cup brown sugar or honey

1/4 teaspoon Tabasco

1/4 cup Worcestershire Sauce

2 teaspoons prepared horseradish

2 lemons, thinly sliced

2 oranges, thinly sliced

2 sweet onions, thinly sliced

Preheat oven to 400 degrees. Cut ribs into serving pieces and place bone side down in baking pan. Bake 30 minutes.

Mix together lemon juice, orange juice, ketchup, salt, paprika, Tabasco, Worcestershire sauce, horseradish and brown sugar.

Lower oven temperature to 325 degrees. Drain fat from ribs. Place bone side up in baking pan. Layer lemon, orange and onion slices on top of the ribs. Pour sauce over ribs. Cover with aluminum foil and bake for 2 hours, basting often. Uncover and continue baking for 20 minutes.

Turkey Meatloaf

Damien Anderson, 2002, Football

YIELD: 3 TO 4 SERVINGS

This is healthier than traditional meatloaf. Oats are a nice replacement for bread-crumbs.

INGREDIENTS

1 pound ground turkey

1/4 cup barbecue sauce

2 egg whites, lightly beaten

1/2 green bell pepper

1 small onion, chopped

3 tablespoons chopped fresh parsley

1/2 cup old fashioned quick oats

1/2 teaspoon pepper

Preheat oven to 350 degrees. Combine ingredients and mix thoroughly. Place mixture into lightly buttered loaf pan. Bake uncovered approximately 1 hour.

casserole

Chicken Artichoke Casserole

Carole Tye

INGREDIENTS

3 pounds chicken pieces
   (thighs or breasts)
1-1/2 teaspoons seasoned salt
1/4 teaspoon pepper
6 tablespoons butter, divided
8 ounces sliced mushrooms
1 can (12 ounces) artichoke heart
   quarters
2 tablespoons flour
2/3 cup chicken broth or bouillon

Preheat oven to 375 degrees. Salt and pepper chicken pieces. Brown in 4 tablespoons of butter. Transfer into a large casserole. Sauté mushrooms in 2 tablespoons of butter using the same pan; sprinkle flour over them and stir in the broth. Cook for 5 minutes. Arrange artichoke hearts in the casserole dish over the chicken. Pour the mushroom sauce over the chicken and mushrooms, cover and bake for 40 minutes.

Serve with rice. This can be fixed the day before and refrigerated.

Chicken and Broccoli

Mary Ann Graham

YIELD: 8 SERVINGS

INGREDIENTS

2 whole chicken breasts
6 chicken thighs
1-1/2 packages (10 ounces each)
   frozen chopped broccoli
2 cans (10-3/4 ounces each)
   condensed cream of
   chicken soup
1 cup mayonnaise
1 tablespoon lemon juice
3/4 teaspoon curry powder dissolved
   in a little hot water
3/4 cups crushed Pepperidge Farm
   herb dressing
1/4 cup butter

Cook broccoli. Boil chicken and cut into bite-sized pieces. Place in a shallow 9x13 inch greased baking dish. Top with broccoli. Mix soup, mayonnaise, lemon juice and curry powder and pour over broccoli. Sprinkle stuffing on top and pour melted butter over all. Bake at 350 degrees for 1/2 hour. To prepare ahead, do not add stuffing and refrigerate. Next day, add the stuffing and melted butter.

Dave Henri's Chicken Divan *a la* Alpha Kappa Alpha

Adrianne Hayward, 1971

YIELD: 10 SERVINGS

Great with corn muffins and wine!

INGREDIENTS

- 1 package (20 ounces) of frozen broccoli stalks and pieces (defrosted, uncooked)
- 10 skinless, boneless chicken breast halves, cooked
- 2 cans (10-3/4 ounces each) condensed cream of chicken soup (undiluted)
- 1 cup mayonnaise
- 1 tablespoon lemon juice
- 1 package dry onion soup mix
- 1/2 cup shredded sharp cheddar cheese
- 1 tablespoon butter, melted
- 1/2 cup bread crumbs

Preheat oven to 350 degrees.

Coat a large casserole dish with cooking oil spray. Evenly distribute broccoli across bottom of casserole dish. Layer cooked chicken over broccoli.

In a separate bowl, combine canned soup, mayonnaise, lemon juice and dry soup, blending well. Pour blended mixture over chicken. Top with an evenly sprinkled layer of shredded cheese.

Melt butter in skillet and brown bread crumbs. Sprinkle browned bread crumbs over cheese. Bake for 30 to 35 minutes until cheese is bubbly.

Baked Chicken and Broccoli

Denise & Coach Jerry Brown, Assistant Head Coach, Football

YIELD: 4 SERVINGS

INGREDIENTS

- 4 boneless, skinless chicken breast halves
- 1 pound broccoli spears, trimmed
- 1 can (10-3/4 ounces) condensed cream of mushroom soup
- 1/2 cup milk
- 1 tablespoon Worcestershire sauce

Serve with long grain/wild rice mixture and dinner rolls.

Preheat oven to 350 degrees. Place seasoned chicken breasts in baking dish and bake for 45 minutes.

Remove chicken from oven, gather chicken into center of baking dish, surround chicken with broccoli spears.

Mix soup, milk and Worcestershire and pour mixture over broccoli. Return dish to oven and bake for an additional 30 minutes.

COACHES QUOTES

Tracey Fuchs,
Women's Field Hockey:

"Respect all, fear none."

Green Chili Enchiladas

Patsy Emery,
Director, FA Operations — retired

YIELD: 6 TO 8 SERVINGS

INGREDIENTS

1 pound Monterey Jack or Pepper Jack
cheese, shredded

1 bunch green onions (about 12),
chopped

1 can (4 ounces) diced green chilies or
1 diced jalapeño

1 can (10-3/4 ounces) condensed
cream of chicken soup

1 cup Daisy's light sour cream

2 cups cooked, diced chicken

hard or soft tortillas

toppings such as lettuce, tomato, salsa,
avocado, shredded cheddar and
sour cream

Preheat oven to 325 degrees. Mix shredded cheese, green chilies (or jalapeños) and green onions. In a separate bowl, mix the soup, sour cream and chicken.

Spray a 9x12 inch glass casserole dish with non-stick spray. Place chicken mixture in casserole dish; cover with cheese mixture. Bake for approximately 30 minutes or until hot and bubbly.

Serve with hard or soft shell tortillas.

Chicken Enchiladas — 1

Claudia Crawford,
Men's Basketball Mom — Drew #1

YIELD: 6 SERVINGS

INGREDIENTS

1 medium onion, diced

2 tablespoons cooking oil

2 teaspoons chili powder

1 can (15 ounces) tomato sauce

1 can (15 ounces) diced tomatoes

3 cups chopped cooked chicken
(about 5 boneless breasts)

1 can (4 ounces) chopped green chilies

8 ounces sour cream

8 flour tortillas (8 inches)

1 cup shredded cheddar or other
cheese

Preheat oven to 350 degrees. Cook onion in oil until tender, stir in chili powder and cook 1 minute. Add tomatoes and tomato sauce, heat to boiling, then reduce to simmer for 10 minutes or until sauce thickens slightly.

In a large bowl, mix chicken, green chilies, sour cream and 1/2 teaspoon salt. Place about 1/3 cup chicken mixture along one edge of each tortilla, roll jelly-roll fashion.

Spoon half of tomato sauce into 9x13 inch baking dish, sprinkle half of the cheese. Place enchiladas, seam side down, on top of cheese. Spoon remaining sauce over enchiladas and top with remaining cheese. Bake, uncovered, 30 minutes or until hot and bubbly.

Chicken Enchiladas — 2

Debbie Hinchcliff Seward, 1974

YIELD: 4 TO 6 SERVINGS

INGREDIENTS

SAUCE:

2 tablespoons corn or canola oil

1 can (8 ounces) tomato sauce

1 teaspoon salt

1/4 teaspoon garlic powder

2 tablespoons flour

2 tablespoons chili powder

1 teaspoon ground cumin

1 can (14 ounces) chicken broth

ENCHILADAS:

3 cups enchilada sauce

2 cups cooked chicken breast, shredded

1/2 cup thinly sliced green onions

3/4 cup cheddar cheese, shredded

3/4 cup Monterey Jack cheese, shredded

1/4 cup sour cream

1 can (4 ounces) diced green chilies

corn oil (or canola) to fry tortillas

1/4 cup chopped fresh cilantro

12 corn tortillas (6 inch)

salt and pepper, to taste

SAUCE: Heat oil in large saucepan. Stir in flour and chili powder. Cook for 1 minute. Add remaining sauce ingredients; bring to boil and simmer for 10 minutes.

ENCHILADAS: Heat oven to 350 degrees. In a medium bowl, mix chicken, green onions, 1/2 cup cheddar, 1/2 cup Monterey Jack, sour cream, chilies & cilantro. Stir in 1/2 cup sauce. Season with salt and pepper. Set aside. Heat 1/2 inch corn oil in small fry pan. Fry tortillas, one at a time, until soft (10 seconds per side). Drain on paper towels. Spray 9x13 inch baking dish with cooking spray. Spread small amount of sauce in bottom of dish. Spread 2 heaping tablespoons of chicken mixture in each tortilla. Roll up tortilla and place seam side down, side by side in dish. Pour remaining sauce over tortillas and top with remaining cheeses. Bake until bubbling, 15 to 20 minutes. Optional: Garnish with extra sour cream, sliced green onions and chopped cilantro.

Mexican Casserole

Tammy Walker,
Athletic Department; Widow of NU Football Coach Randy Walker

YIELD: 10 TO 12 SERVINGS

My late husband, Coach Randy Walker (Head football coach 1999-2005), loved this for dinner with a crisp green salad.

INGREDIENTS

1 large jar (about 15 ounces) salsa (medium or hot)

1 package (10 to 12) flour tortillas (small size)

1 large can (7-1/2 ounces) boned chicken white meat

1 can (10-3/4 ounces) condensed cream of chicken soup

1 can (4 ounces) green chilies, chopped

1 can (4 ounces) stems and pieces mushrooms

2 cups shredded sharp cheddar cheese

Preheat oven to 350 degrees. Layer one-half of each of the ingredients, in order listed above, in a 9x13 inch pan. Repeat the layering with the other half of each of the ingredients. Bake until brown, about 45 minutes.

Chicken and Spinach Lasagna

Catie Kannenberg, 2004,
Women's Cross Country

YIELD: 6 TO 8 SERVINGS

INGREDIENTS

1/2 cup butter

1/2 cup flour

1/2 teaspoon salt

1/2 teaspoon dried basil

3 cups chicken broth

2-1/2 cups cooked cubed chicken breast meat

1 pint cottage cheese

1 large egg, slightly beaten

8 ounces lasagna noodles, cooked, or no-boil kind

10 ounces chopped frozen spinach, thawed, drained, or use fresh

4 ounces grated mozzarella cheese

1/2 cup grated Parmesan cheese

Preheat oven to 375 degrees. Melt butter in medium saucepan. Blend flour, salt and basil. Stir in chicken broth with a whisk and cook, stirring constantly. Mixture will thicken and come to a boil. Remove from heat and add the chicken. Combine cottage cheese with egg and mix well. In a greased 9x13 inch dish, place 1/3 of the chicken mixture. Layer 1/2 of noodles, 1/2 of the cottage cheese mixture, 1/2 of the spinach and all of the mozzarella. Repeat chicken, noodles, cottage cheese layers, ending with last 1/3 of chicken mixture. Top with Parmesan cheese and bake for 45 minutes.

Tortilla Pie with Chicken

Chris Martin, 1996,
**Football — Rose Bowl (1996);
Big Ten Network**

YIELD: 9 INCH PIE

*Here is one of my absolute favorites that
does wonders for my palate. I'm not a fan of
sour cream so I typically take that out of the
preparation. I do have decent cullinary skills
and can bang some pots and pans. I'm one
of 7 children and I have 3 older sisters
(Lisa, Ruby and Patrice) that taught me to
cook and iron my own clothes starting at the
age of 10, and to this day I still do both!
At the age of 10 it was more like fried
bologna but the following dish I picked up
later in life.*

COACHES QUOTES

Randy Walker,
Former Football Head Coach:

"Trust Yourself"

This phrase was on a 2x4 that the team always
touched as they left practice on Thursday and
it was posted in the locker room and brought
to the sidelines on game day. They still use it
to this day.

INGREDIENTS

Vegetable oil
1 large onion, chopped
1 jalapeño, minced, optional
1 clove garlic, minced
1/2 teaspoon cumin
2 cans (15 ounces each) black beans
12 ounces beer (or chicken broth)
1-1/2 cups frozen corn
6 to 8 scallions, chopped
1 cup shredded rotisserie chicken or
    other cooked chicken
1-1/2 cups shredded cheddar cheese
salt and pepper, to taste
whole wheat tortillas

GARNISHES:

salsa
scallions

*[Editors' note: we tried to estimate how
much is in a 'Chris handful'. Adjust as
you wish.]*

Preheat oven to 400 degrees. Heat a little
vegetable oil in a skillet over medium
heat. Add onion, jalapeño, garlic, cumin,
salt and pepper, to taste. Cook about
5 minutes, stirring occasionally.

Add black beans and beer to skillet.
Simmer until the liquid has almost
evaporated, about 10 minutes. Stir in a
handful of shredded cooked chicken,
corn, a handful of scallions and remove
from heat. Start layering your pie dish
with whole wheat tortillas (you may have
to trim a little to make them fit), then a
layer of shredded cheddar, then chicken
and bean mix. Repeat three times, using
about a cup of cheese on the very top.
Bake for 20 to 25 minutes until cheese is
melted. Top with more chopped scallions,
cut into wedges and serve with sour
cream and salsa.

Chicken Parmesan Casserole

Stacy & Coach Pat Fitzgerald,

Head Coach, Football

YIELD: 4 TO 6 SERVINGS

Football players love when Coach and Mrs. Fitz serve this dish.

INGREDIENTS

1 pound penne pasta, uncooked

1 pound boneless chicken breasts or thighs

1 pint heavy cream

1 pint cherry tomatoes

4 cups shredded mozzarella cheese, divided

1 clove garlic

1 teaspoon oregano

2 teaspoons basil

2 eggs

3 tablespoons oil

breadcrumbs

Cut chicken into strips. In a bowl beat 2 eggs. Dip chicken strips into eggs. In a large resealable bag add breadcrumbs. Place chicken strips into bag and shake to cover chicken with bread crumbs.

In a skillet, heat 2 tablespoons oil. Place chicken strips into skillet, cooking chicken until breading on both sides is crispy and chicken is cooked.

Cook penne according to instructions on package. Drain penne. Preheat oven to 350 degrees.

Cut cherry tomatoes in half. Wilt tomatoes and garlic in skillet in 1 tablespoon oil. Remove from heat and add cream and oregano.

In large bowl add chicken, penne, tomatoes with cream and 3 cups mozzarella cheese.

Spray bottom of 9x13 inch pan with cooking spray. Add mixed ingredients to pan. Sprinkle top with remaining 1 cup cheese. Sprinkle basil over cheese. Cover pan with foil. Bake 20 to 25 minutes. Remove foil and cook another 5 minutes to melt top cheese. Let sit 2 minutes after removing from oven. N

Mediterranean Chicken

April Bertin,
Assistant Coach, Field Hockey

YIELD: 4 SERVINGS

INGREDIENTS

1 tablespoon olive oil

1/2 teaspoon salt

1/4 teaspoon pepper

8 to 10 chicken thighs

1/4 cup chicken broth

1/4 cup white wine

2 cloves garlic, sliced into thin rounds

3 to 4 sprigs fresh thyme

8 to 10 canned artichoke hearts, halved and rinsed

1 lemon, sliced into thin rounds

1 cup whole-wheat couscous

1/2 pound fresh asparagus

1/2 teaspoon lemon zest

Italian herb seasoning

Preheat the oven to 450 degrees. Heat olive oil in a large ovenproof skillet over medium-high heat. Sprinkle chicken with Italian herb seasoning; add to pan, meaty side down. Cook for 5 minutes. Turn and cook for 2 minutes more.

Pour out any excess fat. Return pan to burner; stir in broth and wine, scraping up any brown bits. Scatter garlic, thyme and artichokes on and around chicken. Lay one lemon round on each piece of chicken. Place skillet in oven. Roast chicken for 17 to 20 minutes, or until juices run clear.

Prepare couscous according to package directions. Salt and pepper asparagus and steam until crisp-tender.

Serve chicken over couscous; place steamed asparagus on the side and sprinkle with lemon zest.

Chicken Tetrazzini

Joann Skiba

YIELD: 12 SERVINGS

INGREDIENTS

1 pound thin spaghetti, cooked and drained

1/4 pound sliced mushrooms

1/2 cup butter or margarine

2 cups cooked and diced chicken

2 cans (10-3/4 ounces each) condensed cream of chicken soup

16 ounces sour cream

1 cup shredded cheddar cheese, divided

1 teaspoon salt

pepper, to taste

Preheat oven to 350 degrees. Sauté mushrooms in butter. Combine with chicken, soup, sour cream, salt and pepper and 1/2 cup cheese. Add to spaghetti and mix well. Pour mixture into a greased 9x13 inch pan. Top with 1/2 cup cheese. Bake for 35 to 40 minutes.

Layered Vegetable Cheese Bake

Jean Block, 1949

YIELD: 6 SERVINGS

INGREDIENTS

1 tablespoon oil

1 large onion

1 large green pepper cut to 1-inch squares

1 small eggplant, peeled and cut into 1-inch cubes

1/2 pound fresh mushrooms, sliced

1 large chopped tomato

1 teaspoon salt

3/4 teaspoons dried thyme

1/8 teaspoon pepper

1 cup croutons

2 cups shredded Swiss cheese

Heat oil in large skillet. Sauté onion and green pepper for three minutes. Add eggplant and mushrooms. Sauté 3 minutes, stirring. Add tomato, salt, thyme and pepper and cook 1 minute. Spread croutons over bottom of buttered 2 quart casserole dish. Layer one half the vegetable mixture and cover with 1 cup of the shredded cheese. Top with remaining vegetables. Bake, uncovered, at 350 degrees for 30 minutes. Sprinkle the rest of the cheese over the vegetables. Bake 10 more minutes or until cheese melts.

Pastitsio (Greek Pasta & Ground Beef Casserole)

**Diane Antonopoulos &
Luke Donald,**
**Diane 2004 and Luke 2001,
Men's Golf/PGA Tour**

YIELD: 16 TO 20 SERVINGS

Resembles lasagna

INGREDIENTS

4 pounds ground beef

4 cups finely chopped onions

3 to 4 tablespoons olive oil

1 to 2 cloves garlic, mashed

1 tablespoon salt

1 teaspoon black pepper

2 cups chopped Italian parsley

1/2 teaspoon ground cinnamon

1/4 teaspoon sugar

pinch ground cloves

1 can (15 ounces) tomato sauce

1 can (28 ounces) tomatoes

2 cups grated Parmesan or Romano
　　cheese, divided

2 large eggs, separated

SAUCE:

6 tablespoons butter

6 to 7 tablespoons flour

3 cups hot milk

1/2 teaspoon salt

pinch of nutmeg and pinch of white
　　pepper, optional

2 pounds elbow or other small pasta,
　　cooked al dente

2 tablespoons butter

*This recipe is for a large 14x17x4 inch
pan; it can be easily halved for a 9x13x4
inch pan. Be sure it is at least 4 inches
deep.*

MEAT SAUCE: In a large heavy pot, sauté the onions with the olive oil until clear. Add the beef, mix and break the beef into pieces; stir until it browns. Add the spices and herbs, stir; add the tomato sauce and tomatoes. Bring the mixture to a boil, lower heat and simmer for about an hour, stirring from time to time, or put in a preheated 350 degree oven for about an hour (covered in oven-proof pot), until most of the water has evaporated. Let it cool slightly. Cook the pasta al dente according to package instructions, drain, return to the pot and add the butter while hot.

WHITE SAUCE: Heat the milk in a pot. In another large heavy pot melt the butter and add the flour making a roux (cook slowly stirring constantly with a wooden spoon until it develops a toasty smell and you can't smell raw flour, but before it starts to darken.) Slowly pour the hot milk, whisking it with a wire whisk until half of the milk is added. Stir until smooth and add the remaining milk and cook until it is thick and smooth. Add the salt and nutmeg; let cool slightly; add 1 cup grated cheese. Beat the egg whites until stiff; gently fold into the meat sauce. Slightly beat the yolks; add to the white sauce, mix thoroughly.

ASSEMBLY: Preheat oven to 350 degrees. Mix about 1 cup of the meat sauce, 1 cup of the white sauce and 1/2 cup of the grated cheese with the pasta. DO

NOT OVERFILL the pan; make sure the pan has at least one-half inch room at the top. Place half of pasta mixture on the bottom of the pan, smooth with a wooden spoon; sprinkle with cheese. Add the meat sauce and smooth; sprinkle with cheese. Add the remaining pasta, smooth; sprinkle with cheese. Add the white sauce mixture, smooth; sprinkle with cheese. Bake for 1 hour.

Mexican Lasagna — 1

Diane Keuth

I have frozen after assembling for heating another day.

INGREDIENTS

1 pound ground meat (beef, turkey, chicken)

1/2 cup chopped onions

28 ounces stewed tomatoes

10 ounces enchilada sauce

1 teaspoon salt

1 teaspoon pepper

10 medium flour tortillas

8 ounces cream cheese

8 ounces sour cream

4 ounces canned diced green chilies

1 cup Monterey Jack cheese

I have also made the tortillas with sauce inside without putting sauce on the bottom.

Preheat oven to 350 degrees. Brown the meat and onion, draining fat. Stir in the enchilada sauce, tomatoes, salt and pepper; cover and simmer for 15 minutes. Mix cream cheese and sour cream in a small bowl.

Pour half of the sauce in a 9x13 inch greased pan. Take each tortilla and fill with cream cheese mix (down the middle) adding a few chilies, then roll up and line up in the sauce. Complete with all the tortillas. Add the remaining sauce and top with shredded cheese.

Cover and bake for 15 minutes, then uncover and bake for another 15 minutes.

Mexican Lasagna — 2

Steve Schnur, 1996, Football, Rose Bowl (1996)

YIELD: 4 TO 6 SERVINGS

INGREDIENTS

1 pound hamburger meat

1/2 cup diced onion

1 can (15 ounces) refried beans

1/2 cup chopped green pepper

1 can (8 ounces) tomato sauce

1 can (4 ounces) diced green chilies

1 package taco seasoning

6 large tortillas

2 cups shredded cheddar cheese

Preheat oven to 350 degrees. Brown onions and hamburger. Drain liquid from meat. Stir in refried beans, tomato sauce, green pepper, chilies and taco seasoning. Layer 1/2 of tortillas on bottom of 7x11 inch pan. Spread 1/2 of meat mixture, then 1/2 of cheese. Layer second half of tortillas, then meat, then cheese again. Bake 30 minutes until bubbly.

Wildcat Lasagna

Carrera Harris Romanini,
Women's Swimming and Diving

YIELD: 12 SERVINGS

INGREDIENTS

3 tablespoons chopped onion

1 pound ground beef

1/2 teaspoon garlic salt

1 tablespoon parsley flakes

1 tablespoon oregano

2 bay leaves

1/2 teaspoon salt

1 can (28 ounces) chopped tomatoes

12 ounces tomato paste

10 ounces lasagna noodles

3 cups cottage cheese

2 eggs, beaten

2 teaspoons salt

1/2 teaspoon pepper

2 tablespoons chopped parsley

1/2 cup grated Parmesan cheese

1 pound mozzarella cheese, sliced thin

Preheat oven to 375 degrees.

Brown onions in 2 tablespoon fat. Add meat and brown slowly in frying pan. Add next 8 ingredients and simmer uncovered 30 minutes stirring occasionally.

Cook noodles in boiling salt water until tender; drain, soak in cold water. Combine cottage cheese, eggs, seasonings and Parmesan cheese. Place 1/2 noodles in 9x13 inch dish. Spread half cottage cheese mixture over; add half mozzarella and half meat mixture. Repeat layers. End with mozzarella cheese on top. Bake at 375 for 30 minutes. Let stand for 10 to 15 minutes before serving.

Lasagna

Kathy Newcomb

YIELD: 8 SERVINGS

INGREDIENTS

1-1/2 pounds Italian sausage

1/2 cup chopped onion

1 can (15 ounces) tomato sauce

1 can (6 ounces) tomato paste

1/2 cup tomato juice

1/2 teaspoon salt

1/4 teaspoon pepper

1 teaspoon brown sugar

1/8 teaspoon basil, or to taste

1/8 teaspoon oregano, or to taste

1/8 teaspoon garlic salt, or to taste

1/8 teaspoon parsley flakes, or to taste

1 package (15 ounces) ricotta cheese

3 cups grated mozzarella cheese

1 cup grated Parmesan cheese

1 pound lasagna noodles

Preheat oven to 350 degrees. In a large skillet, brown, then drain sausage and onion. Add all other ingredients, except cheeses. Simmer sauce for 35 minutes. While simmering, cook lasagna noodles and rinse in cold water. Mix cheeses together. Grease a 9x13 inch pan. Layer half of the noodles, half of the sauce and half of the cheese in the pan. Repeat. Bake for 40 to 60 minutes until sauce is bubbly and cheese has melted.

Cool 15 minutes before cutting. May be made ahead and refrigerated or frozen.

Lasagna with Sausage Meat Sauce

Mary Ellen Baker,
Football Mom — Hayden #68

YIELD: 6 TO 8 SERVINGS

INGREDIENTS

1 tablespoon olive oil

1 medium onion

2 tablespoons minced garlic

1 pound Italian sausage, casing removed

1/2 teaspoon each salt and pepper

1/4 cup heavy cream

1 can (28 ounces) tomato purée

1 can (28 ounces) diced tomatoes, drained

15 ounces ricotta cheese

2-1/2 ounces grated Parmesan or Romano cheese

1/2 to 1 cup chopped fresh basil, to taste

1 large egg, beaten

1/2 teaspoon salt

1/2 teaspoon pepper

12 no-boil lasagna noodles

16 ounces mozzarella, shredded (4 cups)

Preheat oven to 375 degrees.

MEAT SAUCE: Heat oil in a Dutch oven over medium heat. Add onion and garlic and cook until soft but not browned. Increase heat to high and add sausage, salt and pepper. Break into small pieces with wooden spoon. Cook until it loses color but before it has browned, about 4 minutes. Add cream and simmer until the liquid evaporates and fat remains. Add both cans of tomatoes. Reduce heat to low and simmer until flavors are combined, approximately 3 to 5 minutes. Set aside.

FILLING: Combine ricotta, 1 cup Parmesan, basil, egg, salt and pepper in a bowl until well combined/creamy.

ASSEMBLY: Spread 1/4 cup meat sauce on bottom of 9x13 inch baking dish. Place 3 noodles on top. Drop 3 table-spoons of ricotta mixture down center of each noodle, level with the back of the spoon. Sprinkle evenly with 1 cup shred-ded mozzarella. Spoon 1-1/2 cups of meat sauce evenly over the cheese/noodles. Repeat layering of noodles/ricotta/mozzarella/sauce two more times. Place remaining 3 noodles on the top and spread remaining sauce over noodles, sprinkle with remaining cup of moz-zarella and 1/4 cup Parmesan. Spray a large sheet of foil with nonstick spray and cover lasagna. Bake for 15 minutes. Remove foil and bake until cheese is melted and lightly brown and sauce is bubbling, approximately 25 minutes. Cool lasagna 15 minutes and serve.

Linebacker Helper

Nick Roach, 2006,
Football, Chicago Bears

YIELD: 6 SERVINGS

The cooking process is simple, but goes a lot faster when you have some help.

INGREDIENTS

2 pounds lean ground beef

1 large red onion

2 tablespoons minced fresh garlic

2 or more bell peppers (any color)

salt and pepper, to taste

Lawry's Seasoned Salt or your house blend

garlic salt

1/4 teaspoon cumin

2 cups macaroni noodles

8 ounces Velveeta (the fiesta kind makes it really good)

1/2 to 1 cup milk (less for thicker cheese sauce)

1 tablespoon all-purpose flour

1/4 cup butter

1 package of your favorite blend of cheeses (2 cups) I like jack and cheddar

1 large bag of Cheddar 'n' Sour Cream Ruffles (more if you like to snack while you cook).

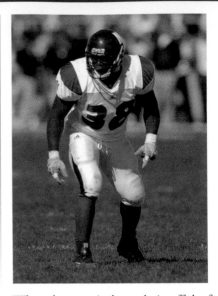

I like to start by cooking the noodles, just to get them out of the way. Cook only to al dente since they'll cook more with the whole thing. Open your Ruffles (eat a couple) and crush the whole bag, just like massaging it through the bag. Set aside until it's time for baking. Start browning the meat, while in a separate pan sauté the chopped and diced veggies with the garlic. I like my veggies pretty soft and wilted, but cook them as you prefer.

When the meat is done, drain off the fat; combine the meat with the veggies in the pot you used to boil the noodles. Now, mix in all your seasonings, then add the noodles and set aside.

Next, in a saucepan, melt the butter on low heat so it doesn't turn brown. If it's bubbling, turn down the heat. Add the flour. Stir it for a couple minutes, until there aren't any big lumps from the flour. Now you can add your milk and let that go for about 5 minutes to heat up, then add the Velveeta (it'll melt faster if it's cut up into chunks). When all the cheese is melted, your sauce is ready. Transfer the meat and noodles to your baking dish, then combine with cheese sauce. Mix it together and cover with the shredded cheese blend. Bake it covered with foil in a 350 degree, preheated oven for the first 15 minutes. When the 15 minutes is up, remove the casserole and cover it with the delicious chips. Put it back in, UNCOVERED for 15 more minutes, or until you see the tips of your chips getting dark. Once the time is up, remove it from the oven and let it rest for about 5 minutes. Eat!

Pizza Casserole

E C Rapp, 1961,
Football

YIELD: 8 TO 10 SERVINGS

INGREDIENTS

1-1/2 pound ground beef
1/2 cup chopped onion
1 can (4 ounces) mushrooms
2 cans (8 ounces each) pizza sauce
1 can (8 ounces) tomato sauce
1 cup pepperoni pieces
1/8 teaspoon oregano
1 cup whole milk
3 cups cooked egg noodles
1 cup shredded mozzarella

Preheat oven to 350 degrees. Brown ground beef with onion. Add mushrooms, pizza sauce, pepperoni, oregano and milk. Mix well. Fold in noodles. Put into greased 9x13 inch casserole. Bake covered for 45 minutes, uncover and bake for 10 minutes.

Sprinkle on mozzarella, bake another 5 minutes.

Alumni Sausage & Peppers

Charles Katzenmeyer, 1985,
President, Northwestern Alumni Association

YIELD: 4 SERVINGS

INGREDIENTS

3 green peppers, cut in large chunks
3 tablespoons olive oil
1/2 teaspoon salt
1/4 teaspoon pepper
1 pound hot Italian sausage links
1/3 cup red wine

Preheat oven to 350 degrees. In a baking dish that can be used on top of the stove, sauté green peppers in oil until they begin to soften. Sprinkle with a little salt and pepper, to taste. Lift the green peppers out of the dish and set aside. Brown the sausages in the same baking dish. When browned, add red wine. Cover the pan with foil and bake sausage in wine for 35 to 40 minutes (ovens vary so cook until sausage is no longer pink). Uncover and add the sautéed green peppers. Bake up to 30 minutes, checking every few minutes to avoid overbrowning. Serve in the same baking dish.

COACHES QUOTES

Arvid Swan, Men's Tennis:

"Give more of yourself than you receive."

NoNo's Quick Jambalaya

Noah Herron, 2004,
Football

Yield: 6 to 8 servings

Ingredients

2 cups uncooked rice

2 pounds shrimp

1 pound smoked sausage, chopped

1 to 2 cans (10-3/4 ounces each)
    Campbell's French Onion Soup

1 can (15 ounces) chicken or beef
    broth

1 can Rotel tomatoes, chopped

1/4 pound butter

1 bunch green onions, chopped

1 whole Spanish onion, chopped

1 bell pepper, chopped

3 stalks celery, chopped

garlic, to taste

salt and pepper, to taste

1 tablespoon crab boil

Tony Chachere's Creole Seasoning,
    to taste

Combine vegetables and rice in baking dish. Pour cans on top and add meat. Slice butter and layer on top evenly. Cook at 350 degrees for 1-1/2 hours, remove and cover with foil for 30 minutes to rest.

G's Spam Casserole

Sue Little, 1960

Yield: 6 servings

G gave me this recipe over 40 years ago. We love it.

Ingredients

1 can (12 ounces) Spam

1 can (14 ounces) peas, drained

1 can (10-3/4 ounces) condensed
    cream of mushroom soup

1/2 cup milk

1 tablespoon Worcestershire sauce

1/2 cup Italian seasoned bread crumbs

1/2 pound elbow macaroni

Preheat oven to 350 degrees. Cook macaroni and drain.

Slice Spam into 8 slices. Mix soup, milk and Worcestershire sauce together.

Put macaroni in greased casserole, add peas, then Spam. Pour soup mixture over all.

Top with crumbs. Bake, uncovered, for 30 minutes.

Spinach Pie

Jaime & Coach Adam Cushing,
Offensive Line Coach, Football

YIELD: 8 TO 10 SERVINGS

INGREDIENTS

1 pound Italian sausage, cooked and crumbled

1 package (20 ounces) frozen spinach, thawed and well drained

1 pound shredded mozzarella cheese

2/3 pound cottage cheese or ricotta

1/2 teaspoon salt

5 eggs, reserve 1 yolk

1/8 teaspoon pepper

1 teaspoon garlic powder

2 deep dish pie crusts

Preheat oven to 375 degrees. Mix sausage, spinach, cheeses, spices and 4 and 1/2 eggs. Place 1 pie crust in deep dish pie pan. Fill with sausage mixture. Top with second crust, trimming and crimping edges. Beat reserved egg yolk with a few drops of water and brush on the top crust. Cut 4 slits in top crust and bake for 75 minutes.

Great for tailgating!

Yummy Tuna Noodle Casserole *a la* Alpha Kappa Alpha

Debra Hill, 1971

YIELD: 4 TO 6 SERVINGS

INGREDIENTS

1 can (12 ounces) white tuna

1 can (5 ounces) white tuna

1 bag (8 ounces) dumpling noodles

1 box (10 ounces) frozen peas and carrots

1 pound Velveeta

1 bag (1-1/2 cups) shredded cheddar cheese

1 medium bag of regular potato chips

1/2 cup dried minced onions

2 cups milk

1/4 pound butter

1 cup chopped celery

salt and pepper, to taste

paprika for color

Preheat oven to 350 degrees. Prepare noodles to al dente stage.

Melt approximately 1/4 of the Velveeta with the milk. Shred the rest of the Velveeta and mix with the cheddar.

Drain, then mix the two cans of tuna, celery, onions, frozen peas and carrots, salt, pepper and milk/cheese mixture. The mixture should be somewhat soupy and not dry. Add more milk if necessary.

Pour one layer in a lightly greased 2 quart or larger baking dish. Cover the mixture with cheese; add another layer and cover with cheese. Finish the top with a layer of crushed potato chips and sprinkle with paprika. Bake for 45 minutes.

Serve with cranberry or apple sauce.

Hot Crossed Tuna Casserole

Nancy Tierney,
Director, Fitness/Wellness, NUDAR

YIELD: 6 TO 8 SERVINGS

INGREDIENTS

2 cans (7 ounces each) tuna, drained
10 ounces frozen peas, thawed
1 cup shredded sharp cheddar cheese
1 cup sliced celery
1/2 cup bread crumbs
1/4 cup chopped onion
1/4 teaspoon salt
1/8 teaspoon pepper
1 cup Miracle Whip or plain yogurt
8 ounce can refrigerated crescent
    dinner rolls

SAUCE:
1/2 cup sour cream
1/2 cup chopped, seeded cucumber
1 tablespoon chopped chives
1 teaspoon chopped parsley
1/4 teaspoon salt
1/4 teaspoon dill weed

TUNA: Preheat oven to 350 degrees.
Combine tuna, peas, cheese, celery,
crumbs, onion, seasonings and Miracle
Whip dressing. Mix well. Spoon into
6x10 inch baking dish. Separate dough
into two rectangles; press perforations to
seal. Cut dough into four long and eight
short strips; place strips over casserole in a
lattice design. Brush lightly with dressing;
sprinkle with sesame seeds if desired.
Bake 35 to 40 minutes or until crust is
golden brown. Serve with cool cucumber
sauce.

SAUCE: Combine all ingredients, mix
well and chill. **N**

Wild Rice and Turkey Casserole

Jean Yale, 1957,
Athletic Development/Special Events

YIELD: 8 TO 10 SERVINGS

INGREDIENTS

1-1/2 cups cooked wild rice
1 pound bulk pork sausage
8 ounces mushrooms (fresh or canned,
    drained)
2 cans (10-3/4 ounce each) condensed
    cream of mushroom soup
1 teaspoon Worcestershire sauce
12 slices cooked turkey
1-1/2 cups Ritz cracker crumbs
1/4 cup melted butter
1 cup cooked peas or green beans,
    optional
1 to 2 tablespoons chopped parsley for
    garnish, optional

Preheat oven to 375 degrees. Cook rice
according to package directions. Brown
sausage and drain off fat. Stir in mushrooms, soup, Worcestershire sauce and
vegetables. Lightly stir in rice.

Spoon half of mixture in greased 8x12
inch baking dish. Put a layer of turkey
slices on top, cover with remaining rice
mixture. Sprinkle with cracker crumbs
and melted butter. Bake for 30 minutes.

Dish can be made ahead of time and refrigerated. To serve, bake for 45 minutes. **N**

grilled/broiled

Horseradish Sauce for Grilled Beef

Lisa & Jeff Weiss

YIELD: 1 CUP

INGREDIENTS

1/2 cup sour cream
1/2 cup mayonnaise
1 tablespoon fresh dill
1 tablespoon fresh chives
2 tablespoons hot horseradish
1/2 teaspoon salt
1/2 teaspoon pepper

Mix all ingredients in a bowl and chill. Serve as a side to grilled flank steaks, roasts or tenderloin.

Beef Satay

Kelle Frymire,
Football Mom — Kevin 2009

These are fabulous, easy to eat at a tailgate and gone in a flash.

INGREDIENTS

1/4 cup soy sauce
1/4 cup fresh orange juice
1/4 cup wine
1/4 cup Thai fish sauce
4 cloves garlic, finely chopped
2 tablespoons fresh lime juice
2 tablespoons finely chopped
     fresh ginger
1 teaspoon ground cumin
1 teaspoon ground coriander
1 tablespoon natural peanut butter
1 tablespoon brown sugar
1 pound flank steak cut crosswise at
     an angle into 3/4 inch strips

At home: In a medium bowl, mix together the soy sauce, orange juice, wine, fish sauce, garlic, lime juice, ginger, cumin, coriander, peanut butter and brown sugar. Thread a slice of steak onto a skewer, weaving it back and forth several times so the meat is not flopping and is close to the stick. Place the skewers in a sealable container just big enough to hold them. Pour the marinade over them and make sure the meat is coated on all sides. Refrigerate until you are ready to pack for the game — at least 1 hour and up to 6 hours.

At the Tailgate: Grill the beef for 6 to 7 minutes, turning once and brushing with the remaining sauce.

COACHES QUOTES

Pat Fitzgerald, Football:

"Wildcat Effort –
 Go as hard as you can
 for as long as you can."

Sunshine Salmon

Top Chef Stephanie Izard,
Top Chef (Season 4) and chef/owner of
the Girl and the Goat Restaurant,
Chicago

Yield: 4 servings

Ingredients

1 cup soy sauce

juice and zest of 2 oranges

3 tablespoons light brown sugar

4 cloves garlic, peeled and left whole

1 tablespoon fresh ginger, finely
chopped

1 tablespoon white sesame seeds,
optional

4 skinless salmon fillets (about 6
ounces each)

Combine soy, orange zest and juice,
brown sugar, garlic and ginger in sauce
pan. Bring to a boil and simmer slowly
until reduced and syrupy, about 15 minutes. Remove from heat, stir in sesame
seeds and cool. Transfer to baking dish,
add fish, turn to coat and marinate for an
hour. Preheat broiler or outdoor grill. (If
using a grill, use enough cooking spray
on grate to avoid breaking fish.)
Broil/grill until done, approximately 4
minutes per side.

Grilled Balsamic Chicken

Mary Pat Watt,
Football Mom — Kevin #42

Yield: 4 servings

Ingredients

1/4 cup balsamic vinegar

2 tablespoons olive oil

1 tablespoon fresh oregano
(1 teaspoon dry)

1 tablespoon fresh rosemary
(1 teaspoon dry)

1/2 teaspoon pepper

1 clove garlic

4 boneless, skinless chicken breast
halves

2 red onions, quartered

2 red, orange or yellow peppers
quartered

Mix first 6 marinade ingredients.
Marinate chicken in marinade for 1 hour.
Preheat grill. Drain and reserve marinade,
boiling for 5 minutes. Grill vegetables
and chicken, basting with boiled marinade. Chicken takes about 5 minutes per
side. Vegetables take a bit longer. Can
serve with focaccia bread or angel hair
pasta.

Investment

Grilled Chicken for a Crowd

Kim & Coach Tim Cysewski,
Associate Head Coach, Wrestling

YIELD: 12 SERVINGS

INGREDIENTS

1 can (10-3/4 ounces) condensed
    cream of tomato soup
1 cup virgin olive oil
3/4 cup vegetable oil
3/4 cup cider vinegar
3/4 cup sugar
2 tablespoons chopped onion
1 tablespoon Worcestershire sauce
2 medium cloves of garlic, peeled
1 teaspoon dry mustard
12 skinless, boneless chicken breast
    halves

Place tomato soup, olive oil, vegetable oil, cider vinegar, sugar, onions, Worcestershire sauce, garlic and dry mustard in a blender or food processor fitted with a steel blade and blend until smooth. Rinse chicken breasts under cold running water and pat them dry with paper towels. Cut chicken breasts in half and, using a meat pounder, pound them to an even 1/2 inch thickness. Arrange the pounded chicken in a single layer in two 9x13 inch glass or ceramic baking dishes and pour 1 cup of the marinade in each pan. Cover the baking dishes with plastic wrap and marinate the chicken in the refrigerator overnight. When you're ready to cook, preheat the grill to medium heat. Remove the chicken from the marinade, putting the marinade aside. Grill the chicken pieces until the juices run clear, 4 to 5 minutes per side. If you'd like you can heat up some of the remaining marinade to boiling and serve with the chicken.

Apricot Honey Chicken Poupon

Megan Anderson, 1976

YIELD: 4 SERVINGS

Great for last minute preparations.

INGREDIENTS

1/3 cup Grey Poupon honey mustard
3 tablespoons apricot preserves
1 teaspoon ground ginger
4 boneless chicken breasts
    (about 1 pound)

Blend mustard, apricot preserves and ginger. Brush on chicken breasts. Grill for 6 to 8 minutes on each side or until done. Continue to brush with mixture while cooking to keep chicken moist.

Erryn's Finger Lick'n Chicken and Chimichurri Sauce

Erryn Cobb,
2006,
Football and contestant on Fox's MasterChef

INGREDIENTS

CHICKEN:
chicken quarters or drumsticks
mustard
salt
black pepper
garlic salt
Cajun seasoning
cumin
paprika
cayenne pepper
ground ginger
ground allspice

SAUCE:
1/2 cup chopped fresh cilantro
1 cup olive oil

This sauce is simple but awesome. Traditionally a chimichurri sauce would have some parsley in it as well, but I went all cilantro for this one.

Coat the chicken in mustard (don't get crazy with it, just use enough to cover the meat). You want to be generous with the garlic salt, Cajun seasoning and cumin. Dust all of the other ingredients lightly over the chicken. Adjust the seasoning according to your taste (add more cayenne for extra heat). Once the chicken is seasoned, place on a medium low grill. Cook the chicken low and slow over charcoal, it should stay on for at least an hour.

SAUCE: Roughly chop the fresh cilantro and add it to a mortar and pestle. Add the diced garlic, olive oil, salt and pepper and white wine vinegar. Grind until garlic and cilantro are incorporated into the sauce. Taste and adjust. (You can use a food processor too, the motar and pestle is just cooler!)

Rib and Pulled Pork Rub

Nick Pauly,
Softball Dad — Nicole 2010

YIELD: ENOUGH FOR 6 RIB SLABS

This is the first time Nick has shared the recipe for his popular barbeque dish.

INGREDIENTS

1/2 cup brown sugar
1/4 cup paprika
1-1/2 tablespoon black pepper
1 tablespoon salt
1 tablespoon chili powder
1 tablespoon garlic powder
1 tablespoon onion powder
1 teaspoon cayenne pepper

Mix all ingredients together in a bowl.

For Ribs: Rub mixture on the ribs and grill using the indirect method, cooking until done.

For Pulled Pork: Rub mixture on top of pork shoulder. Wrap in foil and cook at 200 degrees for 8 hours. Cooking overnight before the tailgate works great.

Get your favorite BBQ sauce ready with buns and coleslaw!

Chimichurri Steak Marinade/Sauce

Nicole & Zak Kustok, 2002,
Football

YIELD: 4 TO 6 SERVINGS

This recipe (along with the Shrimp Tacos) is Zak's favorite … he calls it the The Spicy Surf and Turf although upon further inspection, it should probably be called, garlic, garlic and more garlic. And yes, it's a lot of food for two people :) but somehow he always manages to finish it!

INGREDIENTS

2 to 3 pounds of steak

1 cup olive oil

2 limes, zest and juice

1-1/2 cups packed finely chopped fresh parsley

8 cloves garlic, finely chopped

2 tablespoons crushed red pepper

2 tablespoons finely chopped fresh basil

2 tablespoons finely chopped fresh thyme

2 tablespoons finely chopped fresh oregano

Salt and pepper, to taste

Combine the ingredients except steak in a bowl and season with salt and pepper, or use food processor to pulse all into a thick purée. Divide the chimichurri between 2 bowls. Use half as the marinade and half as the dipping sauce. We like to marinate the beef for at least 4 hours. Works either on the grill or over stove top.

Marinated Wildcat Flank Steak

Matthew Goren, 1987,
Asst. Prof. Clin. Ophthalmology, Feinberg School of Medicine

YIELD: 3 TO 4 SERVINGS

INGREDIENTS

2 pounds flank steak

1 cup soy sauce

1/4 cup teriyaki sauce

1/4 cup honey

6 cloves garlic, finely chopped

1 teaspoon liquid smoke

3 tablespoons lime juice, sherry or red wine

1 bunch cilantro, finely chopped

Finely chop garlic cloves and cilantro just before mixing it with all other ingredients except meat. Marinate the flank steak in mixture for at least an hour but longer if possible. Periodically turn the meat so that both sides are well-marinated.

Preheat grill to very hot and throw the flank steak on the grill for about 2 minutes each side for rare to medium-rare. Allow flank steak to rest at least 5 minutes before cutting and serving.

This steak will make you roar!

Marinated Flank Steak with Ginger

Laura & Coach Joe McKeown,
Head Coach, Women's Basketball

YIELD: 4 SERVINGS

INGREDIENTS

1/4 cup soy sauce

3 tablespoons honey

2 tablespoons vinegar

2 teaspoons garlic powder

2 teaspoons powdered ginger

3/4 cup salad oil

1 small onion

2 pounds flank steak

Place flank steak in a non-metal dish. Combine all the marinade ingredients and pour over steak. Marinate in refrigerator overnight, changing meat position occasionally so all sides are well coated in marinade. Bring steak to room temperature before cooking. Grill 5 minutes per side for medium rare. Slice thinly on the diagonal and serve.

Marinated Flank Steak

Kenan & Coach Paul Stevens,
Head Coach, Baseball

YIELD: 4 TO 6 SERVINGS

INGREDIENTS

2 flank steaks

1 cup brown sugar

1 cup honey

1 cup soy sauce

1/2 cup vegetable oil

3 tablespoons red wine vinegar

chopped garlic, to taste (I use lots!)

4 to 5 chopped green onions, to taste

Mix all the ingredients, except the steaks, in a bowl. Divide the marinade into 2 large gallon-size zippered bags. Pierce the flank steaks with a fork all over. Put 1 steak in each bag and let marinade overnight in the refrigerator; occasionally turn the bags.

Grill over medium heat for approximately 5 minutes per side. Remove steaks from grill and let them rest for 5 minutes before cutting. Slice into thin pieces with the grain and serve.

Grilled Lime Marinated Flank Steak

Zach Strief, 2005,
Football/NO Saints

YIELD: 8 TO 10 SERVINGS

INGREDIENTS

1/4 cup olive oil

juice of 2 limes

1/4 cup orange juice

2 cloves garlic, minced

2 tablespoons low sodium soy sauce

1 tablespoon Cajun seasoning

1/8 cup chopped fresh parsley,
(1/2 tablespoon if dried)

1/8 cup chopped fresh mint
(1/2 tablespoon if dried)

1 tablespoon garlic salt

1/2 teaspoon salt

1 tablespoon freshly ground pepper

2 flank steaks, 2 pounds each

You can serve this hot off the grill, cold the next day as a sandwich or over a salad with a vinaigrette dressing and blue chees crumbles.

In a small bowl, add all of the ingredients except the steaks; whisk. Place the flank steaks in a large, shallow non-aluminum dish. Pour marinade over the steaks, cover and refrigerate for at least 2 hours or overnight.

Remove from refrigerator, turn in marinade and let sit for about 15 minutes before grilling. Fire up grill and remove the steaks from the marinade; discard the marinade.

Grill the steaks to your liking, about 5 to 7 minutes, turning once. Slightly undercook; remove from grill, cover with aluminum foil and let rest for about 10 minutes; it will continue to cook. Transfer to a carving board and thinly slice across the grain.

COACHES QUOTES

Joe McKeown, Women's Basketball:

"My Recipe for Success:
I can't cook like my wife, who is tremendous, but my "Wildcat" soup would include a little dash of point guard, a touch of power forward, and a kitchen full of quickness.
Put it all in a pot, let it simmer for an entire pre-season and freeze it 'til the NCAA Tournament."

roasts

Grandpa's Drunken Pot Roast

Tim Hayden,
Athletics Compliance

YIELD: 5 TO 6 SERVINGS

INGREDIENTS

1 pot roast
5 potatoes, peeled, cut into chunks
5 carrots, peeled & coarsely chopped
1 onion, cut in half
1 bottle (16 ounces) chili sauce or ketchup
1 bottle beer
1 cup brown sugar

Place pot roast, potatoes, carrots and onion in roasting pan. Mix chili sauce, beer and brown sugar and pour over roast. Cover and bake at 325 degrees for 3 to 4 hours. Best if made in a slow cooker — on high for approximately 8 hours.

Beef Tenderlion

Denise Munday,
Lacrosse Mom — Lindsey 2006

YIELD: 8 TO 10 SERVINGS

INGREDIENTS

5 to 6 pounds tenderloin
1 cup soy sauce
1 cup port wine
1/2 cup olive oil
1 teaspoon thyme leaves
1 bay leaf
1 teaspoon pepper
4 cloves garlic, crushed
1 teaspoon hot sauce

SAUCE:
1/4 cup heavy whipping cream
1/2 cup mayonnaise
1/2 cup prepared horseradish, drained
2 tablespoons Dijon mustard
pinch of salt
freshly ground pepper, to taste

First cut meat into 3 pieces — the end or skinny piece, the middle, and the big end as cooking times vary by size, or cook whole. Combine all ingredients (except beef). Place beef in roasting pan and cover with marinade. Cover and place in fridge overnight, turning once or twice.

Next day: Make some boats out of heavy duty foil. Use 3 pieces for each piece of beef (enough to cover meat completely when you are ready). The boats will prevent the marinade from running out. Remove beef from marinade, but keep marinade. Place beef in another pan.

Preheat oven to 500 degrees. Put beef in oven and cook.; if whole, 5 to 7 minutes per pound. If cooking in 3 pieces, cook the skinny 20 to 25 minutes; middle 35 to 40 minutes; big end 45 to 50 minutes. When the first piece is ready to take out, place it in a boat (put the rest back in the oven) and pour some marinade on it, wrap tightly and place in a cooler (no ice). Finish the other pieces the same way. You may want to put the bigger pieces on the bottom of the cooler. The meat will finish cooking in the wrap and be ready to slice later in the day or evening.

Serve with horseradish cream sauce and/or caramelized onions, on a roll or not.

SAUCE: Whip the heavy cream in a bowl until it forms soft peaks. In another bowl, combine the mayonnaise, horseradish and mustard. Fold in the whipped cream. Add sugar, salt and pepper. Stir well and transfer to serving bowl.

Weber Corned Beef

James Wagner, 1961

YIELD: DEPENDS ON SIZE OF ROAST

INGREDIENTS

1 large corned beef
1 cup orange marmalade
1 cup brown sugar
1/2 cup brandy

Put six pieces of charcoal on either side of the Weber. Put the corned beef in the middle, over a drip pan.

Add three pieces of charcoal every half hour. Cover and cook for three hours.

In the last half hour mix the other ingredients and baste frequently until the mixture is gone.

Serve with Champagne mustard. Typical side dishes are cabbage and boiled potatoes.

Salt and Herb Rub for Poultry

Daniel R Barron, KSM

YIELD: 1 CUP

INGREDIENTS

3/4 cup kosher salt
1 tablespoon dried sage
1 tablespoon dried rosemary
1 tablespoon dried thyme
2 tablespoons freshly ground
    black pepper

Mix salt and seasonings well. Rub bird inside and out with the mixture. Place in a plastic bag and refrigerate in a dish or roasting pan overnight. To cook the bird, remove from plastic bag and rinse well inside and outside. Pat bird dry and cook as you would any bird.

Rack of Nittany Lion

Jack Griffin, 1990,
**Wrestling, Assistant A.D.,
Director of the Wildcat Fund**

INGREDIENTS

4 Frenched racks of lamb (7 to 8 bones each)

1-1/2 cups finely chopped pine nuts or bread crumbs

3 tablespoons Dijon mustard

2 tablespoons chopped fresh thyme

2 teaspoons chopped fresh rosemary

Salt and pepper

Prepare the grill for direct heat. Trim all but a thin layer of fat off the lamb. Season the lamb with salt and pepper, to taste. When grill is nice and hot, sear the lamb on both sides (4 to 5 minutes per side). Do NOT close the lid while searing. Remove the lamb from the grill; keep the grill at the same temperature.

Place the pine nuts on a sheet of aluminum foil on the grill and close the lid for about 4 minutes to toast (or toast on stove). While pine nuts are toasting, in a bowl mix the rosemary and thyme. Add pine nuts when toasted. Re-set grill for indirect grilling. Coat the lamb generously with Dijon mustard and pat with

herb mixture. Intertwine the bones of 2 racks to make a single roast; repeat for the other two racks. Place in a roasting pan in the center of the grill (or directly on the grill) for approximately 30 minutes or until the internal temperature reaches 125 degrees for medium-rare. Let rest uncovered for 10 minutes and cut into chops (if it's cold outside, cover with aluminum foil while resting).

COACHES QUOTES

Andrew Pariano, Men's Wrestling:

"One thing I have learned as a competitor is that there are clear distinctions between what it takes to be decent, what it takes to be good, what it takes to be great, and what it takes to be among the best."
–Josh Waitzkin, the Art of Learning

Rack of Lamb Persillade

Laurie & Mark Murphy,

Former NU Athletic Director and current President & CEO of the Green Bay Packers

YIELD: 4 SERVINGS

This rack of lamb is an easy dish for entertaining. You can prepare the persillade ahead and just do the last part when the guests are around.

INGREDIENTS

2 racks of lamb, Frenched
Olive oil
1-1/2 teaspoons kosher salt
1/2 teaspoon ground pepper
2 cups loosely packed flat parsley
1 tablespoon chopped garlic cloves
4 tablespoons unsalted butter, melted
1 cup fresh white bread crumbs
2 teaspoons grated lemon zest

Preheat oven to 450 degrees. Put the racks in a roasting pan with the fat side up. Rub the tops with olive oil and salt and pepper. Roast for ten minutes. Put parsley, garlic and butter in food processor and process until minced. Add bread crumbs and lemon zest and process for a second or two. Take the lamb out of the oven and press the mixture on top of the meat. Return to the oven and roast for 15 more minutes. Tent the meat with foil and let it rest 15 minutes or so. Cut it into double chops.

Roasted Lamb Shanks

Stephanie & Coach Neil Jones,
Assistant Coach, Men's Soccer

YIELD: 4 SERVINGS

INGREDIENTS

4 lamb shanks
2 cloves garlic
1/4 teaspoon basil
1/4 teaspoon rosemary
1/4 teaspoon thyme
1/4 teaspoon oregano
pinch each salt and pepper
1/2 teaspoon curry powder
1 bay leaf
4 large onions, thinly sliced
2 tablespoons soy sauce
1/4 cup dry white wine
1/4 cup water

Preheat oven to 400 degrees. Rub the lamb shanks with the crushed garlic, sprinkle with salt and pepper, and place them in a roasting pan. Mix together herbs, curry powder and crushed bay leaf, then sprinkle over the lamb shanks. Place the onion slices on top of the lamb shanks and pour the soy sauce over the meat.

Roast uncovered for 15 minutes, then reduce heat and roast (uncovered) for 2 hours (or until done) at 300 degrees.

Pour off the fat and add the wine and water. Cover and roast for one additional hour at 300 degrees.

Cherry Almond Glazed Pork

Liz Luxem

YIELD: 8 SERVINGS

INGREDIENTS

4 pounds pork loin roast, rolled, boned and tied

1 cup cherry preserves (12 ounce jar)

2 tablespoons light corn syrup

1/4 cup red wine vinegar

1/4 teaspoon salt

1/4 teaspoon cinnamon

1/4 teaspoon nutmeg

1/4 teaspoon ground cloves

1/4 cup slivered almonds, toasted

Rub roast with a little salt and pepper. Place the roast on a rack in a shallow baking pan. Roast uncovered at 325 degrees for 2 to 2-1/2 hours.

Combine cherry preserves, corn syrup, vinegar, salt, cinnamon, nutmeg and cloves. Heat to boiling, stirring frequently; reduce heat and simmer for 2 more minutes. Add toasted almonds. Keep the sauce warm.

Spoon enough hot cherry sauce over the roast to glaze. Return the roast to the oven for about 30 minutes more or until the meat thermometer registers 170 degrees. Baste the roast several times during the last 30 minutes.

Pass remaining sauce with the served roast.

Iowa Pork Loin with Sherry and Red Onions

Bruce Paynter, 1973, 1976, NUMB

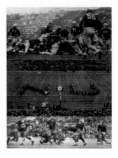

YIELD: 8 SERVINGS

INGREDIENTS

3 large red onions, thinly sliced

1 cup pearl onions, peeled

2 tablespoons unsalted butter or margarine

2-1/2 pounds boneless pork loin, tied

1/2 teaspoon salt

1/2 teaspoon black pepper, freshly ground

1/2 cup cooking sherry

2 tablespoons parsley, fresh chopped

1-1/2 tablespoons cornstarch

2 tablespoons water

Sauté red onions and pearl onions until soft. Rub the pork loin with salt and pepper. Place in slow cooker with cooked onions, sherry and parsley. Cook on low 8 to 10 hours or on high 5 to 6 hours. Remove loin and let stand for 15 minutes before slicing.

To create a sauce, strain drippings, if desired. Mix cornstarch and water until smooth then add to the drippings and heat until thickened.

Italian Sausage with Peppers, Potatoes and Apples

Ruth Anne Velaer-Wheeler, 1988

YIELD: 4 SERVINGS

INGREDIENTS

1 pound sweet Italian sausage (about 4 links)

2 red bell peppers

2 to 3 medium to large yellow/gold potatoes

2 apples (Braeburn or Empire work best)

1/2 tablespoon kosher salt

1/2 tablespoon freshly ground black pepper

2 tablespoons extra-virgin olive oil

Preheat oven to 425 degrees. Cut potatoes in half lengthwise, then cut into wedges, approx 1/4 to 1/2 in thick. Core and slice apples to approximately same width as potatoes. Slice red bell peppers into strips. Place potatoes, apples and peppers into a roasting pan and toss with the olive oil until evenly coated. Top with salt and pepper.

Place in oven and roast for about 15 minutes. Add Italian sausages to roasting pan and stir potato, peppers and apples around and over the sausages. Continue to roast another 25 minutes until sausages are browned.

sandwiches

Mom's Beef Brisket

Cathy Strief,
Football Mom — Zach 2005

YIELD: 35 TO 40 SERVINGS

Serve on rolls with cole slaw; but when serving to the players, all they want is the meat.

INGREDIENTS

2 large beef briskets (6 to 8 pounds each)

1 bottle (28 ounces) of BBQ sauce

12 ounces beer

1 can (15 ounces) beef stock

1 large onion, sliced

8 cloves garlic, minced

1 tablespoon salt

1 tablespoon pepper

1-1/2 tablespoons Cajun seasoning

Season the briskets with salt and pepper and place on a piece of foil large enough to wrap each brisket separately; place side by side in a baking pan. Cut small slices in the top of the beef; cover with garlic pieces then the onion slices. Combine the BBQ sauce, beer, beef stock and Cajun seasoning; mix well. Pour 1/3 of the marinade on one brisket, 1/3 on the second brisket and reserve 1/3 for later. Seal the briskets in the foil and place in a 300 degree oven. Slow cook for 6 to 8 hours. Remove from oven and let cool for about 15 minutes. Open the foil, remove and shred the meat. Place the shredded meat in a foil pan, pour the remaining marinade on top and seal well for transportation.

Burgers with a Kick

The Spice House,
Evanston — Owners Patty and Tom Erd

YIELD: 8 SERVINGS

Provided to The Spice House by Mabel Menard, Chicago.

INGREDIENTS

2 pounds ground meat (or ground vegetarian product)

1 small onion or shallot, finely chopped

1/2 to 1 fresh jalepeño pepper, seeded and finely chopped

1/2 inch fresh ginger, shredded or ground to a paste

1 tablespoon finely chopped garlic

1 tablespoon ground coriander

1 teaspoon ground cumin

2 teaspoons salt, or to taste

freshly ground black pepper, to taste

2 tablespoons vegetable oil, if making veggie burgers

8 small squares of pepper jack or other cheese, optional

Rather than making burgers, shape the meat around soaked bamboo skewers and grill as mini kebobs.

Mix all ingredients together. Shape into 8 patties. When the grill (or broiler) is hot, grill (or broil) burgers until done.

If using cheese, instead of laying cheese on top of the burger patties, make 16 patties, then shape two patties around the cheese, pressing the edges together so the cheese is completely hidden.

Easy Barbeque Hamburgers

Marietta Paynter

YIELD: 4 SERVINGS

Marietta was married to John Paynter, a Northwestern alum who served as director of the NU Marching Band from 1953 to1996.

INGREDIENTS

1 pound ground beef

2 tablespoons ketchup

2 tablespoons prepared mustard

1 tablespoon brown sugar

1 can (10-3/4 ounces) condensed chicken gumbo soup

1/2 cup chopped onion

salt, to taste

Brown beef, breaking into small pieces. Add onion and cook until softened. Add rest of ingredients and simmer for 30 minutes. Salt, to taste. Serve on buns.

Crunchy Sloppy Joes

Jim Zilka, 1969 and 1971

YIELD: 8 SANDWICHES

INGREDIENTS

1 pound ground beef

1 medium onion chopped
(about 1/2 cup)

1/2 cup or more chopped
green pepper

1/2 cup or more chopped celery

1/2 cup or more ketchup

1/4 cup water

1 tablespoon Worcestershire sauce

1 teaspoon salt

1/8 teaspoon hot red pepper sauce

8 hamburger buns split and toasted,
if desired

Cook and stir ground beef with onion in a 10 inch skillet until beef is browned and broken into small pieces. Thoroughly drain.

Stir in remaining ingredients except red pepper sauce. Cover and cook over low heat for 5 to10 minutes. Add red pepper sauce, to taste and stir. Fill buns with beef mixture.

Italian Beef

Beth Trumpy,
Football Mom — Mike #29

YIELD: 10 SERVINGS

INGREDIENTS

3 to 4 pounds beef roast

1 tablespoon garlic powder

1 tablespoon onion salt

1 tablespoon oregano

1 tablespoon chili powder

3 cups water

3 beef bouillon cubes

Place roast in slow cooker with all ingredients. Cook 8 to 10 hours on low until meat falls apart. Serve on buns. Good with peppers and onions.

Slow Cooker Beef

Kelly Deiters,
Football Mom — Neal #79

YIELD: 8 SERVINGS

INGREDIENTS

4 pounds rump roast

16 ounce jar of sliced pepperoncini

1 envelope dry onion soup mix

Cut off any strings and place meat into large slow cooker. Pour in whole jar of sliced pepperoncini (not drained) and dry onion soup mix (no need to mix together). Cover and cook 10 hours on high. When cooking is done, take two forks and shred the meat. Serve on your favorite hard rolls.

Betsy's Brisket

Betsy Wheelan, 1962

YIELD: 6 TO 8 SERVINGS

INGREDIENTS

2-1/2 pounds beef brisket
1 bottle Open Pit BBQ sauce (16 ounces)
3/4 cup sugar
MARINADE:
1/4 cup Worcestershire sauce
1/4 cup liquid smoke
1 teaspoon celery salt
2 teaspoons sugar
1 teaspoon garlic salt or powder
1 teaspoon onion salt

You will make the marinade twice, once on the first day and again on the second day.

Combine marinade ingredients. Put beef on a large sheet of aluminum foil, pour on the marinade mixture. Wrap brisket in foil and refrigerate overnight.

Unwrap brisket, put in roasting pan. Repeat the marinade, combining all ingredients except sugar and pour over meat. Cook brisket at 250 degrees 1/2 hour per pound. Remove from oven and cool.

Thinly slice brisket against the grain and cover with BBQ sauce mixed with the sugar. Serve in a hamburger bun.

Brisket can be reheated in the microwave.

Longbranch Sloppy Marys

Kitty Horne

YIELD: 4 SERVINGS

INGREDIENTS

1 pound ground beef
1 green pepper, chopped
1 medium onion, chopped
1 teaspoon salt
1 tablespoon black pepper
2 cups Longbranch Bloody Mary Zinger

Since Longbranch contains no added sugar, artificial flavors, artificial colors or thickeners, the success of this recipe cannot be guaranteed with the use of another bloody mary mix.

In a large skillet, brown ground beef with green pepper and onion until beef is no longer pink. Add salt, brown sugar, black pepper and Longbranch. Stir to combine. Simmer, uncovered, for about 30 minutes, or until mixture is reduced to desired consistency. Serve on buns or rolls.

Execute

Italian Beef Sandwiches

Patsy Pace,
Football Mom — John Henry #58

YIELD: 12 TO 16 LARGE SANDWICHES

The boys seem to love this and it is easy to assemble and forget. The house smells great while cooking! It can be made several days in advance and is great to feed a crowd.

INGREDIENTS

4 to 5 pounds beef roast (tip or rib roast)

1 envelope dry Lipton Onion Soup mix

2 packages dry Good Seasons Italian salad dressing

1-1/2 teaspoons rosemary

1-1/2 teaspoons basil

1-1/2 teaspoons thyme leaves

1/2 teaspoon celery salt

2 tablespoons Worcestershire sauce

1 can (15 ounces) beef broth

Mix all together and cook in slow cooker 12 to 18 hours on low. Break apart the meat (shred with 2 forks) and serve on French rolls with mozzarella cheese and peppers on the side.

Chicken Caesar Burgers

Beth Miller,
Assistant Coach, Womens Golf

YIELD: 4 SERVINGS

INGREDIENTS

1/2 cup finely chopped onion

2 tablespoons lemon juice

3 teaspoons dried parsley

2 cloves garlic, minced

4 tablespoons fresh shredded Parmesan cheese, divided

1/2 teaspoon salt

1/2 teaspoon pepper

2 teaspoons Worcestershire sauce

4 slider size buns

4 teaspoons fat-free creamy Caesar salad dressing

1 pound ground chicken

1/2 cup Romaine lettuce

In a small bowl, combine the onion, lemon juice, parsley, garlic, 2 tablespoons cheese, salt, pepper and Worcestershire sauce. Mix in the chicken so sauce is evenly dispersed. Shape into 4 small patties.

On a grill pan, heat small amount of olive oil. Place patties onto pan and cook approximately 5 to 7 minutes on each side. Sprinkle with the remaining cheese.

Serve on buns with romaine lettuce and salad dressing on bun.

Pork Barbecue

Jayne Donohoe,
Lacrosse Mom — Casey 2009

YIELD: 3 TO 4 SERVINGS

A favorite of the lacrosse families.

INGREDIENTS

1 whole (2 pound) pork tenderloin

2 cups water

5 tablespoons margarine

2 onions, chopped

2 tablespoons vinegar

2 tablespoons Worcestershire

1 lemon, juiced

3/4 cup ketchup

3/4 cup water

1 tablespoon chili powder

1/2 cup light brown sugar

1 teaspoon salt

1 teaspoon dry mustard

Put tenderloin and water in a pot. Bring to a boil, then simmer the tenderloin for an hour or more, until it falls apart. Cool, then pick/tear into small strands.

Sauté the onions in the margarine. Add the vinegar, ketchup, Worcestershire sauce, water and lemon juice. Cook for a few minutes until the sauce thickens. Then stir in the chili powder, brown sugar, salt and dry mustard. Blend the seasoned sauce with the pulled pork. Salt and pepper, to taste. Heat the pork mixture and serve on buns.

This dish freezes well.

Oven Roasted Pulled Pork

Don Skiba

YIELD: 12 SERVINGS

INGREDIENTS

5 to 7 pounds pork roast, preferably shoulder or Boston butt

1-1/2 cups cider vinegar

1 cup yellow or brown mustard

1/2 cup ketchup

1/3 cup packed brown sugar

2 cloves garlic, smashed

1 teaspoon salt

1 teaspoon cayenne

1/2 teaspoon freshly ground black pepper

RUB:

3 tablespoons paprika

1 tablespoon garlic powder

1 tablespoon brown sugar

1 tablespoon dry mustard

3 tablespoons coarse salt

GARNISHES:

coleslaw

pickle spears

Mix the dry rub ingredients together in a small bowl. Rub the spice blend all over the pork and marinate for as little as 1 hour or up to overnight, covered, in the refrigerator.

Preheat oven to 300 degrees. Put the marinated pork in a roasting pan and bake for 6 hours, until the meat is falling apart and an instant read thermometer inserted into the thickest part registers 170 degrees.

SAUCE: Combine the vinegar, mustard, ketchup, brown sugar, garlic, salt, cayenne and black pepper in a saucepan over medium heat. Simmer gently, stirring, for 10 minutes until the sugar dissolves.

Remove the pork roast from the oven and transfer to a large platter. Allow the meat to rest for about 10 minutes. While still warm, take 2 forks and shred the pork by holding the meat with 1 fork and pulling it away with the other. Put the shredded pork in a bowl. Discard fat pieces. Pour half of the sauce on the shredded pork and mix well to coat. Serve with the remaining sauce on the side. 🐾

Luau Style Pulled Pork

Clem West, 1973,
Women's Swimming

YIELD: 10 TO 12 SERVINGS

INGREDIENTS

6 pounds pork butt roast (bone-in)
2 tablespoons Hawaiian sea salt
Hawaiian rolls or other

Requires an electric smoker to cold smoke the roast prior to slow cooking it.

Pierce the pork butt with a fork or small knife. Rub the Hawaiian salt over the roast making sure to get salt into the holes left by piercing. Place the roast in the electric smoker and cold smoke for 80 minutes with no heat (I use Hickory). Immediately remove roast and place into a slow cooker for 12 hours taking care to turn the roast after six hours. Be sure to watch the liquid level as the roast should not become dry. Add water if necessary. Remove the roast and shred the pork, discarding the bone and fat. Return to the juices and serve hot. 🐾

Kalua Hawaiian Pig

Kenan & Coach Paul Stevens,
Head Coach, Baseball

YIELD: 10 TO 12 SERVINGS

INGREDIENTS

1 pork shoulder roast, about 6 pounds
1 to 2 tablespoons Hawaiian sea salt
1 tablespoon liquid smoke flavoring
Hawaiian bread or buns

Pierce pork all over with a sharp knife. Rub salt and then liquid smoke over meat. Place in slow cooker with fat side up. Cover and cook on low for 16 to 20 hours. Turn roast occasionally. Remove meat from pot and shred. Remove fat from drippings and put meat back in the juice. Use Hawaiian bread or buns for sandwiches. 🐾

COACHES QUOTES

Paul Stevens, Baseball:

PAUL CALLS:

"Never give in, never give up."

"Analysis causes paralysis"

"5 P's"

"Believe"

"Get to it and through it!"

*"Attitude and Hustle.
Things you can control."*

Shrimp Tacos

Nicole & Zak Kustok, 2002,
Football

YIELD: 4 SERVINGS

This recipe (along with the Chimichurri Steak Marinade/Sauce) is Zak's favorite ... he calls it the The Spicy Surf and Turf although upon further inspection, it should probably be called, garlic, garlic and more garlic. And yes, it's alot of food for two people :) but somehow he always manages to finish it!

INGREDIENTS

3 limes

1 cup chopped tomato

2 diced avocados

1/2 cup fresh cilantro, chopped

salt and pepper, to taste

1 teaspoon paprika or smoky chipotle
  seasoning

3 cloves garlic, minced

1 pound cooked and peeled
  medium shrimp

12 (6 inch) corn tortillas

Adjust cilantro, to taste.

Zest limes and squeeze juice in a large bowl. Add remaining ingredients including zest; toss well to combine. Cover and chill for 15 minutes. Serve on warm tortillas.

Chipotle Turkey Taco Filling

Jason Wright, 2003,
Football/Arizona Cardinals

YIELD: 10 TACOS

This recipe is a staple in our household. It is easy, healthy and (most importantly) so frickin' tasty. The recipe makes about ten wonderfully flavored, unique tasting tacos.

INGREDIENTS

1 tablespoon extra virgin olive oil

1-1/3 pounds ground turkey breast

1 small onion, chopped

2 cloves garlic, chopped

2 canned chipotles in adobo sauce,
  chopped

1 cup tomato sauce

1 tablespoon (rounded) chili powder

salt, to taste

10 tortillas, toasted if desired

Remove seeds from peppers if you don't want it spicy. We like the heat.

In a skillet preheated over medium-high heat, add oil and ground turkey meat. Brown meat 2 or 3 minutes, then add onions and garlic. Cook onions and meat together for another 3 to 5 minutes. Stir in chipotles, chili powder and tomato sauce. Season with salt, to taste. Reduce heat to medium low and simmer until ready to serve.

The most popular toppings at our place are sour cream (a great compliment to the heat), avocado, lettuce and tomato. Warning: you will likely be tempted to lick your plate clean, so exert some self-control if you have company!

stove top

Cuban Dinner

Ellen Aiello

YIELD: 6 SERVINGS

INGREDIENTS

1 pound ground beef

1 medium green pepper, diced

1 medium onion, diced

2 cloves garlic, crushed

1 can (14 ounces) diced tomato or
    1 large tomato, diced

1 bay leaf

1 teaspoon oregano

1/2 teaspoon cumin

2 teaspoons cinnamon

1/2 cup raisins

1/2 cup chopped walnuts

1 cup cooked rice

salt and pepper, to taste

Sauté garlic, onions and pepper in olive oil. Add ground beef and spices; brown thoroughly and drain fat. Add tomatoes, raisins and walnuts. Cover and simmer until warm. Serve over rice.

Laurie's Beans and Franks

Cathleen & Coach Laurie Schiller,
Head Coach, Women's Fencing

YIELD: 4 SERVINGS

INGREDIENTS

1 can (28 to 31 ounces) pork & beans
1 package all beef franks
    (6 or 8 count)
2 tablespoons relish
1 tablespoon Grey Poupon mustard
    (or equivalent)
4 teaspoons or more of molasses
1 medium onion, chopped

Boil the franks per the directions on the package. In a separate pot, mix the rest of the ingredients, cover, and simmer on low for 10 minutes. When the franks are boiled, cut them into 1/2 inch pieces and add them to the bean mixture. Cover and cook at low heat for at least 10 minutes until frank pieces have absorbed some of the flavor of the bean mixture.

Easy Chicken Tikka Masala

Larry Villella, 2000

YIELD: 12 SERVINGS

INGREDIENTS

4-1/2 pounds boneless skinless
    chicken breast, cubed
3 tablespoons Dijon mustard
6 ounces skim milk
15 ounces Greek yogurt
6 tablespoons lemon juice
3 cans (8 ounces each) tomato sauce
15 cloves garlic, minced
2 cans (4 ounces each) green chilies
6 tablespoons paprika
6 tablespoons garam masala
3 teaspoons cumin
1-1/2 teaspoons turmeric
4 to 6 cups cooked basmati rice,
    optional

Garnish with fresh cilantro and serve with kheera ka raita (cucumber in spiced yogurt)

Mix all ingredients (except rice) together in airtight container and refrigerate overnight to marinate. Add to slow cooker and cook over low heat for at least 6 hours, or until chicken is fully cooked. Prepare basmati rice per package directions and serve with chicken.

COACHES QUOTES

Laurie Schiller, Women's Fencing:

"Focus on one touch at a time — the score is always 0-0."

Szechwan Pasta

Betty Flowers,
**Lacrosse Mom — Lynda McCandlish,
2006, and Kristin McCandlish, 2009**

YIELD: 6 SERVINGS

INGREDIENTS

1 pound angel hair pasta
3/4 cup soy sauce, divided
1/4 cup peanut oil
3/4 cup mayonnaise
1 tablespoon Dijon mustard
1/4 cup Oriental sesame oil
1/8 cup House of Tsang
    sesame chili oil
2 whole chicken breasts,
    boneless and skinless
2 tablespoons olive oil
6 green onions, thinly sliced
1 red bell pepper, coarsely chopped
1/2 cup fresh parsley
1/2 pound fresh snow peas, trimmed
    and cut into pieces
2 carrots, peeled and coarsely chopped
1 can (6 ounces) sliced
    water chestnuts, optional

*If you don't want crispy snow peas,
blanch them.*

Blanch snow peas if desired. Halve and
sauté chicken breasts in olive oil, cool and
shred or cut into bite-sized pieces. In a
small bowl, combine the mayonnaise,
mustard, sesame oil, 1/4 cup of soy sauce
and chili oil. Refrigerate.

Cook noodles according to package directions. Drain and immediately toss in a
large bowl with 1/2 cup of soy sauce —
noodle will absorb the soy sauce. Next
add the peanut oil and toss. Cool to
room temperature.

Add the chicken, green onions, carrots,
sweet pepper and chopped parsley to the
noodles. Toss gently and add the mayonnaise mixture. Toss again and cover.
Refrigerate overnight. Approximately 30
minutes before serving, remove noodle
mixture from refrigerator and toss in
snow peas, adding a little extra soy sauce,
peanut oil, or mayonnaise if noodles seem
dry.

Pesto Pasta

Aaron Smith,
Assistant Coach, Volleyball

YIELD: 8 SERVINGS

INGREDIENTS

3/4 pound chicken
1/2 pound bulk Italian sausage
2 jars (10 ounces each) prepared pesto
    sauce (to taste)
3 medium tomatoes, coarsely chopped
1 bag (16 ounces) broccoli, chopped
1 pound bow tie pasta
garlic salt, to taste
salt and pepper, to taste
grated Parmesan for garnish

Cook pasta in salted water until done;
drain, reserving 1 cup water.

Pan fry chicken in olive oil, season with
salt and pepper, set aside. Pan fry sausage,
breaking into small pieces, and set aside.
Pan fry broccoli, season with garlic salt,
adding oil if needed.

In large bowl add pesto, add cooked
chicken, sausage, broccoli and tomatoes.
Stir gently, adding a little of the reserved
pasta water if mixture is too stiff. Sprinkle
with Parmesan, to taste.

Serve with bread and salad.

Pasta a la Passion

Maureen Dowd,
Lacrosse Mom — Katrina 2010

YIELD: 4 SERVINGS

INGREDIENTS

2 cloves garlic, minced

1/4 cup extra virgin olive oil

3/4 pound chicken breasts, boned,
   skinned and cut into strips

2 cups broccoli florets

3/4 cup oil packed sun-dried
   tomatoes, cooked, drained and
   thinly sliced

1 teaspoon basil

1 red bell pepper, cut into thin strips

salt and pepper, to taste

1/4 cup white wine

3/4 cup chicken broth

1 to 2 tablespoon butter

1/2 pound bow tie pasta

grated Parmesan cheese for garnish

In skillet or saucepan, sauté the garlic in oil until golden. Add the strips of chicken and sauté until cooked. Push the chicken aside and add the red pepper and broccoli florets. Sauté the broccoli florets until they are crispy tender. Now add the sun-dried tomatoes, the seasonings, the white wine and the chicken broth. To complete the sauce, add the butter, cover and simmer for 5 minutes over low flame. Now add the cooked pasta and toss. Serve with grated Parmesan cheese.

Chicken & Andouille Pasta

Bluestone,
Evanston — Owners Jennifer and John Enright.

YIELD: 6 SERVINGS

INGREDIENTS

2 large chicken breasts, 12 to 16
   ounces, diced 1/2 inch

12 ounces Andouille sausage halved
   lengthwise and diced

4 cloves garlic, crushed or minced

1 tablespoon chopped fresh oregano

1 teaspoon crushed red pepper flakes

2 cups Roasted Red Pepper Sauce
   (below)

1 cup heavy cream

1 cup shredded sharp cheddar cheese

1 pound dried rigatoni pasta, cooked
   al dente

1 tablespoon olive oil

salt and fresh cracked black pepper, to
   taste

SAUCE:

8 large red bell peppers

1 small yellow onion, chopped

1 clove garlic, chopped

1 teaspoon olive oil

SAUCE: Roast the peppers over fire until the skin blackens and bubbles. Steam the hot peppers in a bowl covered with plastic wrap. When cool enough to handle, peel the blackened skin off the peppers and discard along with the stems and seeds. Heat the oil in a pot over medium-low heat. Add onion, garlic and peppers. Cook until the onions are soft and there is no liquid. Purée and set aside.

PASTA: Heat a sauté pan or wide pot large enough to accommodate the entire recipe. Season the raw diced chicken with salt. Add the diced chicken and the sausage, spreading out as flat as possible; turn the heat to high. Let the chicken and sausage cook without stirring for 3 minutes. Using a wooden spoon stir the meats to cook evenly another 3 minutes.

Add the garlic, oregano and red pepper flakes, cook 1 more minute. Add the heavy cream and cook for 3 to 5 minutes until thickening begins. Do not change the heat. Add the red pepper sauce and cook another 3 minutes. Lower the heat to a simmer and slowly add the cheese while stirring. Add the pasta and stir to coat. Continue simmering until the pasta is hot. Season with salt and fresh cracked black pepper, to taste.

Linguine with Clam Sauce

Jacqueline Mafuli,
Football Mom — Niko #93

YIELD: 4 TO 6 SERVINGS

INGREDIENTS

1 can (2 ounces) anchovies in oil

2 to 3 cloves garlic chopped

1 can (28 ounces) chopped tomatoes

2 cans (6.5 ounces each) chopped or minced clams

1/3 cup dried parsley flakes

2 teaspoons black pepper, or to taste

1 to 2 tablespoon olive oil (as needed)

1 pound linguine

Cook linguine to al dente according to package directions. Sauté garlic cloves in large frying pan in small amount of olive oil (just enough to sauté). Add the can of anchovies (including the oil) and sauté until crumbly. Add the cans of clams and tomatoes, parsley flakes and pepper. Allow to simmer on low heat for about 1 hour. Add additional olive oil if it appears too dry. Serve over linguine noodles.

Shrimp and Chicken Jambalaya

Cathy & Coach Mike Hankwitz,
Defensive Coordinator, Football

YIELD: 4 TO 6 SERVINGS

INGREDIENTS

2 tablespoons vegetable oil

1 pound skinless, boneless chicken
thighs, cut into 1 inch pieces

8 ounces andouille sausage, cut into
1/2 inch pieces

1 medium onion, finely chopped

3 stalks celery, finely chopped

1 green bell pepper, cored, seeded, and
finely chopped

6 scallions, green parts only, finely
chopped

4 cloves garlic, finely chopped

1 can crushed tomatoes (28 ounces)

1 can clams with juice (8 ounces)

2 cups chicken broth

1 pound large shrimp, shelled and
deveined

1-1/2 teaspoons salt

2 bay leaves

2 teaspoons dried oregano

2 teaspoons freshly ground
black pepper

1 teaspoon dried thyme

1 teaspoon cayenne

2 cups cooked white rice

Emeril's Kick it Up Sauce, optional

*You can make this really spicy with the
andouille sausage, so have fun.*

Place a Dutch oven over high heat and let it get very hot, about 2 minutes. Add the vegetable oil and spread it evenly over the pot. Add the chicken and cook until it is browned, about 5 minutes. Remove the chicken with a slotted spoon and set aside. Add the sausage and cook until it is crispy, about 5 minutes. Add the onion, celery, bell pepper and scallions; cook until the vegetables are soft, about 8 minutes. Add the garlic and cook for 1 minute more. Return the chicken to the pot along with the bay leaves, oregano, pepper, thyme, salt and cayenne; cook for 1 minute more, stirring continuously. Add the tomatoes, clams with the liquid and chicken broth. Bring to a boil, then reduce the heat and simmer for 20 minutes. Add the shrimp, cover and cook for about 8 minutes more, stirring occasionally. Add the cooked rice and cook 5 minutes more.

Crustless Fried Chicken Drumsticks

John Scott,
WCAS, Ice Hockey Club

YIELD: 40 PIECES

INGREDIENTS

1 gallon peanut oil
40 chicken drumsticks
Cajun or BBQ seasoning, to taste

First wash the drumsticks thoroughly under cool running water. Allow to drain, then pat totally dry with paper towels. Do not season them before you cook them.

Put a full 64 ounces of peanut oil into a deep fryer or a cast-iron pot. Heat the oil to exactly 350 degrees, using a thermometer to measure temperature.

When the oil reaches 350 degrees, gently ease the drumsticks (5 to 8 at a time) into the fryer. Fry 15 to 20 minutes (depending upon sizes of the pieces)… or until the skin is honey brown and crispy. Heat the oil to 350 degrees before adding the next batch.

Drain and generously sprinkle with your favorite Cajun or BBQ seasoning.

Chicken a la Lenny — Chicken with Watercress and Sun-Dried Tomatoes

Tim Lenahan,
Head Coach, Men's Soccer

YIELD: 4 SERVINGS

This is a delicious dish that is protein rich, low fat and very healthy.

INGREDIENTS

1 tablespoon olive oil
2 tablespoons onion, finely chopped
1/2 teaspoon garlic, very finely minced
1 cup white wine
2 tablespoons lemon juice
2 tablespoons tarragon, chopped
1/2 cup sun-dried tomatoes, chopped
4 boneless, skinless chicken breast
  halves
Salt and pepper, to taste
1-1/2 cups chicken broth
1 bunch watercress, washed and
  stemmed

Heat the olive oil in a stockpot on medium heat. Add the onion and garlic; cook for 3 to 4 minutes. Add the wine, lemon juice, tarragon and sun-dried tomatoes; simmer on high heat for 1 to 2 minutes. Salt and pepper chicken, to taste; add to the stockpot; cover with chicken broth. Bring mixture to a boil. Simmer for 10 minutes or until the chicken is cooked through. Remove chicken from the mixture and set aside. Simmer the remaining liquid until it is reduced in half.

Serving: Place the chicken and sun-dried tomatoes on top of the watercress. Drizzle the reduction sauce over the chicken.

Macadamia Nut-crusted Halibut

Chef William King,
**McCormick & Schmick's,
multiple locations**

YIELD: 2 SERVINGS

INGREDIENTS

2 fresh halibut fillets (5 to 6 ounces each)

1 cup macadamia nuts, roasted and crushed

1/2 cup panko bread crumbs

1 tablespoon freshly ground pepper

1/2 cup all-purpose flour

2 eggs

1/4 cup vegetable oil

1/2 cup Lemon Butter Sauce (below)

1/4 cup Major Grey's Chutney

LEMON BUTTER SAUCE:

6 ounces white wine

3 ounces freshly squeezed lemon juice

3 whole black peppercorns

1 shallot, quartered

1 cup heavy cream

6 ounces cold unsalted butter cut into pieces

3 ounces cold salted butter cut into pieces

SAUCE: Combine wine, lemon, peppercorns and shallot in a non-corrosive saucepan. Reduce until the mixture is just 1 to 2 tablespoons and has the consistency of syrup. Add the cream and reduce again until the mixture is 3 to 4 tablespoons and very syrupy. Remove pan from heat. Add the butter, about 2 ounces at a time, stirring constantly and allowing each piece to melt before adding more. Strain and keep warm until ready to use.

HALIBUT: Combine the nuts and bread crumbs; blend well. Place on a large plate or pie pan. Season the flour with the salt and pepper and place on a second plate or pan. Beat the eggs with a tablespoon of water or milk and place in a third plate or pan. First dip the fillets in the flour, coating thoroughly and shaking off the excess. Next dip the fish into the egg mixture, allowing the excess to drip off. Finally roll the fillets in the nuts, pressing them in firmly to ensure that the fish is thoroughly coated. Pan-fry the fillets 3 to 4 minutes per side in oil over medium-high heat. Remove the fillets and allow them to drain briefly on paper towels. Place them on your serving dishes. Combine the butter sauce and the chutney and pour over the halibut.

Fish Fry

Dr. Monica Joseph-Griffin & Jack Griffin,
**Monica 1989 and Jack 1990,
Assistant A.D.,
Director of the Wildcat Fund**

YIELD: 6 SERVINGS

INGREDIENTS

6 walleye, cod or pollack fillets

1-1/2 cups fish breading

red cayenne pepper

corn or vegetable oil

2 eggs

I use Andy's breading and there are others including Shore Lunch.

In a skillet (cast-iron skillet works best) put a layer of a light oil in the pan so it would cover about 1/2 of the thickness of the fish fillet. Get the oil nice and hot (375 degrees if you have a thermometer). Put breading in a bowl and add cayenne, to taste. Crack eggs in a bowl, coat the fish generously with the egg and run it through the breading so it is completely coated. Add the fish to the pan and cook until lightly browned (3 to 4 minutes each side is a good guide).

Serve it with some mac-n-cheese and some mixed veggies and you've got yourself a nice fish fry.

Peppery Cheese Fondue

Helene Bak Slowik, 1973

YIELD: 4 TO 5 SERVINGS

For pepper lovers only: it has a bite. Can also use as an appetizer.

INGREDIENTS

8 ounces sharp cheddar cheese, shredded

8 ounces Swiss cheese, shredded

2 tablespoons flour

1/2 teaspoon salt

4 teaspoons pepper

1 clove garlic, cut in half

12 to 16 ounces beer

1 dash Tabasco

1/2 loaf French bread cut into 2-inch cubes

2 apples, cored, cut into 2 inch chunks, (Granny Smith or your favorite)

1/2 loaf rye bread cut into 2-inch cubes

Cut bread and allow to dry for about one hour.

Mix cheeses, flour, salt and pepper in a large bowl. Rub cut side of garlic halves around bottom and sides of fondue pot. Discard garlic. Pour in 12 ounces beer and heat slowly. Gradually stir in cheese mixture, stirring constantly. Stir in Tabasco.

Fondue may be thin at first but will thicken as it cooks. If it gets too thick, add warmed beer. Dunk bread and fruit chunks.

Tex-Mex Spaghetti

Kelly Deiters,
Football Mom — Neal #79

YIELD: 6 SERVINGS

INGREDIENTS

16 ounces spaghetti

1 tablespoon vegetable oil

1 small yellow onion, chopped

1 teaspoon minced garlic

1 can (14-1/2 ounces) Mexican-style stewed tomatoes, undrained

1 cup mild picante sauce

1 teaspoon ground cumin

1/2 teaspoon dried oregano

1 can (16 ounces) pinto beans, drained

1 cup shredded cheddar cheese

Cook pasta according to directions on package. While it is cooking, heat oil; add chopped onion to pan with garlic and cook for about 2 minutes. Add tomatoes, picante sauce, cumin and oregano. Cover and bring to a boil. Reduce heat, uncover, and simmer for 5 minutes. Stir beans into tomato mixture. Continue to simmer until thickened. Drain pasta and top with sauce and cheese.

Mediterranean Pasta

Julie & Chloe Eades

Yield: 4 to 6 servings

Ingredients

1 tablespoon olive oil

1 onion, sliced very thin

10 to 15 kalamata olives, chopped

2 cans (14.5 ounces each) fire roasted
  tomatoes

1 bag fresh spinach, (12 ounces),
  stems trimmed

cooked pasta (approximately 2 to 3
  ounces dried per serving)

salt and pepper, to taste

shredded Parmesan or other cheese for
  topping

*Experiment: add oregano, garlic, feta or
other flavorful ingredients*

In a medium saucepan, sauté the sliced
onion in olive oil. Next add the fire
roasted tomatoes, kalamata olives and
fresh spinach. Simmer just until the
spinach is wilted.

Serve over your favorite pasta. Top with
shaved Parmesan or your favorite kind of
cheese!

Penne with Vodka Sauce

Dagmar Porcelli,
Football Mom — Chuck #74

Yield: 6 to 8 servings

Ingredients

2 cans (28 ounces each) crushed
  tomatoes

1-1/2 cups vodka

1 cup heavy whipping cream

1 cup grated Romano cheese

8 ounces marscarpone cheese

Boil pasta to al dente. In 6 quart pan add
tomatoes and vodka. Stir occasionally
bringing to a boil. Add heavy whipping
cream and continue boiling slowly. Stir
occasionally until the sauce starts to
thicken. Add cheeses and allow to melt
stirring constantly. Bring to a simmer,
then remove from heat. Pour vodka sauce
over pasta, stir and serve immediately.

Veggie-Basil Pasta

Julie Swieca, 1994,
WNUR

YIELD: 10 SERVINGS

This dish makes great use of garden favorites plus it's enjoyable cold, too!

INGREDIENTS

6 ounces farfalle or other pasta

1 can (14 ounces) quartered artichoke hearts

1 can (14 ounces) hearts of palm, sliced

2 cups chopped bell peppers, mixed colors

1/3 cup finely chopped red onion

2 cloves garlic, minced

1 tablespoon olive oil

1 cup chopped and seeded tomato

1/4 cup snipped fresh basil or
2 teaspoons crushed dried basil

2 tablespoons grated Parmesan cheese

Cook pasta until tender but firm, approximately 8 to10 minutes. Drain and keep warm.

Heat oil in a large skillet or sauté pan. Sauté peppers, onions and garlic until tender, about 5 minutes. Add artichoke hearts and hearts of palm and cook 1 to 2 minutes. Stir in tomato and basil; cook and stir about 2 minutes or until heated through. Add pasta to vegetable mixture and toss gently to mix. Sprinkle each serving with Parmesan cheese and serve.

Marie's Gnocchi

Sandy Orlandino

YIELD: 6 TO 8 SERVINGS

INGREDIENTS

2 egg yolks

2 pounds ricotta

4 cups flour

1/2 teaspoon salt

Mix all ingredients together. Separate dough and roll (by hand) into long 1-inch thick strands. Cut strands into 1-inch pieces and roll (by hand) into dumpling shape. Cook in salted boiling water; remove as they rise to the top of the boiling water. Drain but do not rinse; cover with your favorite pasta sauce.

Meatballs for Pasta

Ling & Ed Albrecht,
Lacrosse Parents — Sarah 2006

YIELD: 15 TO 20 PIECES

*From: The North End Italian Cookbook:
Marguerite Buonopane*

INGREDIENTS

1 pound ground beef

1/2 pound ground pork

2 medium eggs

2 cups soft bread crumbs or enough to
hold the mixture together

1/2 cup chopped fresh parsley

1/2 cup freshly grated Parmesan or
Romano cheese

1 large garlic clove, finely chopped

salt and pepper, to taste

*Serve with your favorite tomato sauce
over pasta.*

Combine all ingredients in a large bowl.
Toss gently with your hands until thoroughly blended. The mixture should be
fairly moist.

To form the meatballs, wet your hands in
lukewarm water and then pick up about
1/3 cup of the meatball mixture. Roll it
in the palm of your hands to form a
smooth ball about 2-1/2 inches in
diameter.

Drop the meatballs directly into your
basic tomato sauce recipe. Or, if you prefer a crusty meatball, fry in approximately
3 tablespoons of olive oil on medium
heat for about 5 minutes, turning to
brown evenly. Then drop them into gently boiling tomato sauce. Meatballs take
20 minutes to cook well. Remember to
scrape the bottom of the skillet and pour
meat particles into the meat sauce.

Potato Curry

Maret Thorpe, 1984,
Daily Northwestern

YIELD: 6 SERVINGS

INGREDIENTS

7 medium white potatoes (about 2-
1/2 pounds)

1 pound cauliflower

1-1/2 to 2 cups plain yogurt (full fat is
better, more yogurt gives very
creamy texture)

3 tablespoons curry powder

1 teaspoon salt or more, to taste

1 cup frozen peas

2 tablespoons butter or peanut oil

*Sweet curry powder from The Spice
House is best.*

Peel potatoes and cut into 3/4 inch cubes.
Wash cauliflower and break into florets.
Beat yogurt in a bowl until smooth. Set
aside to allow yogurt to get to room
temperature. Heat oil in a large, thick-
bottomed pot. When hot, add potato
cubes and brown slightly on all sides.
Then stir in curry powder to coat the
potatoes.

Add 1-1/2 cups water, bring to a boil
then simmer covered for about 3 to 5
minutes. Add cauliflower and simmer
until all vegetables are tender but not
mushy. Add salt, to taste and frozen peas.
When frozen peas are heated, stir a little
of the hot liquid into the yogurt, then
add the yogurt to the pan and stir gently.
Cook on low until yogurt is just heated,
then serve with basmati rice.

Italian Sausage Pasta

Maren & Coach Keylor Chan,
Head Coach, Volleyball

YIELD: 6 TO 8 SERVINGS

INGREDIENTS

1 pound Italian sausage
1 can (32 ounces) whole San Marzano
   tomatoes
4 cloves garlic, finely diced
1/2 red onion, diced
1/2 cup red wine
olive oil, to taste
Salt and pepper, to taste
1 bag (12 ounces) egg noodles
1 cup Italian parsley, chopped
1 cup grated Parmesan cheese

Heat a large skillet, then add olive oil to
pan. Take casing off sausages and place in
pan along with onions, garlic, wine, salt
and pepper. Break sausage into small
pieces. Cook until meat is brown, approximately 8 to 10 minutes. Add
tomatoes. Bring to simmer and cook for
20 minutes. Boil egg noodles according
to instructions on box. Drain the noodles
and place in large serving plate. Add the
sausage and sauce over the noodles, add
the parsley and cheese over the sausage
sauce. Serve.

Pasta with Italian Sausage, Sun Dried Tomatoes and Mushrooms

Erica Westrich Scullion, 2000,
Women's Soccer

YIELD: 4 SERVINGS

INGREDIENTS

1 pound rigatoni
1 tablespoon olive oil
2 cloves garlic
1 pint mushrooms
1 cup sundried tomatoes
4 spicy Italian turkey sausages
1 yellow onion
1 can diced tomatoes (14 ounces)
1 cup chicken broth
1 tablespoon Italian seasoning
salt and pepper, to taste
grated Parmesan cheese

Cook rigatoni according to the package
directions. Meanwhile, cook the sausages
over medium heat and then slice. Using
the same pan, add olive oil and sauté
onions until translucent. Add mushrooms
and sundried tomatoes, cook for 3 to 5
minutes. Add garlic and sauté for 30 seconds or until fragrant, but not brown.
Add cooked sausage back to the pan and
cook for 2 minutes. Then add chicken
stock and simmer until stock is reduced
by half. Add diced tomatoes, Italian seasoning, salt and pepper. Simmer for 10 to
15 minutes letting all of the flavors
combine. Toss with pasta and serve with
Parmesan cheese.

Creole Style Jambalaya

Tara Gregus,
Football Mom — Jake #42

YIELD: 8 TO 10 SERVINGS

This is a family favorite.

INGREDIENTS

3 to 4 tablespoons olive oil

1 large red onion, chopped

6 ribs of celery, chopped

6 green onions, white and green, sliced

5 to 6 cloves garlic, minced

3 cups uncooked long grain rice

46 ounces chicken broth
plus more if needed

2 cans (15 ounces each) diced
tomatoes

2 medium chopped fresh bell peppers,
any color

1 pound frozen cooked shrimp,
thawed, tails off

1-1/2 pounds thinly sliced smoked
sausage

4 to 5 bay leaves

1 tablespoon dried thyme

1 tablespoon Cajun seasoning

1/4 cup Louisiana hot sauce, to taste

1 teaspoon Cayenne, to taste

*If using frozen peppers, add with
tomatoes*

In a large pot with a lid, sauté onion, peppers and celery in olive oil over medium-high heat until soft, approximately 5 minutes. Add garlic and green onions and stir for a minute. Add rice and chicken broth a cup or two at a time stirring until the contents of the pot get hot again. Add remaining broth, tomatoes, bay leaves, thyme, Cajun seasoning, Louisiana hot sauce and sausage. Lower heat to medium low and cover. Cook for 45 to 50 minutes, stirring occasionally, but minimizing lifting the lid of the pot. Add more broth if it seems dry and is sticking to the bottom of the pot. Add in shrimp, taste for seasonings; adjust if necessary. Cook 5 minutes longer and check to see if the rice is soft. Serve.

Can be made up to a day ahead of time and chilled overnight in the refrigerator, though the rice can get mushy. If needed, add a bit of chicken broth to reheat.

Shrimp Fra Diavolo

Kathy Quinlan,
Director, Operations & Strategy, NAA

YIELD: 4 SERVINGS

INGREDIENTS

1 pound large shrimp, peeled and
deveined

1 teaspoon salt, plus more, to taste

1 teaspoon dried crushed red pepper
flakes

3 tablespoons olive oil

1 medium onion, finely chopped

1 can (14-1/2 ounces) diced tomatoes
with juices

1 cup dry white wine

3 cloves garlic, chopped

1/3 teaspoon dried oregano

3 tablespoons chopped fresh flat-leaf
parsley

3 tablespoons chopped fresh basil

In a medium bowl, toss the shrimp with 1 teaspoon of the salt and the red pepper flakes. In a large, heavy skillet, heat the oil over a medium-high flame. Add the shrimp and sauté until just cooked through, about 2 minutes. Using a slotted spoon, transfer the shrimp to a large plate and set aside. Add the onion to the same skillet and sauté until translucent, about 5 minutes. Add the tomatoes with their juices, wine, garlic and oregano; simmer until the sauce thickens slightly, about 10 minutes. Return the shrimp and any accumulated juices to the tomato mixture and toss to coat. Remove from the heat and stir in the parsley and basil. Season with more salt, to taste. Spoon the shrimp mixture into shallow bowls and serve.

Steak Diane

Marilyn Zilka, 1975

YIELD: 2 SERVINGS

INGREDIENTS

1/2 cup thinly sliced fresh mushrooms

2 tablespoons minced onions

1 clove garlic

1/8 teaspoon salt

1 teaspoon lemon juice

1 teaspoon Worcestershire sauce

1/4 cup butter

2 tablespoons snipped parsley

1 pound beef tenderloin or rib eye steak

Sauté and stir mushrooms, onion, garlic, salt, lemon juice and Worcestershire sauce in butter until mushrooms are tender. Stir in parsley. Add a little wine to the mixture if desired. Season the meat with salt and pepper. Add tenderloin/steaks; cook over medium-high heat, about 3 to 4 minutes each side. Serve with sauce.

Pepper Steak

Joe Slowik,

YIELD: 6 TO 8 SERVINGS

INGREDIENTS

8 ounces bacon, cut into 1/4 inch strips

1 cup onion, coarsely chopped

3 to 4 cups green and/or red bell peppers, cut into strips

1-1/2 cups ketchup

1-1/2 pounds flank or round steak, cut into strips

1/2 to 1 teaspoon dry sage

prepared rice or noodles

Fry bacon until just starting to crisp. Remove from pan and drain on paper towel.

Remove excess fat from pan — need just enough to cover the bottom of the pan (or add oil if not enough). Sauté onion in the same pan until slightly softened. Add peppers, sautéing until tender crisp. Remove from pan and place in bowl.

In pan, brown meat, a few pieces at a time, moving cooked pieces to a bowl. (If too crowded, meat will not brown.) Return meat and vegetables to pan (including any juice that accumulated).

Add bacon, ketchup, sage. Stir to mix well. Add salt and pepper, to taste. Cover, cook slowly for 15 to 20 minutes until meat is tender.

Serve over rice or noodles.

Coffee Rubbed Filet Mignon with Ancho Mushroom Sauce

Iron Chef Bobby Flay,
**Mesa Grill, N.Y. and his wife,
Stephanie March, 1996**

YIELD: 4 SERVINGS

INGREDIENTS

RUB:

1/4 cup ancho chili powder

1/4 cup finely ground espresso

2 tablespoons Spanish paprika

2 tablespoons dark brown sugar

1 tablespoon dry mustard

1 tablespoon kosher salt

1 tablespoon ground black pepper

1 tablespoon ground coriander

1 tablespoon dried oregano

2 teaspoons chile de arbol powder

2 teaspoons ground ginger

4 cuts fillet mignon, 12 ounces each

MUSHROOM SAUCE:

4 cups homemade chicken stock

3 tablespoons olive oil

1-1/2 pounds thinly sliced assorted
    wild mushrooms (shiitake,
    cremini, portobella, oyster)

4 shallots, finely diced

4 cloves garlic, finely chopped

2 tablespoons honey

salt and pepper, to taste

1/4 cup chopped cilantro leaves

3 dried ancho chilies

ANCHO CHILI PURÉE: Pour boiling water over dried ancho chilies, weigh down to submerge and soak for 30 minutes. Remove chilies from liquid, remove stems and seeds. Purée in blender with some of the soaking liquid until smooth to make about 1/4 cup.

WILD MUSHROOM SAUCE: Place stock in a medium saucepan over high heat and cook until reduced to 2 cups. Heat oil in a large sauté pan over high heat. Add mushrooms, shallot and garlic; cook until the mushrooms are golden brown and liquid has evaporated. Whisk the ancho purée into the reduced chicken stock, then add to the pan with the mushrooms. Bring to a boil and cook until the sauce is reduced by half, stirring occasionally, approximately 15 to 20 minutes. Season with honey, salt and pepper then fold in the cilantro.

RUB: Combine all spices in a bowl.

FILLETS: Season one side of each fillet with a heaping tablespoon of the rub. Heat 2 tablespoons canola oil in a large sauté pan over high heat until smoking. Place the fillet in the pan, rub-side down and cook until a crust has formed, 2 minutes. Turn the steak over, reduce heat to medium and continue cooking to medium-rare, about 6 to 7 minutes. Remove from the pan and let rest 5 minutes before serving.

SERVE: Ladle mushroom sauce onto plates, top with steak and drizzle with smoked red pepper sauce and sprinkle with chopped chives.

Sidelines

TENNIS

Men's:

Head Coach Arvid Swan (2008–present)

- It has been a varsity sport at NU since 1897 and has an all-time record of 937–624.

- Prior to Coach Swan, Paul Torricelli served as head coach from 1984–2007, winning 342 matches, leading NU to nine NCAA Tournaments and winning Big Ten Coach of the Year honors three times.

- There has been 17 Big Ten Singles champions, including eventual Grand Slam finalist Todd Martin (1990).

- There were 28 Academic All-Big Ten honorees over the last five seasons.

Women's:

Head Coach Claire Pollard (1998–present)
– 5th head coach

- It became a varsity sport in 1976 with Coach June Booth.

- There were 85 Academic All-Big Ten honorees in the years 1984-2011.

- Back to back (2009–2010) Intercollegiate Tennis Association (ITA) National Indoor Team Champions.

- There were 13 straight Big Ten Tournament titles.

beans

Bourbon Baked Beans

Marietta Paynter

YIELD: 16 TO 20 SERVINGS

Marietta was married to John Paynter, a Northwestern alum who served as director of the NU Marching Band from 1953 to1996.

INGREDIENTS

4 cans (16 ounces each) B & M
    Boston baked beans

3/4 teaspoon dry mustard

1 cup chili sauce

1 tablespoon molasses

1/2 cup bourbon

1/2 cup strong black coffee

1 can (16 ounces) crushed pineapple,
    drained

4 tablespoons dark brown sugar

Combine all ingredients in a 4-1/2 quart casserole. Bake uncovered for one hour at 350 degrees. Stir once or twice. Any more stirring and you bruise the bourbon.

Teddyboy's Touchdown Green Beans

Ted Albrecht,
WGN Radio Color Analyst for Wildcat Football

YIELD: 6 TO 8 SERVINGS

INGREDIENTS

2 pounds green beans (ends trimmed)

1 pint cherry tomatoes

1/3 cup shredded Parmesan cheese

2 tablespoons extra virgin olive oil

Sea salt

Preheat oven to 450 degrees.

Lightly oil a large, rimmed roasting pan. Add green beans and tomatoes to pan and drizzle with olive oil. Make sure they are coated well — use your hands! (Now wash your hands!)

Roast for 15 minutes until they are browned. Gently shake pan every 5 minutes for even browning. Remove after 15 minutes and salt, to taste.

Sprinkle with Parmesan cheese and return to oven for 1 to 2 minutes.

Old Fashioned Picnic Baked Beans

Ann Marie Bernardi,
Field Hockey Mom

YIELD: 12 TO 14 SERVINGS

INGREDIENTS

5 cans (16 ounces each) Great
    Northern beans, drained, rinsed
2 cups ketchup
1 cup water
1/2 pound brown sugar
1 pound bacon, cut up
1 bottle light corn syrup
1 handful dried onion flakes
1 teaspoon dry mustard

Mix all ingredients in a roasting pan.
Bake at 350 degrees for about 3-1/2
hours. Stir approximately every 30 minutes throughout cooking.

Green Beans a la Greco

Mark Hassakis, 1973

YIELD: 6 SERVINGS

INGREDIENTS

1 to 1-1/4 pounds fresh green beans,
    trimmed
1 tablespoon oil
2 medium onions, coarsely chopped
    (about 1 cup)
1 can (15 ounces) chopped tomatoes
1 can (15 ounce) tomato sauce
1/4 cup light brown sugar
1 teaspoon dried oregano
1 teaspoon dried basil
salt and pepper, to taste
1/4 cup red or white wine
water to cover

Sauté onions in oil; add chopped tomatoes, tomato sauce, brown sugar, wine,
salt, pepper, oregano and basil. Cook
simmering for 1/2 hour. Add fresh beans
and water to almost cover; cook until
sauce has reduced and thickened and
beans are done.

Finish

Allen Beans

Clare Jorgensen,
Football Mom — Paul #78

YIELD: 8 TO 10 SERVINGS

INGREDIENTS

1 can (30 ounces) Campbell's
    Pork and Beans
1 can (15 ounces) butter beans,
    drained
1 can (15 ounces) lima beans or
    black beans, drained
1 can (15 ounces) kidney beans,
    drained
1 medium onion, chopped
1 cup brown sugar
1/2 cup ketchup
1 teaspoon garlic powder
1 teaspoon dry mustard
1/2 pound cooked bacon or ham,
    chopped

*Light brown sugar will work but dark
brown gives more flavor.*

Preheat oven to 350 degrees. Combine all
ingredients and pour into greased 9x13
inch pan and bake for about 1 hour or
until top is browned and bubbly.

Roasted Green Beans

Arlene Koester,
Lacrosse Mom — Courtney 2005

INGREDIENTS

Fresh young, tender green beans
olive oil
onion salt
garlic salt
Parmesan cheese, shredded

*The amounts for all the ingredients are,
to taste. Use as many green beans as
needed for your meal.*

Preheat oven to 400 degrees.

Remove the ends of the beans, rinse and
pat dry. In a large bowl toss the beans
with olive oil, garlic salt and onion salt.
Place the beans in a single layer on a
cookie sheet. Roast for 10 to15 minutes.
Remove the beans as they begin to turn
golden, continue roasting remaining
beans. Garnish with shredded Parmesan
cheese.

California Baked Beans

Mary & Coach Gary Barnett,
**Former NU Football Head Coach
(Rose Bowl 1996);
Mary is a Founder of CatBackers**

YIELD: 8 TO 10 SERVINGS

INGREDIENTS

1 can (16 ounces) kidney beans

2 cans (16 ounces each) pork & beans
(I use Bush's)

1 can (16 ounces) small white beans
(canelli) or black beans

12 slices bacon, partially cooked and
chopped

1-1/2 cups ketchup

1 cup brown sugar

1/2 teaspoon cumin

1 large onion, chopped

1 teaspoon chili powder

Drain beans and combine all the ingredients. Bake at 400 degrees in uncovered bean pot for 45 minutes. Cover pot and continue cooking for 15 more minutes.

rice

Wild Rice Casserole

Bonnie & Dan Wefler,
Bonnie 1950 and Dan 1950

Don't skip the olives; for some reason, they are very important. Our family has been serving this Minnesota recipe on holidays for about fifty years. It can be a meal by itself, or a wonderful side dish.

INGREDIENTS

1 cup wild rice

1 cup diced sharp cheddar cheese
(about 6 ounces)

1 cup chopped ripe (black) olives

1 can (14-1/2 ounces) diced tomatoes,
including juice

1 cup sliced fresh mushrooms (button
or Baby Bella), optional

1 cup chopped onion

1/3 cup olive oil

1 cup water

1/3 teaspoon salt

black pepper, to taste

Wash rice in cold water. Add 3 cups water to a saucepan and heat to boiling. Stir rice into the boiling water; parboil for 5 minutes. Remove from heat and let stand for one hour. Drain. Preheat oven to 350 degrees. Mix all ingredients together and put mixture into a casserole. Pat down so liquid is visible. Bake for at least an hour or until rice is tender. Time depends on freshness of rice and soaking time. When casserole is done, water will have evaporated and top will be browned with onions slightly caramelized.

This dish can be prepared ahead of time. It reheats well or can be eaten at room temperature.

Denise's Foolproof Risotto

Denise Norton,
Executive Chef/Owner,
Flavour Cooking School

YIELD: 4 TO 6 SERVINGS

The secret to this recipe is a pressure cooker; it eliminates the need to stand and stir for 45 minutes.

INGREDIENTS

1 tablespoon extra virgin olive oil

1 medium onion, diced

1 clove garlic, minced

1-1/2 cups arborio rice

1/2 cup dry white wine

3 cups chicken stock

1 cup finely grated Parmesan cheese

1 tablespoon minced fresh herbs
(chives, oregano, thyme, basil, etc)

salt

pepper

Heat pressure cooker over medium-high heat. Add oil. Add onions and sauté for about 3 minutes. Add garlic and sauté until aromatic — about 1 minute. Add rice and stir to combine. Add wine and sauté until absorbed, about 2 minutes. Add stock. Secure the lid and bring the cooker to pressure using high heat. Reduce heat to just high enough to maintain pressure. Cook for 10 minutes. Release pressure and turn off heat. Remove lid. Stir in Parmesan and herbs. Taste and adjust seasonings.

fruit

Minnie's Apples and Potatoes

Lorraine Morton,
Former Evanston Mayor

YIELD: 6 TO 8 SERVINGS

INGREDIENTS

6 baking apples, cored

6 white potatoes

1/4 teaspoon salt

1/4 teaspoon cinnamon

1/4 teaspoon sugar

1/4 pound butter or margarine

Cut unpeeled apples and potatoes in round slices about 2 inches thick. Brush potato slices with butter and bake in 375 degree oven until done. Place the apples in a frying pan. Cover with 1/2 to 3/4 cup of water and cook until softened, saving the juice.

Put potatoes in a baking dish and place apple pieces on top. Dot pieces with butter and sprinkle with salt, sugar, cinnamon and juice from apples. Bake until brown and juices have been absorbed. Brown in broiler for additional color.

Homemade Applesauce

Jid Kratz, 1971

INGREDIENTS

5 pounds apples, mixture of Granny
    Smith, Gala and Golden

1/4 cup apple cider (or water)

1 to 2 teaspoons cinnamon

1 to 1-1/2 teaspoons nutmeg

1 teaspoon ground cloves, optional

1 teaspoon honey or maple syrup,
    optional

1/2 to 1 cup raisins, dried cranberries
    or toasted nuts, optional

Peel, core and slice apples. (I use the
Apple Peeler; you can core and slice 5
pounds of apples in 5 minutes.)

Place slices in pot on medium heat. Add
cider or water; bring to boil then lower
heat and simmer for 30 to 40 minutes
until apples are soft. Add cinnamon and
nutmeg, to taste. Add other flavorings, to
taste.

Cranberry Relish

Karen Laner &
Pete Friedmann, 1980,
NUMB Announcer

YIELD: 4 TO 6 SERVINGS

INGREDIENTS

1 package fresh or frozen cranberries

1 cup sugar

3 oranges, peeled and sectioned

1 package frozen raspberries, thawed

Cut or add sugar, according, to taste.

Wash raspberries. Combine with other
ingredients in food processor and pulse
until evenly minced. Refrigerate until
ready to serve.

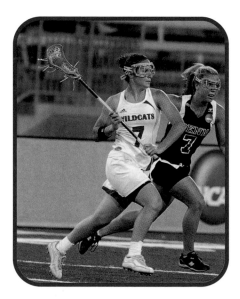

Squash and Fruit Medley

Helene Bak Slowik, 1973

YIELD: 8 TO 10 SERVINGS

INGREDIENTS

1 tablespoon molasses

1 teaspoon cinnamon

1/4 teaspoon ground ginger

1/8 teaspoon nutmeg

1/8 teaspoon mace

1/8 teaspoon kosher salt, to taste

4 cups peeled butternut squash,
    cut in 1-inch cubes

3 cups fresh pears, cut in 1 inch cubes

2 cups peeled baking apples,
    cut in 1-inch cubes

1 cup fresh cranberries

2 tablespoons melted unsalted butter

Preheat oven to 350 degrees. In a small bowl, stir together the melted butter, molasses, cinnamon, ginger, nutmeg, mace and salt. Set aside. In a large bowl, toss together the squash, pears, apples and cranberries. Pour butter mixture over and toss until well mixed. Spread into a 9x13 inch baking dish and bake for 30 minutes. Remove from oven, stir. Return to oven and bake an additional 15 minutes or until the squash and pears are tender.

other

Antipasto Bowl

Mary Ellen Baker,
Football Mom — Hayden #68

YIELD: 20 SERVINGS

INGREDIENTS

3 cups sliced asparagus cut into
    2-inch pieces

3 cups quartered mushrooms

1 cup red bell pepper strips

3 ounces mozzarella, cubed

3 ounces salami or pepperoni strips

1 can (14-1/2 ounces) artichoke
    hearts, quartered and drained

1 jar (11-1/2 ounces) pepperoncini
    peppers, drained and sliced

1/4 cup cider vinegar

1/4 cup finely chopped fresh flat leaf
    parsley

2 tablespoons olive oil

2 teaspoons dried oregano

1 teaspoon sugar

1/4 teaspoon salt

1/4 teaspoon pepper

3 cloves garlic, minced

Steam asparagus for 2 minutes. Drain and plunge into ice water; drain again. Combine asparagus with the rest of the vegetables. In a separate bowl, combine vinegar, parsley, oil, oregano, salt, pepper and garlic with a whisk. Pour over veggies and refrigerate for at least 2 hours for flavors to combine. Can add more salt/pepper/garlic, to taste.

Yorkshire Pudding

Audrey Toelke

YIELD: 6 SERVINGS

INGREDIENTS

2 eggs

1 cup milk

1 cup flour (3/4 cup for delicate pudding)

1/4 teaspoon salt

Preheat oven to 450 degrees. Beat eggs and milk together until well blended. Stir in flour and salt. Beat by hand until evenly blended but do not overbeat. Pour into greased cupcake/muffin pan or 9x9 inch cake pan. Batter should be 1/2 inch deep. Bake for 30 minutes or until puffed and brown. Remove from pan and cut in squares. Serve with roast beef and gravy. Pudding should be served over noodles with gravy.

Shon Morris:

"The meek shall inherit the earth, but they aren't going to get an offensive rebound."

Said during a television brodcast of a Northwestern Men's Basketball game.

pasta

Macaroni and Cheese — Not the Box Stuff

Mike Deneen, 1990

If all your mac&cheese intake has come out of a narrow, rectangular box, you have to try this stuff. It's an indispensible comfort food.

INGREDIENTS

3 or 4 cups cooked macaroni

2 cups evaporated milk

1/2 teaspoon paprika

1 teaspoon salt

2 tablespoons minced onion

1 egg, beaten, optional

2 cups cubed cheese (sharp cheddar or add others for a combination)

2 tablespoons butter

Put all sauce ingredients in a slow cooker; stir well. Cover and cook on high 1 hour, stirring occasionally. Add egg if using; mix. Add cooked and drained macaroni; stir. Cover and cook on low for 3 to 5 hours without stirring. There will be a nice crust on top.

Mom's Mac N Cheese

Greg Kameika, 1977

YIELD: 16 SERVINGS

INGREDIENTS

1 pound rigatoni

8 tablespoons flour

1/4 pound butter

1 tablespoon Worcestershire sauce

2 teaspoons garlic powder

1 tablespoon dried minced onions

1 tablespoon dried mustard

2 teaspoons lemon-pepper

1 quart whole milk

1 pound grated extra-sharp cheddar cheese

1 pinch paprika

1 teaspoon freshly grated horseradish, optional

Preheat oven to 350 degrees. Cook the rigatoni and drain.

Make a roux with the flour and butter, stirring constantly over low heat until thoroughly mixed. Remove from heat and add Worcestershire sauce, garlic powder, minced onions, dried mustard and lemon-pepper; continue stirring for 1 to 2 minutes. Add milk, return to heat and keep stirring until mixture thickens. Watch closely since the mixture will thicken quickly. Do not let boil over.

Remove from heat and add grated cheese. Grease casserole dish and pour a little sauce on bottom. Add half the cooked rigatoni then add more sauce and rest of rigatoni, top with remaining sauce and mix so rigatoni is evenly coated.

Sprinkle a little paprika on top for color. Bake for 45 to 60 minutes.

Baked Macaroni and Cheese

Denise & Coach Jerry Brown, Assistant Head Coach, Football

YIELD: 6 SERVINGS

INGREDIENTS

2 cups elbow macaroni

2 cups milk

2 tablespoons all-purpose flour

3 tablespoons butter

2 cups shredded sharp cheddar cheese

1/2 teaspoon salt

Cook macaroni according to package directions. Drain. Preheat oven to 350 degrees.

Melt butter in saucepan. When melted, add flour and stir until well blended. Gradually add milk and continue to stir over low heat until mixture thickens. Remove from heat and stir in cheese until melted. Add cheese sauce to cooked macaroni and stir until macaroni is evenly covered.

Pour mixture into a 2-quart baking dish that has been sprayed lightly with cooking spray.

Bake until bubbly, for 20 to 25 minutes.

Running Back Macaroni and Cheese

Damien Anderson, 2002,
Football

YIELD: 4 TO 6 SERVINGS

INGREDIENTS

1 pound elbow macaroni
1 tablespoon vegetable oil
1 tablespoon butter
1/2 cup grated mild cheddar cheese
1/2 cup grated sharp cheese
1/2 cup grated Monterey Jack cheese
1 cup grated Velveeta
2 cups half-and-half
2 eggs, lightly beaten
1/4 teaspoon seasoned salt

Preheat oven to 350 degrees. Lightly butter a casserole dish. Cook the macaroni according to box instructions to al dente. In a large bowl, mix butter and cooked macaroni thoroughly. Mix in shredded cheeses, adding the Velveeta last. Mix in half-and-half and seasoned salt. Pour macaroni in buttered casserole dish. Place in oven and bake 30 to 35 minutes.

Coach Carmody's Pesto

Barbara & Coach Bill Carmody,
Head Coach,
Men's Basketball

YIELD: 4 CUPS

Adapted from an authentic Ligurian recipe.

INGREDIENTS

1/2 pound unsalted cold butter,
    cut into pieces
1 clove garlic, peeled
2 bunches (about 6 cups) fresh basil,
    thick stems discarded, rinsed
    and dried. (This is the hardest
    part!)
3/4 cup olive oil
1/3 cup walnuts
1/4 cup pine nuts
1/4 pound Pecorino cheese
1/4 pound Parmesan cheese
3 tablespoons cream cheese
1/4 cup heavy cream
freshly ground pepper

Pesto should be stored in tightly closed containers, and will keep for about 3 weeks. Take from refrigerator 30 minutes or more before using. (DO NOT heat it.) Add to hot pasta, vegetables, whatever just before eating. It can be frozen, but will lose some flavor.

Get out your food processor — the only way to make it quickly. Cut Parmesan and Pecorino into 1 inch cubes and process until completely grated. Add pine nuts, walnuts and garlic and process briefly. Add rinsed and dried basil to food processor and process until blended — stop and start to ensure the leaves get completely incorporated. Remove processor cover, and distribute butter pieces and cream cheese on top of basil mixture. Process until smooth. Combine olive oil and heavy cream in measuring cup and slowly, in a steady stream, pour into running processor, blending completely until thick and creamy. Add pepper, to taste.

Betty Ruben's Noodle Kugel

Betty & Fred Ruben, 1957

YIELD: 12 SERVINGS

Noodle Kugel (noodle pudding) is a traditional dish in Jewish cooking. Kugel can be savory or sweet. A savory kugel might contain onions and mushrooms but no cottage cheese. This sweet version is unique because the noodles are not boiled before being added to the pudding, but instead cook in the liquid as the kugel bakes.

INGREDIENTS

3 large eggs
1/4 cup sugar
1 teaspoon vanilla
2 cups milk
1 cup small curd cottage cheese
1 can (8 ounces) crushed pineapple in juice
1 package (8 ounces) medium noodles
1/4 pound butter
1 cup crushed cornflake crumbs
1 teaspoon cinnamon, to taste

Preheat oven to 350 degrees.

Make topping by combining cornflake crumbs and cinnamon in small bowl. Set aside.

In large bowl whisk eggs with sugar until well blended. Add vanilla, milk, cottage cheese and pineapple with juice; mix thoroughly. Add uncooked noodles, mix gently.

Melt butter in a 9x12 inch baking dish; fold butter into noodle mixture, then pour mixture into the pan. Sprinkle topping over kugel. Bake for one hour.

Orzo Risotto

Daniel R Barron, KSM

YIELD: 6 SERVINGS

INGREDIENTS

3 cups water
2 cups chicken broth
2 tablespoons olive oil
1-1/2 cups finely chopped onion
1-1/2 cups orzo pasta
1/2 teaspoon dried thyme
1/2 cup dry white wine
1/2 cup grated Parmesan cheese
2 tablespoons butter
salt and pepper, to taste

Mix water and chicken broth in a saucepan and bring to a boil, then simmer covered. Add olive oil to a larger pan and add onions. Cook until onions begin to soften. Add orzo and thyme and stir just until orzo begins to darken a bit. Add white wine and stir until absorbed. Add 1 cup of the water/chicken broth mixture and stir. Continue adding liquid 1/4 cup at a time as absorbed by the orzo.

When the orzo has absorbed as much liquid as possible, turn off heat. Some liquid may be left over. Add Parmesan and butter, stir to mix and season with salt and pepper, to taste. Serve.

To re-heat, cool risotto and refrigerate in a resealable bag. Add a bit of water or broth and heat gently in the microwave.

potatoes

Gourmet Potatoes

P J Sinopoli,
Cheerleading Mom — Jenny

YIELD: 8 TO 10 SERVINGS

INGREDIENTS

8 medium potatoes

2 cups shredded cheddar cheese

1/2 cup butter, cut in pieces

1-1/2 cups sour cream

1/3 cup chopped onion

1 teaspoon salt

1/2 teaspoon pepper

2 tablespoons butter,
    cut in small pieces

paprika

Cook potatoes in skins, cool, peel and shred (I chill the cooked potatoes overnight in the refrigerator and shred in the food processor the next day). Combine cheese and 1/2 cup butter. Melt over low heat, stirring constantly. Remove from heat and blend in sour cream, onion, salt and pepper. Fold in shredded potatoes. Put in a greased casserole, dot with butter and sprinkle with paprika.

Bake in a preheated 350 degree oven for 45 minutes.

Potato Cheese Soufflé

Megan Anderson, 1976

YIELD: 4 TO 6 SERVINGS

INGREDIENTS

4 servings prepared instant
    mashed potatoes

4 eggs, separated

8 ounces shredded cheddar cheese

1 teaspoon Worcestershire sauce

2 drops Tabasco sauce

Preheat oven to 350 degrees. Prepare potatoes according to package directions. Stir in egg yolks, cheddar cheese, Worcestershire sauce and Tabasco sauce. Beat egg whites until stiff. Fold gently but thoroughly into potatoes. Pour into a greased 1-1/2 quart casserole or soufflé dish. Bake 40 to 45 minutes until brown. Serve immediately.

Texas Ranch Potatoes

Cathy & Coach Mike Hankwitz,
Defensive Coordinator, Football

YIELD: 10 SERVINGS

INGREDIENTS

10 large potatoes with skin

1 bottle ranch dressing (24 ounces)

1/4 pound butter

1 bag sharp cheddar cheese (2 cups)

salt, to taste

pepper, to taste

Boil the potatoes with skin until fork soft. Set aside to cool.

Preheat oven to 325 degrees. Peel if desired and slice potatoes; place in large baking dish. Add salt and pepper, to taste. Mix.

Slice butter on top of potatoes then pour ranch dressing all over them. Make sure the potatoes are covered with dressing. Top with cheddar cheese (generously) so dressing is thickly covered. Cover and bake for 45 minutes or until cheese is browning on edges.

Potato Casserole

Shon Morris, 1988,
Senior Associate AD (Development), Basketball

YIELD: 12 SERVINGS

INGREDIENTS

2 pounds Ore-Ida cubed hash browns

1/2 cup butter, melted

1 teaspoon salt

1/4 teaspoon pepper

1 can (10-1/2 ounces) condensed cream of chicken soup

2 cups grated cheddar cheese

1/2 cup chopped onion

2 cups sour cream

2 cups crushed corn flakes

1/4 cup melted butter

Preheat oven to 350 degrees. Thaw potatoes and combine all ingredients except cornflakes and melted butter. Mix and put in 9x13 inch pan. Top with crushed corn flakes and butter. Cook for 45 minutes until hot and slightly browned.

Mascarpone Mashed Potatoes

Bonnie Bock

YIELD: 12 TO 14 SERVINGS

INGREDIENTS

10 medium Yukon Gold potatoes

1 teaspoon salt

8 cloves garlic, roasted, mashed

2 teaspoons Tuscan Herb olive oil (from The Olive Tap)

1/4 cup butter

8 ounces mascarpone cheese

1 cup Asiago grated cheese

1/4 cup chopped chives

1/2 to 3/4 cup whole milk

You can roast the garlic cloves the day before and refrigerate.

Peel potatoes and boil them in water until they are soft; drain.

Mash potatoes. Then stir in mascarpone, milk, mashed roasted garlic, olive oil, butter and chives.

Add half of the Asiago cheese and mix.

Place mixture in a 9x12 inch glass baking dish and top with the rest of the Asiago cheese. Bake 10 minutes and then put in the broiler for about 3 minutes to brown a little.

Snowy Mashed Potatoes

Mary Ann Graham

<small>YIELD: 8 SERVINGS</small>

INGREDIENTS

4 pounds potatoes (12 medium)

8 ounces cream cheese

1 cup sour cream

2 teaspoons salt

1/2 teaspoon pepper

1 clove garlic, crushed

2 tablespoons chopped chives

1 tablespoon butter,
    cut into small pieces

1/2 teaspoon paprika

May be prepared a day in advance and refrigerated. Let come to room temperature then bake.

Cook, drain and mash potatoes. Beat until smooth adding cream cheese, sour cream, salt, pepper and garlic. Stir in chopped chives. Pour into a 2-quart greased baking dish. Dot the potatoes with butter and sprinkle with paprika. Bake at 350 degrees for 30 minutes.

Peggy's Sesame Potatoes

Tim Sonder, 1983,
Men's Fencing

<small>YIELD: 6 AS A MAIN COURSE OR 10 TO 12 AS A SIDE</small>

Serve with plain yogurt for a yummy low-fat treat.

INGREDIENTS

6 large russet potatoes

2 tablespoons sesame or caraway seeds

1-1/2 teaspoons coarse salt
        (kosher or sea salt)

Preheat oven to 400 degrees. Scrub potatoes and slice in half lengthwise. Mix the seeds and salt in a large flat dish or pie plate. Press the cut potatoes cut side down into the seed mixture so seeds and salt stick; then place cut-side down on ungreased cookie sheet.

Bake for about 20 to 25 minutes or until tender when poked and seeds are nicely browned.

Parmesan Roasted New Potatoes

Don Skiba

YIELD: 8 SERVINGS

INGREDIENTS

2 pounds new potatoes, cut into quarters

1/3 cup olive oil

1 teaspoon dry oregano

1/2 teaspoon dry basil

1 teaspoon dry parsley

salt and pepper, to taste

2 cloves garlic, minced

1/2 to 1 cup grated Parmesan cheese

Preheat oven to 400 degrees. Toss potatoes with oil, seasonings, garlic and cheese. Spread in single layer onto a cookie sheet. Sprinkle with a little additional Parmesan cheese. Bake for 45 minutes or until golden brown.

Half-Finger-Size Dumplings

Harriet Skiba

YIELD: 6 TO 8 SERVINGS

INGREDIENTS

1 cup cold mashed potatoes

1 cup flour

1 large egg

1/2 teaspoon salt

3 tablespoons butter, melted

3 tablespoons seasoned bread crumbs

2 quarts water, salted (or broth)

Mix mashed potatoes, flour, egg and salt. Bring water to a boil. Pinch off small pieces of the potato mixture and roll between hands to form small fingers. Drop fingers into boiling water and boil for 10 minutes. Drain. Toss with melted butter and top with bread crumbs.

Cheesy Hashbrown Casserole

Laura & Coach Joe McKeown, Head Coach, Women's Basketball

INGREDIENTS

1 package Ore-Ida Country Style hash browns (about 30 ounces)

1 can (10-3/4 ounces) condensed cream of chicken soup

12 ounces grated cheddar cheese

8 ounces sour cream

1 teaspoon salt

1/2 small onion, finely chopped

2 cups crushed corn flakes

1/4 pound butter, melted

Preheat oven to 350 degrees. Spray a 9x13 inch dish with non-stick spray. Layer hash browns into dish.

Mix in a medium bowl: soup, cheese, sour cream, salt and onion; put on top of hash browns.

Top with crushed corn flakes, spread evenly and press firmly. Drizzle with melted butter.

Bake for 45 minutes until golden.

Hashbrown Casserole

Abbey Boudreau,
Daughter of Tammy and the late
Coach Randy Walker

YIELD: 8 TO 10 SERVINGS

A favorite holiday side dish in our family.

INGREDIENTS

1 bag (30 ounces) frozen hash browns
1/2 cup chopped green onions
1/4 pound margarine, melted
1 can (10-3/4 ounces) condensed
   cream of chicken soup or cream
   of mushroom
1 cup sour cream
1-1/2 teaspoons salt
1 cup crushed corn flakes
4 teaspoons margarine, melted
salt and pepper, to taste

Thaw potatoes completely. Preheat oven to 350 degrees. Mix the potatoes, onions, margarine, soup, sour cream and salt. Pour into a greased 9x13 inch pan, sprinkle crushed corn flakes on top and drizzle the 4 teaspoons of margarine over the whole thing. Bake uncovered for 45 to 60 minutes.

Old Wisconsin Potato Casserole

Bonita Paynter, 1972, 1974

YIELD: 10 TO 12 SERVINGS

INGREDIENTS

2 pounds frozen hash browns
1/2 cup melted butter
1 teaspoon salt
1/4 teaspoon pepper
1/2 cup chopped onion
1 can (10-3/4 ounces) condensed
   cream of mushroom soup
1 cup cultured sour cream
1 cup grated cheddar cheese
1/2 cup chopped green pepper,
   optional
1 cup buttered bread crumbs
10 slices bacon, cooked and diced
1/2 cup mushrooms, optional

Defrost potatoes and combine all ingredients except the bread crumbs and bacon in a 3 quart casserole dish. Sprinkle the bread crumbs on top. Bake uncovered at 350 degrees about 65 minutes (35 minutes for a 9x13 inch pan). Add sautéed bacon chunks on top and bake another 10 minutes.

Sweet Potato Casserole

Karen Rudel Novak, 1981,
Women's Swimming

YIELD: 10 TO 12 SERVINGS

I always make this recipe by sight. You may want more or less depending on your servings. All the football players love this dish!

INGREDIENTS

3 cups cooked and mashed
    sweet potato
3/4 cup sugar
2 eggs beaten
2 teaspoons vanilla extract
1/2 cup milk
4 ounces melted butter or margarine
1/2 teaspoon salt

TOPPING:

1 cup brown sugar
1 cup all-purpose flour
1 cup chopped nuts
1/2 cup melted butter or margarine

Add to the mashed potatoes the sugar, eggs, vanilla and butter or margarine. Place mixture in sprayed casserole dish. Mix topping and spread over potato mixture. Bake at 350 degrees for 30 to 40 minutes.

stuffing

Wheat Bread Stuffing

Helene Bak Slowik, 1973

YIELD: 8 TO 10 SERVINGS

INGREDIENTS

1/4 pound butter
3/4 cup chopped onion
1 pound sprouted or whole wheat
    bread
1/2 cup raisins
1 cup coarsely chopped walnuts
1 cup coarsely shredded carrots
1 cup chopped celery
3 to 4 cups chicken broth

Makes enough to stuff two chickens or bake separately

In a large Dutch oven, melt butter. Add onion and sauté until soft. Cut bread into cubes; add to onions. Stir until bread cubes are lightly browned on all sides. Stir in raisins, walnuts, carrots, celery and enough broth to thoroughly moisten all the bread. Mixture should hold together. Remove from heat. If stuffing chickens, cool and keep in refrigerator until stuffing birds. Or, pour into buttered casserole, bake at 350 degrees for about 20 minutes. Add broth if too dry; bake another 10 minutes until light brown.

Thanksgiving Dressing

Don Skiba

YIELD: 10 SERVINGS

INGREDIENTS

1 cup unsalted butter

2 cups chopped onions

2 cups chopped celery

1 bag Pepperidge Farm herb seasoned
  stuffing

1 pound pork sausage,
  cooked and drained

2 large eggs, beaten

2 cups chicken broth

1 teaspoon salt

1/2 teaspoon pepper

Sauté butter, onion and celery until tender. Combine stuffing, pork sausage,
eggs, celery, onions, salt and pepper. Add
chicken broth until mixture is moist. Add
more chicken broth, salt and pepper, if
necessary. Pour dressing into a 2 quart
casserole sprayed with non-stick spray.
Bake at 350 degrees for 30 to 35 minutes.

Pride

Grandma Sarah's Old Fashioned Dressing

Natasha Brown Moss, 1992

YIELD: 6 TO 8 SERVINGS

*This southern style dressing was introduced
to me during the first Christmas dinner
with my husband William's family in South
Carolina. His grandmother's dressing never
joined the other leftovers.*

INGREDIENTS

1 pan old fashioned cornbread*

3 slices bread, toasted

1 medium onion, finely chopped

2 stalks celery, finely chopped

1 hard boiled egg, chopped

1 teaspoon dried sage, crushed

1/2 teaspoon salt

1/2 teaspoon freshly ground
  black pepper

3 tablespoons oil drippings

2 to 3 cups juice from baked hen or
  chicken stock

1 egg, beaten

**See Grandma Sarah's Old Fashioned
Cornbread recipe.*

Preheat oven to 350 degrees. Grease
2-quart baking dish and set aside. In a
large mixing bowl, coarsely crumble cornbread and slices of toast. Add boiled egg.
Heat oil in a skillet over medium heat.
Stir in onion, celery and sage. Sauté over
medium heat 4 to 5 minutes, stirring
occasionally. Remove from heat and add
to bowl containing cornbread mixture.
Add juice from hen, beaten egg, salt and
pepper to bowl. Toss mixture until well
blended. Spoon into baking dish. Bake
45 to 60 minutes until golden brown and
liquid is absorbed.

vegetables

Festive Squash

Karen Laner &
Pete Friedmann, 1980,
NUMB Announcer

YIELD: 4 TO 6 SERVINGS

INGREDIENTS

1/2 butternut squash, halved and
    seeded
1 apple, Granny Smith or Golden
    Delicious
1/2 teaspoon cinnamon
1/8 teaspoon allspice
1 teaspoon honey
1 tablespoon butter

Bake squash in oven-safe pan, cut side
down, in 1/2 inch of water, at 350 degrees for about 45 minutes, or until
squash is very tender. Core and grate the
apple. Mash the squash pulp, apple and
the rest of the ingredients in a large bowl.
Serve hot. N

Marinated Mushrooms and Artichokes

Suzanne Calder

YIELD: 4 TO 6 SERVINGS

INGREDIENTS

2 pounds mushrooms,
    clean and remove stems
2 cans (14 ounces each) quartered
    artichokes
1 medium onion, sliced
1/2 cup oil
1 cup vinegar
1 clove garlic
1-1/2 tablespoons salt
1/2 tablespoon pepper
1/2 teaspoon thyme
1/2 teaspoon oregano
1 tablespoon dried parsley
1 tablespoon sugar
fresh spinach

Mix all ingredients together, except
spinach. Marinate overnight, turning
occasionally. Arrange on spinach leaves
and serve.

If you have artichoke lovers in the group,
you can increase to three cans of
artichokes and reduce the mushrooms
to 1 pound. N

Broccoli Casserole

Mary Pat Watt,
Football Mom — Kevin #42

Yield: 8 to 10 servings

Ingredients

2 large eggs

1/4 pound butter or margarine, softened

1 cup mayonnaise

1 can (10-3/4 ounces) condensed cream of mushroom soup

1 cup shredded sharp cheddar cheese

2 tablespoons chopped onion

2 boxes (10 ounces each) frozen chopped broccoli

Ritz Crackers, crushed — enough to top the casserole

Cook broccoli according to package instructions, drain. Mix everything except crushed crackers in a 9x13 inch pan or 2-quart casserole dish. Top with crumbled crackers and bake in 350 degree oven for 1 hour.

Carrot Soufflé

Liz Luxem

Ingredients

1 pound baby carrots

3 large eggs

1/ 2 to 1-1/4 cups sugar

1/2 cup light sour cream or honey yogurt

1/4 cup butter, softened

1/4 cup flour

1-1/2 teaspoons baking powder

Adjust sugar based on the sweetness of the carrots and your taste.

Preheat oven to 350 degrees.

In a large saucepan, cook carrots in boiling water 20 to 24 minutes or until tender. Drain well and cool.

Process carrots with sour cream and butter in a food processor (or use immersion blender) until smooth. Mix eggs with sugar, then add flour, then baking powder. Add to carrot mixture and process until smooth. Pour into a 9 inch square baking pan. Bake for 55 to 60 minutes until set.

COACHES QUOTES

Claire Pollard,
Women's Tennis:

"It's supposed to be fun, ladies!!!"

Grandma J's Corn Pudding

Clare Jorgensen,
Football Mom — Paul #78

YIELD: 8 SERVINGS

INGREDIENTS

1/2 cup butter, softened
1/2 cup sugar
2 eggs
8 ounces sour cream
1 package (8-1/2 ounces) corn bread/muffin mix
1/2 cup milk
1 can (15-1/4 ounces) whole kernel corn, drained
1 can (14-3/4 ounces) cream-style corn

Can make this the day before. Cover and put in the refrigerator. Remove and let stand 15 minutes before baking.

Preheat oven to 325 degrees. In a large mixing bowl, cream butter and sugar until light and fluffy. Add eggs, one at a time, beating well after each addition. Beat in sour cream. Gradually add corn bread/muffin mix alternately with milk, about 1/3 for each addition. Fold in corn.

Pour into a greased 3 quart baking dish (or 9x13 inch pan). Bake uncovered for 45 to 50 minutes or until set and lightly browned.

Scalloped Corn

Julie Wood, 1982

YIELD: 6 SERVINGS

INGREDIENTS

2 cans (17 ounces each) sweet corn, drained
2 eggs, beaten
1 cup cracker crumbs
1 teaspoon sugar
1/2 teaspoon dried thyme
1/4 teaspoon salt
1/4 teaspoon pepper
1/4 cup butter
2 tablespoons chopped onion
1 cup milk

Drain corn (discard liquid) and place in large mixing bowl. Add eggs, cracker crumbs, sugar, thyme, salt and pepper. Melt butter in small saucepan, add onions and cook until transparent. Add milk and heat until warm. Stir into corn mixture. Pour into greased 1-1/2 quart casserole dish. Bake at 350 degrees for 30 minutes or until center of casserole is firm.

Cheesy Creamed Corn

Lori Street, 1981

YIELD: 8 TO 10 SERVINGS

INGREDIENTS

3 packages (16 ounces each) frozen
    corn
11 ounces cream cheese, cubed
1/4 cup butter
2 tablespoons sugar
3 tablespoons milk
6 sliced American cheese, cut up

Mix all ingredients together and place in
slow cooker. Cook on low for 4 hours.
Stir before serving.

Vidalia Onion Casserole

Bonnie & Dan Wefler,
Bonnie 1950 and Dan 1950

YIELD: 6 TO 8 SERVINGS

INGREDIENTS

1/4 cup unsalted butter
7 medium Vidalia onions, sliced
1/2 cup uncooked rice
5 cups boiling water
1 teaspoon salt
1 cup grated Jarlsberg cheese
2/3 cup half-and-half

Preheat oven to 325 degrees. Melt butter
in skillet and sauté onions until soft.
Cook rice in boiling salted water for
5 minutes. Drain well. Blend rice with
onions, cheese and half-and-half. Put in
greased shallow baking dish (such as a pie
plate). Bake for 1 hour.

Festive Onions

Ellen & Ivan Zilka, 1941

YIELD: 4 SERVINGS

INGREDIENTS

2 teaspoons butter
2 large onions, sliced
1 whole egg
2 egg whites
1/2 cup skim milk
1/2 cup light sour cream
1/4 teaspoon salt
1/4 teaspoon pepper
1/2 cup grated Parmesan cheese

Preheat oven to 425 degrees.

Melt butter in stovetop-safe baking dish
(1-1/2 quart). Add onions and sauté for
5 minutes. In a bowl, add all other
ingredients except cheese and whisk
until smooth. Pour over onions.
Sprinkle cheese on top.

Bake until top is golden, about 15 to 20
minutes.

Baked Spinach and Gruyère

Debbie Hinchcliff Seward, 1974

INGREDIENTS

2 tablespoons olive oil, divided

6 shallots, thinly sliced

kosher salt

black pepper

6 large eggs

1 cup heavy cream

1 cup whole milk

1/4 teaspoon grated nutmeg

4 boxes (10 ounces each) frozen chopped or leaf spinach (thawed)

1/2 cup grated Parmesan

2 cups grated Gruyère

1 cup dry white wine

Preheat oven to 400 degrees. Coat a shallow 2-1/2 to 3 quart baking dish with 1 tablespoon oil; set aside.

Heat 1 tablespoon oil in a large skillet over medium-high heat. Add shallots, 1/2 teaspoon salt and 1/4 teaspoon pepper.

Cook, stirring occasionally, until soft, 6 to 8 minutes. Add wine and simmer until evaporated, 4 to 6 minutes.

In a large bowl, whisk together the eggs, cream, milk, nutmeg, 1/2 teaspoon salt and 1/4 teaspoon pepper.

Squeeze excess liquid from thawed spinach. Stir spinach, shallots, Gruyère and Parmesan into the egg mixture. Transfer to the prepared baking dish.

Bake until bubbling and top is golden brown, 45 to 55 minutes.

Winter Vegetable Gratin

Mary Pat Watt,
Football Mom — Kevin #42

YIELD: 6 TO 8 SERVINGS

INGREDIENTS

2 large Russet potatoes (about 1 pound)

1 large sweet potato (1/2 pound)

1 small butternut squash (1 pound)

2 medium onions

1 cup shredded Gruyère cheese

2 tablespoons chopped fresh sage

1/4 pound butter

Preheat oven to 350 degrees. Butter a 9x13 inch baking dish with 1 tablespoon of the butter.

Peel the potatoes and squash and slice as thinly as possible (1/4 inch or less). Peel the onions and finely dice.

Layer everything in single layers in the dish as follows: squash, potato, sweet potato. Top with one quarter of the onion and cheese and sprinkle with sage, dots of butter, salt and pepper. Repeat the layering process until everything is used up. Be sure to end with butter on top.

Bake for 1-1/2 to 2 hours, or until a knife inserted in the middle pierces the vegetables easily. If it starts to brown too much, cover with foil towards the end of the baking time.

Baked Acorn Squash

Kelly Deiters,
Football Mom — Neal #79, 2012

Yield: 2 servings

Ingredients

1 large acorn squash
1/4 cup chopped onion
1/4 cup margarine
1/4 cup grated Parmesan cheese

Preheat oven to 350 degrees.

Cut the squash in half, clean out the seeds, and level the rounded bottoms. Bake the squash halves for 40 minutes upside down on a lightly greased baking sheet. Meanwhile sauté onions in margarine. When squash is done, turn each half over and pour half of onion/margarine mixture and half of Parmesan cheese inside. Continue baking for 15 to 20 minutes until cheese is browned.

Baked Butternut Squash

Judy Kelley

Yield: 6 to 8 servings

Ingredients

1 large butternut squash
1/3 cup olive oil
2 cloves garlic, minced
2 tablespoons parsley, minced
1 teaspoon salt
1/2 teaspoon black pepper
1/3 cup grated Parmesan cheese

Peel squash, remove seeds and cut into chunks. Place in buttered casserole dish with olive oil, garlic, parsley, salt and pepper. Baked covered at 400 degrees for 30 minutes or until tender. Mash in casserole dish with potato masher. Stir in Parmesan cheese and return to oven, uncovered, for 15 to 20 minutes. Can be made a day or two ahead of time and reheated in the microwave. It's a wonderful side dish for a holiday meal.

Brussels Sprouts Pie

Tracey Fuchs,
Head Coach, Field Hockey

Yield: 6 to 8 servings

Ingredients

2 cups Brussels sprouts
1/2 cup Italian seasoned bread crumbs
2 eggs
1 teaspoon crushed garlic
salt and pepper, to taste
extra-virgin olive oil

Boil Brussels sprouts until soft.

Chop and mix sprouts with eggs and bread crumbs (no lumps). Add garlic, salt and pepper.

Heat frying pan with olive oil (cover surface). Add sprouts, mix and pack down (should look like a mini-pizza 1/2 inch thick). Flip onto plate after 3 minutes and return to frying pan 2 to 3 minutes.

Remove and serve.

Celery Casserole

Marian Kurz, MSJ

YIELD: 4 TO 6 SERVINGS

A nice accompaniment at Thanksgiving for those who are not crazy about turkey dressing.

INGREDIENTS

5 cups sliced celery
   (1/2 to 1-inch chunks)
1 cup sliced water chestnuts
1 cup sliced mushrooms
1 can (10-3/4 ounces) condensed cream of chicken or cream of mushroom soup, undiluted
1 cup crumbled savory crackers
1/4 pound butter or margarine, melted
salt and pepper, to taste
1 clove garlic, minced, optional
1/2 cup minced onion, optional

Preheat oven to 350 degrees. Boil celery for 3 to 4 minutes (in water or broth) and drain. (Can also be made without cooking celery.)

Mix celery, water chestnuts and mushrooms (garlic and onion, if using), then mix with soup. Pour into buttered glass baking dish (9x11 inch or 8x10 inch), top with crumbled crackers and pour melted butter or margarine over all. Bake for about and hour or until bubbling. Dish will bake faster in larger dish so check after 45 minutes. Recipe can be doubled.

Tomato Pie

Elizabeth Kurz

YIELD: 2 PIES

Pies are amazingly good as leftovers.

INGREDIENTS

2 deep dish pie crusts
3 to 4 cups fresh tomatoes, sliced and drained (peeled and seeded, if desired)
5 to 6 fresh basil leaves, chopped
3 to 4 green onions, chopped
1 cup mayonnaise
1 cup shredded mozzarella cheese
1 cup shredded sharp cheddar cheese

Preheat oven to 350 degrees. Salt the tomatoes and fill the cooked pie crusts to half. Sprinkle the the basil leaves and green onions evenly over the tomatoes. In a bowl, stir together the mayonnaise, mozzarella and cheddar cheeses. Top both pies with the cheese mixture, smooth and bake for 30 minutes or until lightly browned. Serve warm.

Leadership

Wildcat Ra-ta-tat Hooray

Mary Weed

YIELD: 8 TO 10 SERVINGS

INGREDIENTS

1/2 cup olive oil, virgin or extra virgin
1 medium yellow onion, small dice
2 cloves garlic, crushed
1 cup dry white wine
1 can (28 ounces) crushed tomatoes
1 teaspoon dried oregano
1 teaspoon dried thyme
1 teaspoon dried basil
1 bay leaf
1 red pepper, small dice
1 green pepper, small dice
1 yellow pepper, small dice
1 yellow squash, small dice
1 zucchini squash, small dice
1 small eggplant, small dice
1/2 cup ground pork
8 ounces rotini pasta, optional
salt and pepper, to taste

Can be made ahead and reheated. Should have approximately the same amount of each vegetable.

In a large sauté pan, place 2 tablespoons olive oil and sauté onion over medium heat until translucent. Add garlic and stir for 30 seconds. Add wine and cook until almost evaporated. Add tomatoes, oregano, thyme, basil and bay leaf. Simmer for 30 minutes until thick.

Meanwhile, heat 1 tablespoon olive oil in skillet. Sear the red bell pepper with a pinch of salt, about 1 minute. Empty into a colander to drain. Repeat with each of the vegetables. Avoid crowding in the pan or vegetables will not sear. Discard the juices.

Brown ground pork, set aside. Cook pasta per package directions, set aside.

Add vegetables, pork and pasta to tomato mixture and season with salt and pepper. Stir and simmer for ten minutes. Check seasoning. Remove bay leaf and serve.

Roasted Vegetables

Daniel R Barron, KSM

YIELD: 4 TO 6 SERVINGS

INGREDIENTS

8 cups mixed raw vegetables cut into bite-sized pieces
1/4 cup extra virgin olive oil
Kosher salt
Freshly ground black pepper

Use mixed vegetables that you and your guests enjoy. For example, zucchini squash, bell peppers (any color), onions, broccoli, cauliflower, yellow squash, green beans, mushrooms, radishes, canned whole potatoes, par-boiled baby carrots and/or green beans.

Preheat oven to 400 degrees. Toss the vegetables with the olive oil and salt and pepper. Place on a foil lined rimmed baking sheet (coated with non-stick spray if desired) and cook for 20 minutes. Turn vegetables with a flipper and roast another 20 to 25 minutes. Serve hot, warm or at room temperature.

These may be refrigerated and reheated in a microwave.

Bench Warmers

Soups & Stews

GOLF

Women's:

Head Coach Emily Fletcher (2008–present)

- It became a varsity sport in 1993.

- They play 12 Tournaments with a five or six-women squad coming from as close as Hinsdale to as far as Bangkok, Thailand.

- There were 74 Academic All-Big Ten honorees in the years 1993–2011.

Men's:

Head Coach Pat Goss (1996–present)

- NU won the first of its eight Big Ten Championships in 1925.

- They play in 15 Tournaments with a 5-man squad.

- The world famous Chick Evans attended NU as well as the current (as of July, 2011) No.1 golfer in the world, Luke Donald.

- There were 59 Academic All-Big Ten honorees in the years 1987–2011.

chili

Championship Chili

Laura & Jim Phillips,
Director of Athletics and Recreation

YIELD: 8 SERVINGS

INGREDIENTS

1 large onion, chopped

2 pounds lean ground beef or
ground turkey

1 can (26 ounces) tomato soup

1 can (28 ounces) diced tomatoes

1 can (15 ounces) kidney beans,
drained and rinsed

1-1/2 teaspoons salt

1/2 teaspoon pepper

3 tablespoons chili powder or, to taste

GARNISHES:

oyster crackers

shredded cheddar

sour cream

Brown meat in frying pan. Drain fat
when finished. Transfer meat to 4-quart
saucepan. Begin adding all other ingredients stirring thoroughly with each
addition. Add chili powder (2 to 3 tablespoons is fairly mild). Allow to simmer at
least an hour but for deeper flavor, simmer several hours, stirring occasionally.
Serve plain or with suggested toppings.

Chili Con Carne (Slow Cooker)

Marietta Paynter

YIELD: 6 TO 8 SERVINGS

*Marietta was married to John Paynter, a
Northwestern alum who served as director
of the NU Marching Band from 1953
to 1996.*

INGREDIENTS

4 strips bacon

1 large onion, finely chopped

1 green pepper, finely chopped

1 pound ground beef

1 tablespoon chili powder

1 teaspoon salt or seasoned salt

1/8 teaspoon cayenne pepper

1 teaspoon ground cumin

1 teaspoon dried basil

1 or 2 cans (14-1/2 ounces each) dark
red kidney beans (not drained)

2 cans (14-1/2 ounces each) diced
tomatoes (not drained)

1/4 teaspoon Beau Monde seasoning,
optional

1 tablespoon brown sugar, optional

Fry and crumble the bacon, save drippings. Cook the onion and pepper in the
bacon drippings for 5 minutes. Add the
ground beef and brown for 5 minutes.
Place meat/bacon/vegetables in slow
cooker and mix with all other ingredients.
Cover and cook on low setting for 8 to
12 hours or high setting for 5 to 6 hours.

Brian Kardos' Game Time Chili

Brian Kardos, 1996,
Football, Rose Bowl Team

YIELD: 6 TO 8 SERVINGS

INGREDIENTS

2-1/2 to 3 pounds ground chuck

2 cans (28 ounces each) of whole, peeled tomatoes

1 can (15 ounces) of diced tomatoes (unseasoned)

1 can (15 ounces) kidney beans, optional

1 extra large or 2 medium onions, yellow or white

2 cans (12 ounces each) Spicy Hot V8

2 tablespoons chili powder

1 tablespoon cayenne pepper

1 tablespoon paprika

1 tablespoon cumin

1 tablespoon oregano

1 tablespoon crushed red pepper

garlic powder, to taste

salt and pepper, to taste

TOPPINGS:

cheddar cheese

red onions

sour cream

crackers

Liberally season the meat with salt, pepper and garlic powder. Rough-chop onion. Set 1/4 aside to use as topping later. Add the rest to the meat mixture. Brown the meat and onions together in a large, heavy pot. (Work in batches for good browning.) Drain fat. Return meat and onions to pot. Open up the cans of whole tomatoes. In a food processor, pulse the whole tomatoes with the juice a few times until they're broken up as much as you like. I like big, messy chunks, but you can pulse them more finely if desired. Add all canned goods, including pulsed tomatoes, diced tomatoes, kidney beans and V8 to the pot with the meat. Add chili powder, plus any desired extra garlic, salt and pepper and stir thoroughly. Bring chili mixture to a boil over medium-high to high heat. After the mixture boils, reduce the heat to medium-low and simmer for about an hour, stirring at least every 10 minutes. Add the five spices during this time. Serve immediately if desired — chili can simmer for hours if needed. Chili will be thinner than most chilies.

COACHES QUOTES

Randy Walker,
Former Football Head Coach:

"They have to kill us to beat us."

Quoted before the 11/4/00
54–51 victory over Michigan.

Fr. John's Hotter-Than-Hell Chili

Fr. John Kartje,
Campus Minister — Chaplain, Sheil Catholic Center

YIELD: 10 SERVINGS

INGREDIENTS

1 pound ground beef or cubed steak

1/2 chopped onion

12 ounces canned kidney beans, drained and rinsed

12 ounces petite diced tomatoes

1 tablespoon olive oil

2 cloves garlic

2 tablespoons chili powder

1-1/2 tablespoons cumin

1 tablespoon cayenne pepper

salt, to taste

pepper, to taste

Brown the beef in a tablespoon of olive oil. Add onions and garlic before the meat is completely browned. Once onions are tender, add spices one at a time, making sure to stir after each addition. You can add more or less based on preference to spiciness. Add tomatoes and kidney beans. Fill each can about 1/4 of the way with water and add to the mixture. Add more water if desired. Add spices as necessary until you get the desired flavor. Let simmer for about 30 minutes. Serve with corn bread or tortillas.

Also works well in a slow cooker. Brown all the meat with onions and garlic, then move to the cooker and add spices, tomatoes and beans. Cook on low for 7 to 9 hours or until meat is at the desired tenderness.

Famous Flentye Tailgate Chili

Tim Flentye

YIELD: 4 TO 6 SERVINGS

INGREDIENTS

1 small onion, diced

1 stalk celery, diced

1 pound ground Tallgrass beef

1 can (15 ounces) dark red kidney beans, drained

1 can (15 ounces) crushed tomatoes

1 teaspoon ground cumin

1/4 teaspoon ground cayenne

1/2 teaspoon curry powder

1 teaspoon kosher salt

1/2 teaspoon ground black pepper

6 ounces lager beer (such as Harp)

Tallgrass beef is available at select stores or www.tallgrassbeef.com

Place onion in a slow cooker on high. Add celery and beef; mix. Add beans and tomatoes. Stir in seasoning and beer. Keep on high for 2-1/2 hours, stirring every 30 to 45 minutes. Turn to low to keep warm.

Serve in bowls topped with shredded cheddar cheese, sour cream and oyster crackers.

Tim's Chili

Tim Stoddard,
Assistant Coach, Baseball (former Chicago Cubs & Chicago White Sox)

INGREDIENTS

6 tablespoons butter or margarine

3 cups chopped onions

3 cloves garlic, minced

1 large bell pepper, chopped

1 can (16 ounces) whole tomatoes

1 can (6 ounces) tomato paste

4 to 5 cans (14 ounces each) chopped spicy tomatoes, undrained

3 tablespoons chili powder

3 teaspoons cumin

2 cans (14 ounces each) black beans, drained

2 cans (14 ounces each) light kidney beans, drained

1 can (14 ounces) Northern beans, drained

1 pound loose mild Italian sausage, cooked, crumbled and drained

2 pounds ground beef, cooked, crumbled and drained

In a 6 to 8 quart sauce pan with lid, melt the butter. Then sauté the onions, garlic and pepper until soft. Add the tomatoes, tomato paste, chili powder, cumin and beans. Stir. Add the sausage and ground beef and stir. Bring to a boil, then lower heat and simmer, covered, at least 1-1/2 hours. Garnish as desired.

Cowboy Chili

Sharon Clark,
Football Mom — Colby 2004

YIELD: 20 TO 24 SERVINGS

INGREDIENTS

2 cups diced onion

6 cloves garlic, minced

4 tablespoons oil

2 pounds beef sirloin cubed

2 pounds chili meat (coarsely ground beef)

4 cups chopped tomatoes

4 cups tomato sauce

24 ounces beer

4 cans (6 ounces each) tomato paste

1 cup beef broth

1 cup brown sugar

10 tablespoons chili powder

2 teaspoons cumin

2 teaspoons cayenne pepper

2 teaspoons salt

1 teaspoon black pepper

8 jalapeños, seeded and chopped

Sauté onions and garlic in oil. Add sirloin and chili meat and lightly brown. Mix tomatoes, tomato sauce, beer, tomato paste, brown sugar, chili powder, cumin, cayenne pepper, salt and black pepper. Reduce heat to low and simmer for about 3 hours. Stir in jalapeños and simmer for another 30 minutes. Add additional beef broth for desired thickness. Cool and either refrigerate or freeze depending on how long you are traveling.

Fox in the Henhouse Chicken Chili

Kitty Horne

YIELD: 6 TO 8 SERVINGS

INGREDIENTS

6 tablespoons butter

1/2 large onion, chopped

1/4 cup flour

1 cup low-sodium chicken broth

2 teaspoons chili powder or more, to taste

1 teaspoon cumin

1 teaspoon Tabasco sauce

1 teaspoon salt

1/2 teaspoon pepper

2 cups half-and-half

1 can (4 ounces) diced chilies

8 ounces jalapeño Jack cheese, shredded

6 boneless skinless chicken breasts, cooked and diced or shredded

2 cans (15 ounces each) cannellini beans, drained and rinsed

1/2 cup sour cream

GARNISHES:

chopped cilantro, sliced green onions, sour cream, shredded jalapeño jack cheese

Melt butter in a 14 inch skillet. Add onions, cook and stir 2 minutes until soft. Whisk in flour. Whisk constantly on low heat for 3 minutes. Pour chicken broth into a glass measuring cup and microwave for 1 minute. Stir in chili powder, cumin, Tabasco, salt and pepper. Pour broth mixture and half-and-half into flour mixture, whisking until smooth. Bring to a boil.

Reduce heat and simmer for 5 minutes, stirring occasionally. Stir in chilies. Sprinkle in cheese and stir until melted. Mixture may appear stringy. Add chicken and beans and stir well to combine. Simmer, covered for 20 minutes stirring well every 5 minutes.

Remove from heat and stir in sour cream. Serve with garnishes, if desired. Can be refrigerated overnight and reheated in a slow cooker the next day. This is double-award winning chili!

Football Sunday Chili

Katie Wright, 2007, Women's Soccer

YIELD: 12 SERVINGS

INGREDIENTS

1 pound ground turkey

1 can (15 ounces) diced tomatoes

1 can (8 ounces) tomato sauce

1 can (15 ounces) chili beans

1 can (15 ounces) red kidney beans

1 package chili seasoning

Brown ground turkey. Place turkey and all other ingredients in slow cooker. Cook on low for 6 hours.

Serve with spaghetti, grated onion and grated cheese.

Chicken Chili

*Gordon Newton &
Ramune Kubiliunas*, 1990

YIELD: 10 TO 12 SERVINGS

INGREDIENTS

1 to 1-1/2 pounds chicken tenders or
    breasts, cut into 3/4 inch pieces
1 can (15 ounces) diced tomatoes,
    including liquid
1 can (4 ounces) of sliced black olives,
    drained
1 can (15 ounces) pinto beans flavored
    with jalapeño, drained and
    rinsed
1 envelope taco seasoning mix
1 cup frozen corn
1 green bell pepper, chopped
1 medium onion, chopped
1 red bell pepper, chopped
1 tablespoon instant tapioca
1 teaspoon chicken soup base or
    1 bouillon cube
1/4 cup small pasta, such as ditalini,
    cooked

*Suggested toppings: shredded cheese and
chopped onions*

Combine all ingredients except pasta in
slow cooker. Cover and cook in a on low
for 4 to 6 hours. Check once after 3
hours and add hot water or another can
of tomatoes with juice if mixture is too
dry. If desired, turn heat up and add
cooked pasta. Or, serve over pasta or rice
with suggested toppings.

White Bean Chicken Chili

Joel Childs,
**Account Executive —
Ticket Sales and Service**

YIELD: 6 TO 8 SERVINGS

INGREDIENTS

2 tablespoons vegetable oil
1 onion, chopped
2 cloves garlic, minced
1 pound chicken meat, cooked and
    shredded
1 can (14-1/2 ounces) chicken broth
1 jar (18 ounces) salsa verde
1 can (16 ounces) diced tomatoes
1/2 teaspoon dried oregano
1/2 teaspoon ground coriander
1/4 teaspoon ground cumin
1 can (15 ounces) white beans
1 can (15 ounces) white or yellow
    corn
salt and pepper, to taste

Heat oil and cook onion and garlic until
soft. Stir in broth, tomatoes, salsa verde
and spices. Bring to a boil and simmer for
10 to 15 minutes.

Add corn, chicken and white beans.
Simmer for an additional 10 to 15 minutes. Salt and pepper, to taste. Serve with
tortilla chips, shredded cheese, sour
cream and/or sliced limes.

Texas 2-Alarm Chili

Mary Ellen Baker,
Football Mom — Hayden #68

YIELD: 6 TO 8 SERVINGS

INGREDIENTS

CHILI:

3 pounds round steak,
       cut into 1/4-inch cubes

1/4 cup olive oil

1 quart water

1 large onion, chopped

2 bay leaves

8 tablespoons Mexican chili powder

2 teaspoons salt

1 clove garlic, chopped

4 teaspoons cumin

1 teaspoon marjoram

1 teaspoon black pepper

1 teaspoon Hungarian paprika (hot)

CORN MEAL PASTE:

1 tablespoon sugar

3 tablespoons flour

6 tablespoons corn meal

In a Dutch oven, sear meat in olive oil until gray in color. (Do in batches so meat will sear). Add onions, bay leaves and 1 quart water. Simmer for 2 hours, covered.

Add spices (chili powder, salt, garlic, cumin, marjoram, black pepper, paprika), water if needed and simmer, covered, another 30 minutes. Remove bay leaves.

Make corn meal paste by mixing the three ingredients together, then adding enough water to make a thick but still pourable paste. Add corn meal paste to meat and still well. Cook another 10 minutes until thickened. Serve with pinto beans on side.

To make 3 Alarm Chili, add 1 teaspoon cayenne red pepper.

To make 4 Alarm Chili, add 1 teaspoon cayenne red pepper and 1 teaspoon Tabasco sauce.

Healthy Turkey Chili

Rick Taylor,
Former Athletic Director

YIELD: 6 TO 8 SERVINGS

INGREDIENTS

1 tablespoon olive oil
1 pound ground turkey (93% lean)
1 onion, chopped
1 green pepper, chopped
1/2 teaspoon salt
1 tablespoon Mexican chili powder
2 teaspoons ground cumin
2 cans (14 ounces each) petite diced
    tomatoes
1 can (8 ounces) tomato sauce
1 can (15 ounces) cannellini beans,
    rinsed and drained

GARNISHES:

Non-fat sour cream
shredded Mexican 4 cheese blend
Onions

In a deep 12 inch skillet, heat oil on medium-high until hot. Add turkey, onion, green pepper and salt. Cook 5 to 7 minutes or until turkey loses its pink color, stirring to break meat into small pieces. Stir in chili powder and cumin, cook 1 minute. Add tomatoes with liquid, canned beans, tomato sauce and

1/2 cup of water. Heat to boiling; reduce heat to medium and simmer, uncovered, stirring occasionally, to let sauce thicken. Serve with garnishes.

Vegetarian Chili with Squash

Judith Criswell, 1959

YIELD: ABOUT 9 CUPS

INGREDIENTS

4 teaspoons olive oil, divided
3 cups chopped butternut squash
2 medium carrots, diced
1 medium onion, diced
2 to 3 tablespoons chili powder
1 can (28 ounces) plum tomatoes
1 can (4 ounces) mild green chilies
1 can (14-1/2 ounces) vegetable broth
1/4 teaspoon salt
2 cans (15 ounces each) black beans,
    drained and rinsed
1/4 cup chopped fresh cilantro,
    optional
4 tablespoons sour cream

In 5 quart Dutch oven over medium-high heat, heat 2 teaspoons olive oil. Add butternut squash and cook, stirring occasionally, until golden, remove.

In same Dutch oven heat 2 more teaspoons olive oil; cook carrots and onions until well browned. Stir in chili powder; cook one minute, stirring, Add tomatoes with their liquid, chilies with their liquid, vegetable broth and salt; over high heat, bring to a boil.

Reduce heat to low; cover and simmer 30 minutes, stirring occasionally with spoon to break up tomatoes. Stir in black beans and butternut squash; over high heat,

heat to boiling. Reduce heat to low; cover and simmer 15 minutes or until squash is tender and chili thickens.

Stir in cilantro. Serve with sour cream. ⚡

Vegetarian Chili

Claire Pollard,
Head Coach, Women's Tennis

YIELD: 10 TO 12 SERVINGS

INGREDIENTS

2 cups chopped onion

3 garlic cloves, minced

3 cups water

2 tablespoons sugar

2 tablespoons chili powder

1/2 cup shredded cheddar cheese

2 tablespoons Worcestershire sauce

2 cans (14-1/2 ounces each) diced tomatoes

1 can (15 ounces) garbanzo beans

1 can (15 ounces) black beans

1 can (15 ounces) kidney beans

1 can (15 ounces) cannellini beans

1 can (6 ounces) tomato paste

Drain and rinse the four cans of beans. Combine one cup water with the can of tomato paste. Add tomato paste mixture and all other ingredients into slow cooker. Cook on low for 4 to 5 hours. ⚡

soups

Vegetarian Black Bean Soup

Janet Drohan, 1975,
Mom of Head Coach Kate & Associate Coach Caryl Drohan, Softball

INGREDIENTS

1 pound dried black beans

3 carrots diced

1 medium red onion, diced

1 jalapeño pepper, diced

3 stalks celery, diced

3 cloves garlic, diced

2 tablespoons olive oil

3 vegetable broth cubes

4 ears corn, shucked (about 3 cups)

1/2 cup chopped fresh cilantro

4 cups water

1 dollop sour cream per serving

1 teaspoon chopped scallions per serving

salt and pepper, to taste

Soak black beans overnight in water.

Sauté all vegetables in bottom of soup pot, 4 to 5 minutes in olive oil. Drain beans and add remaining ingredients (except cilantro). Bring to boil, then lower heat to simmer and cook for 3 hours. Add cilantro. Serve with dollop of sour cream and 1 teaspoon scallions. ⚡

Mexican Soup

Susan Izard

YIELD: 4 TO 6 SERVINGS

*Susan is the mother of
Top Chef Stephanie Izard*

INGREDIENTS

SOUP:

4 slices bacon

3/4 cup chopped onion

3/4 cup chopped celery

1/2 cup chopped green pepper

1 clove garlic, minced

1 can (16 ounces) refried beans

1/4 teaspoon pepper

1/4 teaspoon chili powder

2 or more dashes Tabasco, to taste

1 can (14-1/2 ounces) chicken broth

GARNISHES:

shredded cheddar cheese

chopped tomatoes

crushed tortilla chips

*I usually double this so we can eat it two
nights.*

In saucepan, cook bacon until crisp.
Drain the fat, leaving just enough to coat
the pan. Add onion, celery, green pepper
and garlic. Cook, covered, over low heat
about 10 minutes. Add beans, pepper,
chili powder and several dashes of
Tabasco. Stir in chicken broth. Bring to a
boil. Serve with garnishes.

Note: You can also cook bacon in 400 degree oven until crisp; watch so it doesn't
burn.

Heartwarming Navy Bean Soup

Natasha Brown Moss, 1992

YIELD: 10 SERVINGS

*This nutritious recipe is a favorite dish that
my mother has been making for as long as I
can remember. People are often surprised
that the soup is blended. Looking back on
it, I think my mother blended it to make all
the beans and veggies more palatable to us
as kids. To this day, I prefer the smooth
creamy texture of blended bean soup.*

INGREDIENTS

1 pound dried navy beans

4 medium onions, quartered

3 stalks celery, cut in large pieces

2 medium green peppers,
    coarsely chopped

2 cloves garlic, chopped

1/3 cup olive or vegetable oil

3 ounces tomato paste

1 tablespoon sugar

1 tablespoon sage

1 teaspoon freshly ground
        black pepper

salt

1/4 pound butter

Pick through the beans to remove any
blemished beans, as well as any other de-
bris. Place the beans in a colander and
rinse well with cold water. In a large pot,
cover beans with cold water and bring
them to a boil. Let boil for 3 to 5 minutes, turn off heat, leave covered for 1 to
2 hours. (Alternatively you can soak the
beans overnight). Pour water from beans;
rinse in cold water until foam is gone.

In a 6 to 8 quart pot, add beans, onions, celery, green peppers, garlic, oil, tomato paste, sugar, sage and black pepper. Add enough water to cover ingredients by several inches. Cover and bring to a boil. Reduce heat to medium and cook, covered, until beans mash easily (about 3 to 4 hours). Stir occasionally to ensure beans do not stick.

When beans are tender, add salt and butter. Allow butter to melt and then put soup through blender in batches (or use immersion blender). Blend until soup has a smooth, creamy consistency. Adjust salt, to taste. If soup is too thick, add boiling water in small increments to achieve desired thickness.

COACHES QUOTES

Jimmy Tierney,
Women's Swimming & Diving:

"Before you can win, you have to believe you are worthy."
–Mike Ditka

Hearty Cabbage Soup

Nancy Tierney,
Director, Fitness/Wellness, NUDAR

Yield: 4 to 6 servings

Ingredients

1 pound ground beef

1 large onion, coarsely chopped

1/2 medium cabbage, coarsely chopped or shredded

6 cups chicken broth

2 tablespoons Worcestershire sauce

1 tablespoon salt

1 tablespoon sugar

3 whole peppercorns

4 whole allspice berries

1 whole bay leaf

12 ounces can V8 juice

2 cans (6 ounces each) tomato paste

GARNISH: grated cheese or sour cream

Brown the beef in a heavy soup pot, add onions; stir until soft. Tie peppercorns, allspice berries and bay leaves in a small cotton bag or a pouch made from cheesecloth. Combine all ingredients except V8 juice and tomato paste. Simmer for 1 hour. Add V8 juice and tomato paste and simmer for another 30 minutes. Remove allspice berries, peppercorns and bay leaf. Serve topped with grated cheese and/or dollop of sour cream.

Dad's Beef Barley Soup

Jenni Glick,
Assistant Director, Clubs — NAA

YIELD: 10 TO 12 SERVINGS

Add some crusty bread and serve for the perfect Chicago winter lunch.

INGREDIENTS

3 to 4 cloves garlic, chopped or mashed

3 stalks celery, chopped

3/4 cup chopped onion

8 ounces baby carrots

5 to 6 medium potatoes, cubed

1 cup barley

2 to 2-1/2 pounds sirloin steak, sliced

42 ounces canned whole tomatoes

5 cubes beef bouillon

1-1/2 tablespoons dried basil

3 cups tomato juice

4 tablespoons au jus

4 bay leaves

4 cups water (or more)

pepper, to taste

Cook garlic and onion in olive oil in a 10-quart stock pot until transparent. Brown the meat in batches in the same pot. Return all meat to the pot; add the tomato juice, water, au jus, bay leaves and bouillon. Bring to a simmer. Crush the tomatoes and add to the pot with the basil; allow to simmer for 10 minutes. Add the barley and potatoes and cook for another 10 minutes. Add the carrots, celery and pepper, to taste. Allow to simmer for a couple of hours, stirring every 20 to 30 minutes, until the barley is cooked and vegetables are tender. If the consistency is too thick, add more water to thin it out as needed.

Store in an airtight container in the refrigerator for up to 5 days or freeze for up to 30 days. Simply reheat on a stove top. You may need to add some water.

Cauliflower Soup

David Wuellner

YIELD: 20 TO 24 SERVINGS

Good both hot and cold.

INGREDIENTS

1/2 pound bacon, diced

2 cups chopped onions

16 cups chicken stock

2 cups flour

4 cups whole milk

4 cups heavy cream

2 heads cauliflower, cooked

Worcestershire sauce, to taste

salt and pepper, to taste

cooked broccoli and carrots
        for garnish

Can omit bacon and use vegetable broth for vegetarian version. Also try peas for garnish.

Cook bacon and onions in a large stockpot until softened. Add chicken stock and bring to a boil. Mix flour with the milk with a whisk in a separate bowl. Add this mixture to the large pot and stir well. Add cream and cauliflower and bring to a simmer. Mix with an immersion blender but leave some florettes of cauliflower intact. Add Worcestershire sauce, salt and pepper, to taste. Toss in broccoli and carrots. Serve hot or cool and refrigerate overnight. Re-warm gently to serve.

Chicken and Sausage Gumbo

Zoe T Barron

YIELD: 25 TO 30 SERVINGS

INGREDIENTS

ROUX:

1-1/2 cups canola oil

1-1/2 cups flour

GUMBO:

2 large onions, about 2 cups chopped

2 to 3 tablespoons garlic, minced

6 to 8 ribs of celery, chopped, about 3 cups

6 small red bell peppers, seeded and chopped, about 3 cups

19 to 20 cups cooked shredded chicken

3 pounds Kielbasa or smoked sausage, sliced

16 cups chicken broth

1 teaspoon black pepper

cooked rice

hot sauce(s)

ROUX: Heat oil in a large stock pot (or skillet if preparing ahead of time). Add flour gradually, stirring with a whisk. After all of the flour has been added continue stirring until the roux is the color of milk chocolate. Do not stop stirring! Get a friend to help if needed. The browning of the roux can take 45 minutes. Cool roux. It may be refrigerated up to one week. If cold, stir to re-mix before using.

GUMBO: If cooled, heat the mixed roux in a large stockpot for 5 minutes. Add onions, celery and peppers. Stir until vegetables begin to soften. Add broth gradually and keep stirring. Add the chicken, sausage and black pepper and add more broth as needed. Add salt and pepper, to taste. Serve over cooked rice in individual bowls. Encourage guests to add hot sauces, to taste if they wish. Freeze any leftovers.

NU Chabad's Famous Chicken Soup

Rabbi Dov Hillel Klein,
**Campus Minister — Director,
Tannanbaum Chabad House,
Northwestern Jewish Center**

YIELD: 20 TO 30 SERVINGS

INGREDIENTS

1 chicken, 3-1/2 to 4 pounds

1 bunch celery, diced, about 1-1/2 pounds

1-1/2 pounds baby carrots

2 turnips, diced, about 4-1/2 pounds

2 parsnips, diced, about 1/2 pound

2 large onions, diced, about 3 cups

6 zucchini, sliced, about 1 /12 pounds

1-1/2 ounces salt (3 tablespoons)

1/3 ounce black pepper (1 teaspoon)

1/4 ounce dried basil (1/2 tablespoon)

8 to 10 cups water, enough to cover ingredients

Adjust the amount of seasoning, to taste. Put all the ingredients into a 10 quart pot and cook for 2-1/2 hours. Serve with Osem Mini Croutons. Guaranteed to cure what ails you!

Brett's Favorite Pastina Soup

Kristin & Brett Basanez, 2005,
Football

YIELD: 8 TO 10 SERVINGS

I started making this soup for Brett when we were dating at Northwestern. Ten years later he continues to request it! In the winter, I make a double batch every few weeks — it gets better as it reheats. Back at NU he would have 2 big bowls before leaving for a game. Serve it with grated Parmesan cheese and fresh crusty buttered French bread for dipping. It's simple but hearty and delicious. Not to mention the house smells amazing all day long.

INGREDIENTS

2 cups roasted chicken torn into bite-sized pieces (sometimes I buy a rotisserie chicken and use about half of it in the soup)

2 cartons (32 ounces each) chicken broth

1 to 2 tablespoon olive oil

1/2 cup chopped onion

1/2 cup chopped celery

1/2 cup chopped carrots

1-1/2 cups crushed tomatoes

1 teaspoon salt

1/2 teaspoon pepper

1 dried bay leaf

3/4 cup pastina (or another small pasta such as acini de pepe)

2 cups chopped spinach (frozen or fresh)

Heat oil over medium heat. Add onions, carrots, celery, browning 10 to 12 minutes or until tender. Add chicken broth, crushed tomatoes, bay leaf, salt and pepper. Heat to boiling. Add pastina, reduce to low, cover and simmer for 15 to 20 minutes. Add chicken. Stir in spinach until wilted. Remove bay leaf. Serve with grated Parmesan cheese on top and fresh buttery bread for dipping.

Attitude

Wildcat Greek Avgolemono Soup

Mark Hassakis, 1973

YIELD: 8 SERVINGS

INGREDIENTS

1 whole chicken, 3 to 4 pounds
1 cup chopped onions
5 to 6 cups chopped celery with leaves
1/2 cup uncooked rice
4 eggs, separated
2 fresh lemons (juiced)
salt, to taste
lemon slices for garnish

Put chicken, onion and celery into large stockpot and cover with water; boil until chicken is done, about an hour. Add water as needed to keep chicken covered while cooking.

Cut up chicken and strain broth, retaining 8 cups (or use 8 cups of canned chicken broth). Combine broth and rice in stockpot, bring to boil, cover and simmer for 20 minutes.

In separate bowl, beat egg whites until stiff, then beat egg yolks into egg whites; slowly add lemon juice to egg mixture and beat continuously until well blended.

Add 2 cups of the hot broth to the egg mixture and keep beating mixture; mix egg mixture into remaining broth and rice. Add chicken to your liking and salt, to taste. Stir well, but do not boil. Garnish with lemon slices and serve immediately.

Mulligatawny Soup

Janie Varley

YIELD: 6 TO 8 SERVINGS

INGREDIENTS

1 medium onion, diced
1/4 cup butter
1 medium carrot, diced
1 stalk celery, diced
1/2 medium green pepper, seeded and diced
1 medium apple, pared, cored, thinly sliced
1 cup cooked chicken, diced fine
1/3 cup flour
1 teaspoon curry powder, to taste
2 cups chicken broth
2 cups canned stewed tomatoes
salt and pepper, to taste

Add more carrots, celery, pepper, apple or chicken, to taste.

In a 4 quart pot, sauté onion in butter. Add carrots, celery, green pepper, apple and chicken. Mix flour and curry powder in a small bowl; gradually stir into the vegetables, blending well. Dice tomatoes if necessary. Add broth and tomatoes. Salt and pepper, to taste. Simmer slowly with cover on for about 20 minutes.

Can be made ahead and frozen.

Chicken Tortilla Soup

Abby Kurz

YIELD: 8 TO 10 SERVINGS

It's great — and with a touch of spice.

INGREDIENTS

8 chicken breast halves, shredded

1 large onion, diced

2 cloves garlic, minced

3 to 4 jalapeño peppers, diced

1/4 teaspoon ground cayenne pepper

2 teaspoons ground cumin

7 ounces salsa

4 cans (15 ounces each) low sodium
    chicken broth

1 can diced tomatoes
    (28 or 32 ounces)

1 cup frozen corn

Sauté onions and garlic in oil until tender. Add jalapeños (with or without seeds, depends on how hot you like it) and cook for a few minutes. Add spices and remaining ingredients. Bring to a boil and then simmer for 20 minutes to blend flavors.

COACHES QUOTES

Jarod Schroeder, Men's Swimming:

*"Bring an ICE attitude to every practice. **Intensity, Commitment** and **Excellence** in everything you do will separate you from your competitors when you step up on the block."*

Corn Chowder

Liz & Coach Jarod Schroeder,
**Head Coach,
Men's Swimming & Diving**

YIELD: 10 SERVINGS

INGREDIENTS

2 tablespoons butter

1/2 cup chopped onions

1/2 cup chopped celery

1/2 cup chopped carrots

3 tablespoons flour

3 cups vegetable broth

1-1/2 cups peeled, diced potatoes

2 cups corn kernels, fresh or frozen

1/4 teaspoon thyme

1 bay leaf

1/3 cup half-and-half or milk

1-1/2 cups shredded cheddar cheese

salt and pepper, to taste

In a stockpot, melt the butter. Stir in the onions, celery and carrots. Cook, stirring until vegetables are softened. Add the flour and stir until absorbed. Add the broth and bring to a boil. Add the potatoes, corn, thyme and bay leaf; return to a boil. Reduce heat and simmer 15 minutes or until the potatoes are tender. Discard the bay leaf.

Stir in the half-and-half, salt, pepper and cheese. Continue to cook, stirring, until heated through and the cheese is melted.

Lobster Bisque

Janet Drohan, 1975,
**Mom of Head Coach Kate & Associate
Coach Caryl Drohan, Softball**

YIELD: 6 TO 8 SERVINGS

INGREDIENTS

2 medium size lobsters
2-1/2 cups chicken consommé
1 large onion sliced
3 stalks celery and tops
1 bay leaf
2 whole cloves
8 peppercorns
1/4 cup butter
1/4 cup flour
3 cups milk
1 cup hot cream
1 teaspoon dry sherry

Cook lobster. Remove meat and dice. Crush shells and add to consommé along with onion, celery and spices. Simmer for 30 minutes and then strain.

Melt butter, blend in flour and add milk gradually. When smooth and boiling, add the lobster stock. Simmer covered for about 5 minutes. Stir in the hot cream and sherry; add lobster meat. Serve in warm bowls.

Holly's Mushroom Barley Soup

*Contributed In Memory of
Holly Hartle Roberts*

YIELD: 10 TO12 SERVINGS

For mushroom lovers only!

INGREDIENTS

4 ounces fresh mushrooms, sliced
3 tablespoons pearl barley
3 quarts water
2 teaspoons salt
1/4 teaspoon pepper
2 medium onions, diced
2 tablespoons flour
3/4 cup skimmed milk

Combine mushrooms, barley, water, salt and pepper in a 5 quart saucepan and cook over low heat for one hour. Brown onions in a non stick pan and add to soup. Cook for 30 minutes. Mix the flour with milk and add to soup. Cook for another 15 minutes.

Split Pea Soup

Pam Kerr, KSM

YIELD: 8 SERVINGS

INGREDIENTS

1 bag (16 ounces) dried green split
    peas
8 cups water
1 ham bone or ham hock
1 chopped onion
1 cup chopped celery
1 cup chopped or shredded carrots
1 to 2 bay leaves
5 whole pepper corns
1 to 2 teaspoons minced garlic
2 cups (or more) chopped ham meat

Soak dried peas in water for several hours or overnight. Drain peas and discard water. In a large stock pot or deep pan, add peas, ham bone, water and all remaining ingredients. Bring to a boil and simmer for at least 2 hours or until peas are completely softened and soup has thickened. Stir frequently to be sure soup does not stick to the bottom of the pot and burn. Remove ham bone and add ham meat. Add salt and pepper, to taste.

Cream of Pumpkin Soup

Linda Schoeman

YIELD: 8 SERVINGS

INGREDIENTS

1/4 cup chopped onion
2 tablespoons butter
1/2 teaspoon curry powder
2 cups canned pumpkin
2 cans (10-1/2 ounces each)
    chicken stock
1-1/2 teaspoons salt
2 cups half-and-half

Melt butter in small skillet. Cook onion and curry powder in melted butter until onion is soft but not browned. (Covering the skillet will keep the onion soft.) Combine the pumpkin, 1 can of chicken stock, salt and the cooked onion in a blender. Whirl until smooth. In a large sauce pan, combine pumpkin mixture, the remaining can of chicken stock and the half-and-half. Heat slowly. Serve with a sprinkling of finely chopped parsley or a dollop of sour cream in center of each serving.

Respond

Pumpkin Soup

The Spice House,
Evanston — Owners Patty and Tom Erd

YIELD: 12 TO 14 SERVINGS

INGREDIENTS

SOUP:

1/4 cup butter or margarine

1 large onion, chopped (about 3/4 cup)

1 leek, chopped (about 1 cup)

1 pound canned or homemade pumpkin purée

5 cups chicken broth

1/4 teaspoon white pepper

1 teaspoon salt

1/2 teaspoon curry powder

1/4 teaspoon ground nutmeg

1/4 teaspoon ground ginger

1 bay leaf

1 cup half-and-half

1 cup sour cream

1/2 cup chopped chives

PUMPKIN PURÉE:

3 pounds fresh pumpkin, cubed

1 cup sour cream

1/2 chopped chives

PUMPKIN PURÉE: Combine pumpkin cubes with water to cover in a saucepan. Bring to boil; reduce heat. Simmer, covered, for 20 minutes or until fork tender. Drain and press through a sieve.

SOUP: Melt butter in medium saucepan. Add onion and leek; sauté until tender. Stir in pumpkin purée, chicken broth, pepper, salt, curry powder, nutmeg, ginger and bay leaf. Bring to a boil; reduce heat. Simmer for 15 minutes. Remove bay leaf. Purée soup mixture in blender or food processor. Return to saucepan. Add half-and-half. Soup may be served at this point or refrigerated or frozen. Serve hot or cold. Top with a dollop of sour cream. Sprinkle with chives.

Serving suggestion: Hollow out a pumpkin and fill it with soup. Heat at 350 degrees for 45 minutes and serve the pumpkin.

Lemony Turkey Rice Soup

Bruce Paynter, **1973, 1976, NUMB**

YIELD: 8 SERVINGS

INGREDIENTS

6 cups chicken broth, divided

1 can (10-3/4 ounces) condensed cream of chicken soup

2 cups cooked rice (white or brown)

2 cups or more diced cooked turkey

1/4 teaspoon pepper

2 tablespoons cornstarch

1/4 cup lemon juice

1/4 cup minced fresh parsley or cilantro

More turkey is better.

In a large saucepan, combine 5-1/2 cups of broth, undiluted cream of chicken soup, rice, turkey and pepper. Bring to a boil and cook for 3 minutes. In a small bowl, combine cornstarch and remaining broth until smooth. Gradually stir into hot soup, stirring for 1 to 2 minutes or until thickened and heated through. Remove from heat. Stir in lemon juice and parsley/cilantro.

Manhattan Chowder with Salmon and Avocado

Dagmar Porcelli,
Football Mom — Chuck #74

YIELD: 8 SERVINGS

INGREDIENTS

4 cups water

5 slices bacon

1 large onion, finely chopped

2 large carrots, peeled and chopped

2 stalks celery, finely chopped

3 medium potatoes, peeled and chopped

1 bay leaf

1-1/4 teaspoons fresh thyme

2 cans (28 ounces each) peeled whole plum tomatoes

2 roasted red peppers, chopped

2 medium avocados, cut in slices

1 dash cayenne pepper

Preheat oven to 400 degrees. Bake salmon, skin side down, with coating of olive oil, salt and pepper for about 15 minutes until done, to taste. Set aside.

Cook bacon until browned. Add onion, cook until tender. Add carrots and celery and cook another 5 to 8 minutes. Add potatoes, water, bay leaf, thyme, salt, pepper and cayenne pepper. Heat and bring to a boil, lower heat and simmer until potatoes are almost done.

Add tomatoes with juice, squeeze tomatoes to break up. Add roasted red peppers. Cover and simmer for 10 minutes longer. Serve by spooning broth into bowl and adding a piece of salmon and a slice of avocado.

Tuscana Soup

Nancy Lee

YIELD: 6 TO 8 SERVINGS

INGREDIENTS

1-1/2 pound sweet Italian sausage

1 head (large) escarole, chopped

2 large garlic cloves, chopped

2 cans (15 ounces each) chicken broth

2 cups water

2 cans (19 ounces each) cannellini beans, rinsed and drained

3/4 cup freshly grated Parmesan cheese

1 tablespoon olive oil

salt and pepper, to taste

Remove sausage from casings or use bulk.

Place sausage in a 5 quart heavy pot and cook in olive oil over medium heat, breaking into small pieces. Stir until golden. Pour off all but 2 tablespoons of drippings.

Stir in escarole and garlic, sauté over medium-high heat until wilted. Add broth and water and simmer 5 minutes.

Mash 1 can of cannellini beans in blender or food processor. then add all beans to mixture and simmer at least 5 minutes.

Salt and pepper, to taste.

The more it simmers, the more flavor. Just before serving, stir in Parmesan cheese.

Texas Bouilabaisse

Kate Mims,
Football Mom — Kevin 2008

Yield: 8 servings

Ingredients

ROUILLE:

1 head garlic cut across the top

salt

1/2 teaspoon plus 1-1/4 cups olive oil

1 large egg

2 teaspoons lemon juice

1 tablespoon chopped parsley

1/4 teaspoon cayenne pepper

SOUP:

2 to 3 pounds freshwater fish fillets

4 teaspoons salt

3/4 teaspoon cayenne pepper, divided

3 cups chopped onion

1 large chopped bell pepper

2 teaspoons garlic

1/4 pound butter

4 cups canned tomatoes

6 bay leaves

1-1/2 pounds combination of
    snow crab legs, scallops and
    crab claw meat

1/2 cup white wine

1/4 cup chopped parsley

ROUILLE: Place the garlic in foil and sprinkle with salt and 1/4 teaspoon of olive oil. Wrap in foil and roast at 375 degrees for 30 minutes. Place the pulp of the roasted garlic and egg in the food processor. Turn on and slowly add olive oil until thick. Add the remaining ingredients (lemon juice, parsley, cayenne) and pulse a few times to mix. Can be stored for up to 24 hours in the fridge.

SOUP: Season fish fillets with salt and 1/4 teaspoon of cayenne. In a separate bowl put onion, bell pepper, garlic and 1/2 teaspoon cayenne. Melt butter in a large cast-iron pan. Place 1/3 veggie mix on top of butter, stirring to coat, spread along bottom of pan. Place 1/3 tomato and 2 bay leaves on top of the veggie mix. Add 1/3 fish to top the veggie mix and repeat layering 2 more times. Add the shrimp on top of the veggie mix and pour wine down the side of the pot. Cover and reduce heat to medium and cook one hour with lid on. Remove bay leaves. Serve in bowls with 1 tablespoon of the Rouille on top. Serve with crusty bread.

Butternut Squash and Apple Soup

Karen & Dave Eanet,
Voice of the Cats! WGN-Radio

INGREDIENTS

2 tablespoons butter, unsalted

2 tablespoons olive oil

4 cups chopped yellow onion

2 tablespoons mild curry

5 pounds butternut squash, peeled, cut in 1-1/2 inch cubes

1-1/2 pounds sweet or Jazz apples, peeled, cored, chopped

2 teaspoons kosher salt

1/2 teaspoon freshly ground black pepper

2 cups fresh apple cider (from the refrigerated section), warmed

Warm butter and olive oil in stockpot over low heat. Add onions and curry powder. Cook, uncovered, 15 to 20 minutes. Stir occasionally, scraping bottom of pot.

Add apples and squash with salt, pepper and 2 cups of water. Bring to a boil, then cover, reduce heat to low and cook 30 to 40 minutes, until squash and apples are very soft. Purée in pot, using immersion blender, or in bowl of food processor with steel blade.

Add cider and enough water for preferred consistency. Serve hot.

Bloody Mary Soup

Joann Skiba

YIELD: 6 TO 8 SERVINGS

INGREDIENTS

SOUP:

2 cans (28 ounces each) San Marzano tomatoes, with juice

1 cup beef or chicken stock

1/4 cup chopped green onions

1/4 cup Worcestershire sauce

1/4 cup vodka

2 tablespoons horseradish

2 tablespoons liquid honey

1 tablespoon freshly squeezed lemon juice (1 lemon)

2 teaspoons salt

2 teaspoons celery salt

1 teaspoon freshly ground black pepper

1/4 cup chopped fresh cilantro

tortilla chips

4 flour tortillas, each cut into 8 pieces

2 tablespoons olive oil

salt and pepper, to taste

CHIPS: Brush tortilla pieces with olive oil. Sprinkle with salt and pepper. Bake at 400 degrees for 8 to 10 minutes in a silicone or parchment lined jelly roll pan.

SOUP: In a large, deep bowl combine tomatoes with juice, green onions, Worcestershire sauce, vodka, horseradish, honey, lemon juice, salt, celery salt and pepper. Purée with an immersion blender until smooth (or process in batches in a regular blender).

Taste and adjust seasonings with salt and pepper. Thin with more stock or water, if needed. Cover and refrigerate until cold, about 3 hours. Taste and adjust seasonings, if necessary.

Pour into chilled bowl and garnish with cilantro. (Can also garnish with salad shrimp.)

Serve with homemade tortilla chips.

Victory Gazpacho

Don Skiba

YIELD: 16 SERVINGS

INGREDIENTS

2 cans (48 ounces each) tomato juice

4 large peeled and seeded tomatoes

1 large cucumber

1 large onion

2 green peppers

2 cloves garlic

2 tablespoons red wine vinegar

3 tablespoons salad oil

1 tablespoon chopped cilantro

salt and pepper, to taste

Topping options include: sour cream, croutons, scallions, chives, baby shrimp

Chop vegetables into medium chunks, then process tomatoes, cucumber, onions, peppers and garlic until finely chopped. Do not purée. Combine with tomato juice, vinegar, oil and cilantro in a large pot. Salt and pepper, to taste. Chill thoroughly.

Gazpacho

Marilyn Zilka, 1975

YIELD: 8 TO 10 SERVINGS

INGREDIENTS

4 cups ripe tomatoes — cored and cut into 1/4 inch cubes

2 cups red bell peppers, cored, seeded and cut into 1/4-inch cubes

2 cups cucumbers, 1/2 peeled, 1/2 not; seeded and cut into 1/2 inch cubes

1/2 cup minced sweet onion (Vidalia, Maui, etc.)

2 medium garlic cloves, minced

2 teaspoons salt

1/3 cup sherry vinegar

ground black pepper

5 cups tomato juice

1 teaspoon hot pepper sauce, optional

8 ice cubes

Extra virgin olive oil for serving

GARNISH:

garlic croutons, diced avocado, chopped black olives

Can be refrigerated for up to two days.

Combine tomatoes and any juice, peppers, cucumbers, onion, garlic, salt, vinegar and pepper, to taste in large non-reactive bowl. Let stand for 5 minutes.

Stir in tomato juice, hot pepper sauce and ice cubes; cover tightly and refrigerate to blend flavors, at least 4 hours.

Adjust seasonings with salt and pepper; remove any remaining ice cubes.

Serve cold; drizzle with 1 teaspoon extra virgin olive oil. Garnish as desired.

Great Gazpacho

Coach April & Craig Likhite,
Head Coach, Cross Country

INGREDIENTS

2 cups V8 juice, divided

2 tablespoons olive oil

2 tablespoons red wine vinegar

1 chicken bouillon cube

1/2 teaspoon garlic salt

1/2 teaspoon salt

1/8 teaspoon pepper

3 dashes hot pepper sauce

1 ripe tomato, seeded, peeled and
cubed

1 cup diced peeled cucumber,
cut into 1-inch squares

1/4 medium onion sliced

sour cream

cilantro

In blender, combine 1 cup V8 juice and next 7 ingredients at medium speed for a few seconds. Add tomato, cucumber, green pepper and onion. Process until tomato is evenly chopped, but do not purée. Add remaining cup of juice. Pour into covered one quart container and chill 4 hours or overnight. Serve with sour cream and cilantro.

Texas Tortilla Soup

Marilyn Zilka, 1975

YIELD: 6 SERVINGS

INGREDIENTS

2/3 cup finely diced onions

2/3 cup finely diced celery

3 cups seeded, diced tomatoes
(1/2-inch dice)

1/2 teaspoon finely chopped garlic

2/3 cup kernel corn

2 teaspoons canola oil

2 teaspoons chopped fresh cilantro

1/4 teaspoon cumin

1/4 teaspoon ground white pepper

1/2 teaspoon chili powder

1-1/2 quarts chicken stock

1 cup cooked, diced white chicken
meat

GARNISH:

1/3 pound Monterey Jack cheese

1/3 cup chopped or sliced green
onions

2 avocados, chopped in 1/2 inch dice

tortilla strips

Heat oil in soup pot, lightly sauté onions, celery, garlic. Add tomatoes, corn, cumin, pepper, chili powder and chicken stock.

Bring to a boil, lower heat, simmer for 15 minutes.

Add chicken and cilantro. Adjust seasoning to your liking.

Place tortilla strips and avocado in soup bowl and ladle hot soup over it. Sprinkle with green onions and jack cheese.

stews

Madrid Beef Stew

Joe Slowik

YIELD: 4 TO 6 SERVINGS

INGREDIENTS

1-1/2 pounds beef stew meat, cubed

2 slices lean bacon, minced

1-1/2 cups chopped onion

3 cloves garlic, minced

1/2 teaspoon tarragon

1/2 teaspoon thyme

1/2 teaspoon crushed red pepper

1/2 teaspoon curry powder

1 can (15 ounces) diced tomatoes

1 tablespoon chopped fresh parsley

3/4 cup dry white wine

1/4 cup white vinegar

2 beef bouillon cubes, dissolved in
3/4-cup water

2 cups chopped carrots

2 cups chopped potatoes

Heat a large pot on medium-high heat. Cook bacon until soft. Add beef and brown on all sides, doing in batches if pot is crowded. Return all beef to the pot. Add onion and garlic and cook, stirring for about 3 minutes until onion is soft. Stir in all other ingredients and heat to a boil. Reduce heat and simmer, covered, for about 90 minutes until meat is fork tender and vegetables are cooked. Check periodically and add water if necessary to keep meet almost covered in liquid.

Beef or Lamb Stew

Ann Cox

YIELD: 8 SERVINGS

INGREDIENTS

2-1/2 pounds beef or lamb stew meat,
bite sized

1 cup thickly sliced celery

5 medium carrots, thickly sliced

4 medium potatoes, chopped

2 large onions, coarsely chopped

1 cup stewed tomatoes

1 tablespoon sugar

2 tablespoons tapioca

1/2 cup bread crumbs

1 can (14-1/2 ounces) peas, drained

1 pound mushrooms, halved

Combine ingredients in large oven proof pot, cover and bake at 400 degrees for 4 hours.

COACHES QUOTES

April Likhite, Cross Country:

"Success means having the courage, the determination and the will to become the person you believe you were meant to be."
–George Sheehan

Mexican Skillet Beef Stew

Michael Wilson, 2000

YIELD: 6 SERVINGS

INGREDIENTS

3 pounds chuck roast or steak

2 to 3 packets taco seasoning

1 pound crimini or button mushrooms, sliced

1 can (14 ounces) black olives, sliced

8 ounces shredded sharp cheddar cheese

1 to 4 tablespoons minced or sliced jalapeño peppers

TOPPINGS:

diced tomatoes

shredded lettuce

tortillas, corn or flour

sour cream

For canned mushrooms use 8 ounces of sliced mushrooms.

Cut beef into bite-sized cubes. In a large skillet (12 inches), brown beef. Add taco seasoning mix and water according to the directions on the package. Simmer until sauce gets to desired thickness.

Slice olives and mushrooms. An egg slicer works well. Add to the stew. Add jalapeños, amount depending on desired heat. Simmer on low heat until mushrooms are tender.

Heat tortillas. Serve the stew in the tortillas with lettuce, tomatoes, cheese, sour cream, or whatever you like.

Edna's Beef Stew

Mo Harty,
Associate Athletic Director

YIELD: 6 SERVINGS

INGREDIENTS

3 pounds beef stew meat

4 carrots, cut in chunks

2 onions, cut in rings

3 celery ribs, cut in chunks

8 ounces tomato sauce

8 ounces water

4 tablespoons tapioca mix

2 tablespoons brown sugar

dash salt

dash pepper

Place meat in a single layer in the bottom of baking dish. Place carrots, onions and celery over meat. Combine remaining ingredients and pour over the meat. Cover tightly and bake at 250 degrees for 5 to 6 hours. Also stew can be cooked in a slow cooker.

Let's Go Cats

Laurie's African Peanut Stew

Cathleen & Coach Laurie Schiller,
Head Coach, Women's Fencing

YIELD: 4 SERVINGS

INGREDIENTS

1-1/2 pounds stew beef,
      cut into 1-inch cubes
1/4 cup all-purpose flour
1 teaspoon salt
1/8 teaspoon pepper
1/4 cup cooking oil
1 medium onion, chopped
1 clove garlic, minced
1/3 cup smooth peanut butter
1 can (8 ounces) tomato sauce
1 teaspoon sugar
1 teaspoon vinegar
1 teaspoon chili powder
1 cup water

Mix flour, salt and pepper. Dredge beef with mixture and brown on all sides in hot oil. Remove beef and brown onion and garlic lightly in the oil remaining in the pan. Blend in other ingredients and add beef back in. Bring to boil, lower heat, and simmer, covered, for 40 minutes. Stir sauce occasionally and add more water if necessary to prevent sticking.

Five Hour Stew

Catherine Stembridge,
Executive Director, Alumni Association

YIELD: 5 SERVINGS

INGREDIENTS

2 pounds beef stew meat,
      in 1inch cubes
6 carrots, sliced
3 large celery stalks, chopped
3 medium onions, sliced
2 cans (14 ounces each) tomatoes and
      liquid
1 tablespoon salt
1/2 cup fresh bread crumbs
2 cups frozen peas
1 cup red wine

Preheat oven to 350 degrees. Put the beef, onions, celery, carrots, tomatoes, bread crumbs and salt in a covered casserole or Dutch oven and bake for 4 hours. Add the peas and wine and bake for another hour. Serve over rice.

Sumo Wrestler's Stew (Chanko-nabe)

Andrew Pariano, 2000,
Head Coach, Wrestling

YIELD: SERVES 4 REALLY BIG PEOPLE

Chanko is the staple of the Sumo wrestlers diet. Each day, while the senior wrestlers rest after their 6-hour morning workout, the younger ones retire to the kitchen to chop meat or seafood and vegetables. The highest ranking wrestlers eat first. They sit cross-legged, wearing only the wide loincloth-like belts which they wear while training, and help themselves out of great simmering pots of food.

Practically anything can go into a chanko stew; the only rule is that it is based on either meat or fish, but not both. The cause of the sumo wrestlers' vast size is not the contents of the chanko, but the amount that they eat — dieters have no need to worry!

This dish is served during tournaments and features chicken because four-legged animals (down on all fours) and fish (no hands or feet) might be bad luck. The quanties are large; you may halve them.

COACHES QUOTES

Andrew Pariano, Men's Wrestling:

"We must take responsibility for ourselves, and not expect the rest of the world to understand what it takes to be the best that we can become."
—Josh Waitzkin, The Art of Learning

INGREDIENTS

1 medium chicken

2 to 3 leeks, washed and trimmed

4 carrots, peeled

1 daikon radish, peeled

1 large (or medium) potato, peeled

1/2 teaspoon salt

10 to 12 shiitaki mushrooms
   (if using dry ones, soak in warm
   water until soft; drain)

2 medium onions, peeled

1 medium cabbage, washed

1 to 2 cakes deep-fried tofu (aburage),
   optional

1/2 cup soy sauce

1/2 cup mirin

Bone the chicken and cut the meat into chunks 1-1/2 to 2 inches, reserving the bones. (For lower fat stew, skin the chicken and add the skin to the stock.) Cut the leeks and 3 of the carrots into bite-sized pieces. Put the chicken bones, leeks and carrots into a large saucepan, fill it with water and bring it to a boil. Turn the heat to medium-low and simmer, uncovered, for 3 hours to make stock, then strain and discard solids.

Cut the daikon and potato into bite-sized pieces and parboil in lightly salted water in a separate pot; drain. Cut off and discard the mushroom stalks; cut the mushroom caps and the onion into quarters. Chop the cabbage into small pieces and cut the remaining carrot and the deep-fried tofu (if used) into chunks.

Put the chicken meat and all the vegetables except the daikon and the potato into the stock pot, together with the soy sauce. Simmer until vegetables are cooked.

Add the daikon and potato. Season, to taste with mirin and salt; simmer a few minutes more. Serve hot.

When the stew is finished, hungry wrestlers sometimes top up the remaining soup with cooked udon noodles.

Sugo

Top Chef Stephanie Izard,
Top Chef (Season 4) and chef/owner of the Girl and the Goat Restaurant, Chicago

YIELD: 10 TO 12 SERVINGS

Sugo is an Italian gravy or sauce but this recipe is for a stew. Any mixture of meats can be used in this recipe. It is great for left-over corned beef or brisket. The sausage adds flavor as well as texture to the stew. Create your own favorite combination but don't be afraid to try goat. The sausage (including goat sausage) can be any style (breakfast, kielbasa, Italian, etc.). Like many stews, this recipe is better the second day.

INGREDIENTS

2 pounds goat or other meat, cubed

2 pounds goat or other sausage, sliced

2 pounds braised goat (or other cooked meat), cubed

1 pound onion, diced (for purée)

2 ounces garlic, minced (for purée)

1/4 cup Dijon mustard

1/4 cup Worcestershire sauce

1/2 cup canned crushed tomatos

2 tablespoons sambal chili sauce

1 pound onion, small dice

4 cloves garlic, minced

4 apples, peeled, cored, sliced

3 quarts beef stock

In a smoking hot pan with oil, brown all the meat. Remove from heat and reserve.

In a separate pot, simmer the onion, garlic, Dijon, Worcestershire, tomato and sambal together. Remove from heat and purée.

In a large pot, sweat the onion, garlic and apples together. Add in the meat and puréed mixture. Add the stock and bring to a simmer.

Cover and simmer for about 2 hours or until the meat has fallen apart. Uncover during last 30 minutes to thicken the sauce.

Top your favorite pasta, rice, potatoes with the sugo or eat it on its own!

Portuguese Fish Stew

Dagmar Porcelli,
Football Mom — Chuck #74

YIELD: 8 TO 10 SERVINGS

INGREDIENTS

1 can (28 ounces) plum tomatoes

2 cloves garlic, minced

2 tablespoons olive oil

2 cups thinly sliced red onion

1 cup dry white wine

2 tablespoons fresh-squeezed
    lemon juice

2 teaspoons red pepper flakes

1 teaspoon coarsely ground
    black pepper

1-1/4 pounds littleneck clams, cleaned

1-1/4 pounds mussels, cleaned

2 pounds fresh scrod or whitefish

4 tablespoons chopped parsley

All clams and mussels must be scrubbed for sand and beard. Make sure that clams and mussels are closed when going to cook. Keep them cold. Can also add any shell fish desired (lobster, shrimp, crab claws)

Sauté garlic and onion in oil until soft and browned. Add tomatoes, liquid from tomatoes, wine, lemon juice and red and black peppers. Bring to a boil, lower heat, simmer 15 minutes. Add mussels, clams and cover. Simmer 5 to 8 more minutes. Place white fish on top in chunks. Cover and cook for 6 minutes longer or until fish is soft and flaky and the mussels and clams have opened. Sprinkle with parsley. Serve steaming hot. Great with fresh French baguette for dipping.

Hungarian Goulash

Sandy White,
Women's Fencing Mom — Whitney, 2010

YIELD: 10 TO 12 SERVINGS

INGREDIENTS

2 pounds cubed sirloin steak or
    stew beef

1/4 cup flour

2 cans (10-3/4 ounces each) condensed
    tomato soup

1 can (28 ounces) Redpack diced
    tomatoes

1 cup red wine

1 cup water

2 tablespoons tarragon

1 teaspoon spicy paprika

3/4 teaspoon sea salt

3/4 teaspoon freshly ground
    black pepper

8 cloves garlic, crushed

1/2 cup flour

1/8 cup olive oil

1 extra large Vidalia onion, diced

Use high quality beef so goulash is tender. Also use Redpack tomatoes since this brand is much less acidic than its competition.

Preheat oven to 325 degrees. Coat meat in flour, salt and pepper in a mixing bowl. Brown in frying pan with olive oil, onion and garlic. Once beef is browned, put mixture in Dutch oven with soup, tomatoes, paprika, tarragon, wine, water and pepper, to taste. Cover and bake for 1 hour; open Dutch oven to see if mixture is too thick. If it is add another cup of red wine and stir the goulash. (If too thin, bake without cover for part of the time.) Bake 1-1/2 hours more. Serve goulash on wide egg noodles or sliced French or Italian bread.

Veal Stew with Root Vegetables

Nora Teeple

Yield: 6 to 8 servings

Ingredients

1/3 cup olive oil

1/2 cup flour

1/2 teaspoon salt

1/2 teaspoon pepper

1/2 teaspoon paprika

2 pounds lean veal stew meat, cut into
    1-1/2 inch cubes

2 jars (16 ounces each) white onions,
    drained

1/4 pound parsnips, cut into
    1-inch pieces

1/2 pound carrots, peeled, cut into
    1-inch pieces

1/2 pound celery root, peeled, cut into
    1-inch pieces

1 can (28 ounces) whole peeled
    tomatoes

1 can (13-3/4 ounces) chicken broth

2 bay leaves

2 sprigs parsley

1/2 teaspoon thyme

1/2 teaspoon each salt and pepper

NOODLES:

1 pound broad egg noodles

1/2 cup butter, melted

1 tablespoon Dijon mustard

1/4 cup chopped parsley

1/4 teaspoon each salt and pepper

1/4 teaspoon minced garlic

1/2 cup grated Parmesan cheese

STEW: Heat 2 tablespoons oil in a Dutch oven over medium-high heat. Mix flour, salt, pepper and paprika in a bowl and add veal. Toss to coat. Remove veal and remove excess flour. Add veal to Dutch oven in small batches and turn to brown evenly. Remove veal with slotted spoon and drain on paper towel. Add more oil if needed and repeat with remaining veal. Set aside.

Heat 1 to 2 tablespoons of oil in Dutch oven over medium heat. Add onions, parsnips, carrots and celery root. Cook and stir to brown lightly, about 5 minutes. Remove with slotted spoon and set aside.

Preheat oven to 350 degrees. Put veal in Dutch oven, add the rest of the ingredients and stir to mix. Cover and heat to boil. Put in oven and cook until meat is tender, about one hour. Add reserved vegetables (parsnips, carrots and celery root) and stir to mix. Cover and return to oven until vegetables are tender, 20 to 30 minutes. Uncover and cook until liquid has reduced and thickened, about 20 minutes. Stir once or twice during cooking. Serve with buttered noodles.

NOODLES: Cook noodles and drain. Whisk butter, mustard, salt, pepper and garlic in bowl. Pour over hot noodles and toss to mix. To serve, arrange noodles on platter, add veal and sprinkle with Parmesan cheese.

Veal Stew

Ann Marie Bernardi,
Field Hockey Mom

YIELD: 4 TO 6 SERVINGS

INGREDIENTS

1-1/2 pounds cubed veal
1 can (15 ounces) tomato sauce
1 can (15 ounces) water
2 fresh carrots, sliced
    (about 1-1/2 cups)
2 large potatoes, cubed (about 2 cups)
1 tablespoon Italian seasoning
2 cloves garlic, minced
1 medium onion, chopped
oil
salt, to taste
pepper, to taste
cooked pasta

Brown veal in oil, doing in batches if necessary to avoid crowding. Remove meat, then brown onion and garlic in oil. Add carrots, potatoes and browned meat. Then add tomato sauce, water, salt, pepper, Italian seasoning. Cover and cook one hour, until meat is tender. Uncover and allow sauce to thicken.

Boil pasta. Serve stew over portion of pasta or add pasta to stew.

COACHES QUOTES

Keylor Chan, Volleyball:

"The thing we talk about often in our program is family. Our families center us and helps build the foundations necessary to achieve our goals. Families take many shapes and encompass many people from our relatives to a collegiate sport team. 'Family always comes first.' "

All Big Ten

Breads

BASKETBALL

Men's:

Head Coach Bill Carmody (2000–present)
– *23rd head coach*

- The first year there was a recorded team was 1904 with a record of 2-2.

- 1932-1933 was the last team to win the Big Ten Championship. (Albert Wilkins, the father of our cookbook co-chairman Joann Skiba, was on that team!)

- Wildcats have been to the National Invitational Tournament the last three years.

- There were 70 Academic All-Big Ten honorees in the years 1964–2011.

Women's:

Head Coach Joe McKeown (2008–present)
– *6th head coach*

- First season was 1975–76 under Coach Mary DiStanislao with a record of 5–12.

- Coach Don Perrelli led the Cats to a 251-181 record during his time as head coach (1984–1999).

- There were 87 Academic All-Big Ten honorees in the years 1987–2011. There also have been 49 All-Big Ten honorees since 1983.

- This past year Amy Jaeschke was the first Wildcat to be drafted by the WNBA. She also was the fifth Cat named an All-American.

cornbread

Bazlamaca (Serbian Cornbread)

Kristina Divjak Eschmeyer, 1999,
Women's Basketball

YIELD: 9x13 INCH LOAF

*This is my grandmother's recipe originating
in her birthplace, a village in Croatia
named Donji Lapac.*

INGREDIENTS

1/2 pound butter, melted
1 pound cottage cheese
1 pound sour cream
6 eggs
5 tablespoons sugar
6 tablespoons cornmeal
6 tablespoons flour

Preheat oven to 350 degrees. Dust flour
over a greased 9x13 inch baking dish.
Mix all ingredients, pour in pan. Bake for
35 minutes or until slightly browned.
Can be eaten cold or warmed for breakfast, snacks or dessert.

Vegan Flax Seed Cornbread

Ginnie Morrison, 2006

YIELD: 9x9 INCH LOAF

INGREDIENTS

2 tablespoons flax seed
6 tablespoons water
1 cup all-purpose flour
1 cup cornmeal
1/4 cup sugar
4 teaspoons baking powder
1 teaspoon salt
1 cup soy milk
1/4 cup canola oil
1 tablespoon apple cider (or red wine)
    vinegar

Preheat oven to 425 degrees.

Bring water to a boil in a small pot, add
the flax seed, reduce heat and simmer for
about 3 minutes. The seeds will become
gooey and act as a binding agent. Set
aside.

In a separate bowl, combine flour, cornmeal, sugar, baking soda and salt. Stir
vinegar into soy milk. Add the flax seed,
soy milk with vinegar and oil to the dry
mixture. Stir or beat until just smooth—
don't over beat!

Turn into greased cornbread pan or 9-
inch round pan. Bake for 20 to 25
minutes or until a toothpick comes out
clean.

Cool in pan for 10 minutes, turnout onto
a cooling-rack and let cool at least 10
minutes more.

Grandma Sarah's Old Fashioned Cornbread

Natasha Brown Moss, 1992

YIELD: 10 SERVINGS

This cornbread is an essential ingredient for Grandma Sarah's Old Fashioned Dressing

INGREDIENTS

2 cups yellow cornmeal

1/2 cup all-purpose flour

1 tablespoon sugar

2-1/2 teaspoons baking powder

1/4 teaspoon salt

1 cup milk

1 egg, beaten

1/4 cup vegetable oil

Preheat oven to 425 degrees. Place 10 inch cast-iron skillet or 9 inch square baking pan in oven. Mix together cornmeal, flour, sugar, baking powder and salt. In a separate bowl, mix milk, egg and oil. Add wet ingredients to dry ingredients. Beat vigorously until smooth. Pour batter into preheated pan. Bake until golden brown, about 20 minutes. Allow to rest for several minutes before removing from the pan.

packaged plus

Beer Bread Rolls

Kelly Kowalski,
Wife of Ken Kowalski,
Director of Video Football

YIELD: 6 TO 8 PIECES

Shape into a loaf or into footballs, basketballs, etc. using some of the mix to form laces.

INGREDIENTS

1 box hot bread roll with yeast mix, 16 ounces

1 cup shredded sharp cheddar cheese

1-1/4 cups beer

1 egg, beaten

2 tablespoons kosher salt

Hot bread roll mix can be found in the baking aisle, it may also be called quick bread with yeast.

Preheat oven to 350 degrees. In a small saucepan, heat the beer to almost boiling.

In a medium bowl, combine the bread mix and cheese; add the egg and mix. Add heated beer into mixture and knead for 5 minutes. Allow the bread to sit for 5 minutes.

Roll bread into desired shape. Place onto cookie sheet sprayed with cooking spray. Sprinkle with kosher salt.

Bake 25 minutes or until golden brown.

Bubble Loaf

Megan Anderson, 1976

YIELD: 1 TUBE PAN LOAF

INGREDIENTS

20 frozen dinner rolls

1 package (3.4 ounces) butterscotch
pudding (not instant)

1/2 cup butter

1/2 cup brown sugar

1 cup chopped pecans or as desired

Butter a tube pan. Sprinkle heavily with
chopped pecans. Place 20 frozen dinner
rolls in prepared pan (cut in half if you
like). Sprinkle the pudding over the rolls.
Melt the butter and brown sugar together
and pour evenly over the rolls. Let rise
uncovered overnight.

Preheat oven to 350 degrees; bake for
25 minutes. Invert onto a platter
immediately after baking.

Chili Cheese Bread

Zoe T Barron

YIELD: 2 LOAVES

INGREDIENTS

2 loaves French bread

1/4 pound butter

1 tablespoon garlic, minced

2 cans (7 ounces each) mild chopped
green chilies, drained

1 pound Monterey Jack cheese,
shredded

1 cup mayonnaise

Preheat oven to 350 degrees. Slice loaves
of bread lengthwise. Melt butter in a
small saucepan and add garlic and chilies.
Heat until warm. Spoon the chili mixture
evenly over the cut sides of the bread. In
another bowl, mix the cheese and mayonnaise then spread over the chili topped
bread. Bake for 20 minutes or until
lightly browned. Slice into 2 to 3 inch
pieces to serve.

Cheese Bread

Saul L Thomashow, 1957 — MBA

YIELD: 1 LOAF

INGREDIENTS

1 loaf Gonnella Bread (or similar type)

1/4 pound butter or margarine,
softened

1 cup shredded cheddar cheese

1 cup mayonnaise

dash Worcestershire sauce

1 teaspoon dried minced onions

Preheat oven to 350 degrees. In a bowl
combine butter, cheese, mayonnaise,
Worcestershire sauce and onion.

Slice top off bread horizontally. In each
half, cut 1 inch slices almost to the crust,
vertically. Spread the cheese mixture on
both sides of the bread, pushing some
cheese into the slits. Bake for 20 to 30
minutes.

Cornerstone Farm Onion Shortcake

Linda Schoeman

YIELD: 8X8 INCH PAN

Great with the Cream of Pumpkin Soup, or with baked ham or roast chicken. Also good with a green salad for a light supper.

INGREDIENTS

1 large red onion
1/4 cup unsalted butter, melted
1-1/2 cups corn muffin mix
1 egg, slightly beaten
1/3 cup milk
1 can (8-3/4 ounces) cream style corn
4 drops hot pepper sauce
1 cup sour cream
1/2 teaspoon salt
1/2 teaspoon dill
1 cup shredded sharp cheddar cheese

Preheat oven to 425 degrees. Sauté onions until tender. Combine muffin mix, milk, egg, corn and pepper sauce; stir until barely blended. Turn into a buttered 8 inch square pan. Mix sour cream, salt, dill, half of the cheese, onions and butter; spoon carefully over top of batter. Top with remaining cheese. Bake for about 30 minutes. **N**

Pepperoni Bread

Janet Drohan, 1975, Mom of Head Coach Kate & Associate Coach Caryl Drohan, Softball

YIELD: ABOUT 20 PIECES

INGREDIENTS

1 package pizza dough — fresh if you can
8 ounces pepperoni diced and quartered
8 ounces shredded mozzarella
1 egg, beaten

Allow dough to rise to about double in size. Pat down and size to cookie sheet or stretch out like a pizza.

Combine pepperoni, cheese and egg. Fill center of dough; wrap dough and adhere edge of dough with warm water.

Bake in 350 degree oven for 30 minutes. Slice. **N**

Monkey Bread

Joann Skiba

SERVES 22 NU CHEERLEADERS

INGREDIENTS

3 packages Pillsbury Grands! refrigerated flaky buttermilk biscuits
1 cup granulated sugar
2 teaspoons cinnamon, divided
1-1/2 cups butter
1 cup firmly packed light brown sugar

Preheat oven to 350 degrees. In a small bowl, mix together granulated sugar and 1 teaspoon of cinnamon. Set aside.

Cut each biscuit into quarters and roll in sugar/cinnamon mixture. Place coated biscuit balls into a 9x13 inch cake pan, angel food cake pan, Bundt pan or baking dish.

Boil butter, brown sugar and 1 teaspoon of cinnamon for 2 to 3 minutes and pour over biscuit balls. Bake for 25 to 30 minutes.

Cool monkey bread in pan for at least 15 minutes. Turn over onto a tray or large plate and serve.

Easy Poppy Seed Bread

Nancy Lee

YIELD: 2 LARGE OR 3 SMALL LOAVES

INGREDIENTS

1 box yellow cake mix
1 package instant coconut cream pudding
4 large eggs
1/2 cup canola oil
1 cup warm water
2 tablespoons poppy seeds

A moist tasty bread loved by kids and adults alike. Freezes well too.

Preheat oven to 325 degrees. Spray 2 large or three small loaf pans with non-stick cooking spray.

Combine first 5 ingredients and beat with mixer for 3 to 4 minutes. Add poppy seeds and stir in. Pour into pans. Bake for 40 to 50 minutes on an upper rack. Check with toothpick to test if done.

rolls/muffins

Applesauce Muffins

Kathy Newcomb

YIELD: 1 TO 1-1/2 DOZEN

INGREDIENTS

1-1/2 cups sugar
1/2 cup butter or margarine, softened
2 large eggs
2 cups flour
1 teaspoon baking powder
1 teaspoon ground cinnamon
1/2 teaspoon baking soda
1/2 teaspoon ground cloves
1/4 teaspoon salt
1 cup applesauce

In a mixing bowl, cream sugar and butter. Add eggs and beat well. Combine dry ingredients, add to the creamed mixture, alternately with applesauce, approximately one-third at a time. Fill greased or paper-lined muffin cups no more than two-thirds full. Bake at 350 degrees for 20 to 25 minutes until toothpick inserted in center comes out clean.

Passion

Canadian Beer Muffins

Nicole Tilley,
Women's Fencing, Senior Captain

YIELD: 12 MUFFINS

INGREDIENTS

3 cups flour

3 tablespoons white sugar

5 teaspoons baking powder

1/2 teaspoon salt

12 ounces beer (not dark heavy beer)

1/4 cup butter, melted

Preheat oven to 350 degrees. Mix dry ingredients together. Pour beer into dry mix all at once and stir together using approximately 25 strokes. Grease muffin tin. Spoon dough into tin so that the tops of each mound is roughly level with the tin. Lightly baste tops with melted butter. Bake for 20 minutes.

Blueberry Muffins

Suzanne Calder

YIELD: 12 MUFFINS

INGREDIENTS

3/4 cup melted butter

1 cup sugar

2 beaten eggs

2 teaspoons baking powder

1/2 teaspoon salt

1 cup fresh or frozen blueberries
    (no need to defrost)

1/2 cup blueberry pie filling

2 cups + 1 tablespoon flour

1/2 cup milk

TOPPING:

1/2 cup sugar

1/3 cup flour

1/4 cup butter, softened

Grease the bottoms only of a 12-cup muffin pan, or line the cups with cake papers.

Put one tablespoon of the flour in a plastic bag with the blueberries. Shake it gently to coat the blueberries. Melt the butter. Mix in the sugar. Add the eggs, baking powder and salt; mix thoroughly. Add half the remaining two cups of flour and mix it in with half the milk. Add the rest of the flour and milk and mix thoroughly. Add blueberry pie filling and mix it in. Fold in the flour-coated blueberries. Fill the muffin tins three-quarters full and set them aside. If there is leftover dough, grease the bottom of a small tea-bread loaf pan and fill it with the remaining dough.

CRUMB TOPPING: Mix sugar and flour in a small bowl. Add butter and cut it in until it's crumbly. (Or use a food processor and hard butter.) Sprinkle the crumb topping over the muffins and bake them in a 375 degree oven for 25 to 30 minutes. (The tea bread should bake about 10 minutes longer.)

Hint: divide the remaining pie filling into 1/2 cup portions in paper cups and freeze for another day.

Pumpkin Chocolate Chip Mini Muffins

Carol Hackney,
Women's Basketball Mom — Kendall #4

YIELD: 48 MINI MUFFINS

INGREDIENTS

1-2/3 cups flour
1 cup sugar
1 tablespoon pumpkin pie spice
1 teaspoon baking powder
1/4 teaspoon baking soda
1/4 teaspoon salt
2 large eggs
1/4 cup butter, melted
1 cup pumpkin purée
6 to 8 ounces mini chocolate chips

Preheat oven to 350 degrees. Mix first 6 (dry) ingredients in large bowl, then add eggs, butter and pumpkin. Stir together, using mixer on low speed, until well blended. Then stir in mini chocolate chips. Prepare mini muffin pan with spray oil and fill to top of muffin indent with batter. Bake for approximately 17 to 20 minutes. The recipe easily doubles and the muffins freeze beautifully.

No Beat Popovers

Karen Rudel Novak, 1981,
Women's Swimming

YIELD: 12 PIECES

INGREDIENTS

2 eggs
1 cup milk
1 cup flour
1/2 teaspoon salt

Break eggs into bowl. Add milk, flour and salt. Mix well with spoon (disregard lumps). Fill greased muffin tins 3/4 full. Put in COLD oven. Set oven to 450 degrees and turn on heat. Bake 30 minutes.

Secret … cold oven and do not peek for full 30 minutes!

soda bread

Mrs. O'Leary's Irish Soda Bread

Patsy Emery,
Director, FA Operations — retired

YIELD: 1 LOAF

I adapted this recipe from County Kerry, Ireland.

INGREDIENTS

4 cups flour

1 cup sugar

4 teaspoons baking flour

1/2 teaspoon salt

1/4 pound butter, melted*

1-1/2 cups raisins

2 tablespoons caraway seeds

1 egg

1-1/2 cups buttermilk

1/3 teaspoon baking soda

*You may substitute 6 ounces melted Irish butter for 1 stick of regular butter.

Preheat oven to 375 degrees. In a large mixing bowl, sift together the flour, sugar, baking powder and salt. Add the melted butter to the flour mixture; mix first with a wooden spoon, then blend with fork until consistency of coarse crumbs; be sure the butter has been thoroughly incorporated with the flour. Stir in the raisins and caraway seeds. In a small mixing bowl, slightly beat egg; add the buttermilk and baking soda. Stir until well blended.

Make a well in the center of the flour mixture. Pour buttermilk mixture into well and stir until mixture is thoroughly moist. Place in a large well buttered 10-inch cast-iron skillet; brush top with melted butter and bake for approximately 45 minutes or until golden brown.

Irish Soda Bread

Kelly Deiters,
Football Mom — Neal #79, 2012

YIELD: 8 SERVINGS

INGREDIENTS

4 cups flour

1 cup sugar

1 teaspoon baking powder

1 teaspoon baking soda

1/4 teaspoon salt

1-1/3 cups buttermilk

1/3 cup margarine

1 large egg

1 cup golden raisins

Preheat oven to 350 degrees.

Mix flour, sugar, baking powder, baking soda and salt in large bowl. In a small bowl, beat the egg. Melt the margarine in the microwave. In a medium bowl, stir together the egg, buttermilk and melted margarine. Mix wet ingredients into dry ingredients. Stir in raisins. With your hands, shape dough together into a clump. Dough will be dry and crumbly; pat it together the best you can and transfer to a greased and floured cast-iron fry pan or baking sheet. With a knife slash an X on top of the mound of dough. Bake for 55 minutes until slightly browned.

Enjoy warm out of the oven with butter or raspberry jam; also great toasted the next day.

sweet

Chocolate Chip Banana Bread with Nuts

Laura & Jim Phillips,
Director of Athletics and Recreation

YIELD: 1 LOAF

INGREDIENTS

3/4 cup sugar
1/2 cup margarine or butter, softened
2 eggs
1 cup mashed ripe bananas
(2 medium sized)
1/2 cup milk
1 teaspoon vanilla extract
2 cups all-purpose flour
1 teaspoon baking soda
1/2 teaspoon salt
6 ounces chocolate chips, optional
6 ounces chopped nuts

Preheat oven to 350 degrees. Grease bottom only of 9x5 inch loaf pan.

In large bowl, cream butter and sugar until light and fluffy. Beat in eggs. Blend in bananas, milk and vanilla. In small bowl, combine, flour, baking soda and salt. Add dry mixture to creamed mixture, stirring until thoroughly blended. Stir in chocolate chips and/or nuts. Pour into prepared pan and bake 50 to 60 minutes or until toothpick inserted in center comes out clean. Cool in pan for about 5 minutes. Remove from pan by loosening around the edges and inverting pan. Cool on wire rack. Can be stored in freezer for up to a month.

Chocolate Chip Banana Bread

Claire Pollard,
Head Coach, Women's Tennis

YIELD: 1 LOAF

INGREDIENTS

1-1/4 cups sugar
1/4 cup butter
2 eggs
1 teaspoon baking soda
4 tablespoons sour cream
1-1/4 cups flour
1 cup very ripe mashed banana
1 teaspoon vanilla extract
1 teaspoon salt
1/2 cup chocolate chips

Preheat oven to 350 degrees. Mix sour cream and baking soda together. Set aside. Combine butter, sugar, eggs and vanilla. Slowly add in flour and salt. Add banana to sugar mixture. Fold in baking soda and sour cream mixture. Add chocolate chips. Pour into greased and floured loaf pan. Bake for 1 hour.

COACHES QUOTES

Claire Pollard, Women's Tennis:

"You are either getting better or getting worse. Nothing ever stays the same."

Mouthwatering Chocolate Chip Banana Bread

Alice Phillips Topping,
KGSM, Member of NU Women's Board

YIELD: 1 LOAF

INGREDIENTS

2 whole very ripe bananas
1 cup sugar
2 whole eggs
1/2 cup vegetable oil
1 cup unbleached white flour
3/4 cup whole wheat flour
1 teaspoon baking soda
1/2 teaspoon salt
1/2 teaspoon cinnamon
1/4 teaspoon nutmeg
1/4 cup milk
    (add a bit more than 1/4 cup)
1 teaspoon vanilla extract
1/4 to 1/2 cup chocolate chips

Substitute the chocolate chips with fresh strawberries or fresh blueberries. It's mouthwatering with any of these options!

The key to this recipe is the slow bake with the low temperature oven.

Preheat oven to 325 degrees. Mash bananas in a large bowl. Set aside.

In a separate bowl, sift together flour, baking soda and salt. In banana bowl, mix in the flour, baking soda and salt combination. Add remaining ingredients except the chocolate chips (or fruit) and mix. Hand stir in the chocolate chips (or fruit). When thoroughly combined, pour into greased 5x9 inch loaf pan, lined with aluminum foil for easy removal. Bake 1 hour and 20 to 30 minutes until golden brown and the top splits. Cool on rack for 20 minutes before removing from pan.

Banana Chocolate Chip Bread

Lindy & Coach Pat Goss, **1992,**
Head Coach and NU Director of Golf, Men's Golf

YIELD: 1 LOAF

INGREDIENTS

1 cup sugar
1/2 cup butter at room temperature
1 egg at room temperature
2 ripe bananas
2 cups flour
3 tablespoons milk
1 teaspoon baking powder
1/2 teaspoon baking soda
1 cup chocolate chips

Preheat oven to 350 degrees. Cream sugar and butter together at low speed until light and fluffy. Add egg and mix until combined. Set aside. Mash banana in a bowl and add the milk. Combine the banana mixture with the butter/sugar mixture until combined. Set aside. Sift flour, baking soda and baking powder together. Stir by hand into creamy mixture until flour is just moistened. Stir in chocolate chips. Grease 5x9 inch loaf pan. Turn batter into pan and bake for an hour or until toothpick comes out clean.

The Best Banana Bread

Emily Higgins,
Alumni Relations

YIELD: 1 LARGE LOAF OR 2 SMALL LOAVES

INGREDIENTS

2 eggs
1 to 2 cups mashed ripe bananas
4 tablespoons sour cream
1 teaspoon baking soda
1-1/4 cups sugar
1/2 teaspoon baking powder
1-1/2 cups flour
1/2 cup butter
1 dash salt
1 teaspoon vanilla extract
3/4 cup nuts, optional
1/2 cup chocolate chips, optional

To make a healthier version, substitute wheat flour for 1/2 cup of the flour and add about 1/8 to 1/4 cup ground flax seed.

Preheat oven to 350 degrees.

Place all ingredients (except chocolate chips or nuts) into the food processor (or use a mixer but the processor is a lot faster). Blend until smooth, about 1 minute. Add nuts/chocolate chips. Blend about 10 seconds.

Butter loaf pans or muffing tins. Fill no more than 2/3 full. If using small pans or muffin tins, bake for about 30 minutes. For large pans bake 45 to 60 minutes. When toothpick is clean after piercing center, then the bread is done.

Banana Bread

Sisters Cindy Crawford, 1984
& Danielle Skov, 1992

YIELD: 2 LOAVES

INGREDIENTS

1 stick sweet butter (unsalted butter)
1 cup sugar
2 ripe bananas, mashed
1 cup sour cream
2 eggs
1-1/2 cups flour
1 teaspoon baking soda
1 teaspoon baking powder
1/4 teaspoon salt
1 teaspoon vanilla extract

In a mixing bowl, cream butter and sugar until light and fluffy. Add the wet ingredients: bananas, sour cream, eggs and vanilla. One at a time, add the dry ingredients: flour, baking soda, baking powder and salt, mixing after each addition. Pour into 2 loaf pans which have been greased and floured. Bake at 350 degrees for 45 minutes.

Wildcats don't whisper, they ROAR!

Easy-to-Make Banana Bread

Hillary Fratzke,
Assistant Coach, Lacrosse

YIELD: 1 LOAF

INGREDIENTS

3 smashed very ripe bananas
1/3 cup melted butter
1 cup white sugar
1 egg
1 teaspoon vanilla extract
1 teaspoon baking soda
1/4 teaspoon salt
1-1/2 cups all-purpose flour
1/2 cup walnuts or other nuts,
    optional

Preheat oven to 350 degrees. Mix butter and banana together. Mix in sugar, egg and vanilla. Sprinkle in salt and baking soda and mix. Add flour and mix until blended. Mix in nuts if using.

Pour into buttered 4x8 inch loaf pan. Bake for 1 hour or until toothpick stuck in middle comes out clean.

Grandma Pat's Banana Bread

Kerri Schmidt,
Football Mom — Jacob #39

YIELD: 2 LOAVES

INGREDIENTS

1/2 cup shortening
1 cup sugar
1 teaspoon baking soda
2 cups flour
2 eggs
dash salt
3 very ripe bananas mashed
4 tablespoons milk
1/4 cup walnuts or raisins, optional

Preheat oven to 350 degrees.

Combine baking soda and flour; set aside. In a mixing bowl, cream together shortening and sugar. Beat in eggs. Add milk Add dry ingredients. Add bananas, mixing well. Fold in walnuts or raisins, if using. Pour into 2 greased loaf pans and bake for 40 to 45 minutes.

Pump-It-Up Maple-Raisin Pumpkin Bread

Jenn Korducki Krenn, 2009

YIELD: 12 SLICES

INGREDIENTS

1-1/4 cups whole wheat flour
1/4 cup all-purpose flour
1/2 cup brown sugar
1/2 teaspoon salt
1 teaspoon baking powder
1 cup canned pumpkin
1/4 cup extra-virgin olive oil
2 large egg whites
1/4 cup water
1 tablespoon maple syrup
1/4 cup raisins
Cinnamon, to taste

Preheat oven to 350 degrees. Grease a loaf pan with cooking spray. Combine dry ingredients and wet ingredients in separate bowls (except the maple syrup, raisins and cinnamon). Fold wet ingredients into dry and combine until smooth. Top with raisins and mix until they are evenly distributed. Pour mixture into the loaf pan. Evenly distribute maple syrup and cinnamon over the top so that you will get a taste of each with every bite!

Bake for 50 to 60 minutes or until you can stick a toothpick in the middle and it comes out clean. Remove from the loaf pan and allow to cool on a plate or wire rack before slicing.

This bread will pump you up! Each slice has 140 calories, 5g fat, 22g carbohydrates, 2g fiber and 3g protein.

Zucchini Cranberry Bread

Victoria West, 2004,
Women's Swimming

YIELD: 1 LARGE LOAF OR 2 SMALL LOAVES

INGREDIENTS

3 large eggs
3/4 cup vegetable oil
2 teaspoons vanilla
1-1/2 cups sugar
2-1/2 cups grated zucchini
2-1/2 cups all-purpose flour
2 teaspoons ground cinnamon
1 teaspoon baking soda
1/4 teaspoon baking powder
1 teaspoon ground nutmeg
1/2 cup dried cranberries, optional
3/4 teaspoon salt

I frequently use white whole wheat flour or half whole wheat half all-purpose flour in this recipe.

Preheat oven to 350 degrees. Grease two 5x9 inch loaf pans.

In a large bowl, whisk eggs until frothy. Add oil, vanilla and sugar to the eggs; whisk to combine. Add zucchini; mix well.

Sift flour, cinnamon, nutmeg, baking soda, salt and baking power into a bowl. Add the dry ingredients to the wet ingredients mixing until blended. Do not over mix. Fold in the dried cranberries.

Pour into the loaf pans and bake until golden brown, about 1 hour. A toothpick inserted into the middle should come out clean. Let cool for 10 minutes in the pan then turn out onto a wire rack, right side up; allow to cool before slicing.

Zucchini Bread

Debby Zirin

YIELD: 2 LOAVES

INGREDIENTS

1 cup oil

3 cups flour

1-1/2 cups sugar

2 cups grated zucchini

3 eggs, beaten until foamy

1 teaspoon vanilla extract

1 teaspoon baking soda

1 teaspoon cinnamon

1 teaspoon salt

1/4 teaspoon baking powder

1 teaspoon cloves

Preheat oven to 350 degrees. Use towel to squeeze moisture from grated zucchini. Beat all liquid ingredients. Stir in zucchini, then other ingredients just until mixed. Pour into 2 greased 8 inch loaf pans. Bake for 1 hour. Cool on rack in pans for at least 10 minutes before turning out to finish cooling.

COACHES QUOTES

Randy Walker,
Former Football Head Coach:

"Which do you prefer... The pain of discipline or the pain of regret?"

yeast

Multi-Grain Rustic Bread

Tim Sonder, 1983,
Men's Fencing

YIELD: 2 LOAVES

INGREDIENTS

BIGA:

1-1/4 cups (185 grams) mixture of core flours (unbleached bread, stone-ground whole wheat) rolled oats, whole quinoa, etc.

3/4 cup (100 grams) mix of additional grains such as rolled oats, whole quinoa, raw wheat germ, barley flakes, etc.)

7 ounces (210 grams) cool water

2 pinches instant yeast

DOUGH:

1-1/4 teaspoons instant yeast

1-7/8 cups (450 grams) cool water

3 tablespoons (27 grams) barley flakes

2 tablespoons (27 grams) corn meal

2 cups (250 grams) whole wheat flour

2-3/4 cups (350 grams) unbleached bread flour

2 tablespoons sesame seeds or flax seed

4 tablespoons chopped nuts or sunflower kernels

1 tablespoon honey

1 tablespoon (16 grams) salt

1 cup raisins, optional

Instant yeast, such as SAF red label yeast, can be added directly to dry flours or cold water and requires slightly less yeast than dry active. If using dry active increase to 1-1/2 teaspoons in main recipe and pre-proof in a bit of warmed water.

BIGA: Mix together the biga ingredients and let rise in a covered container at room temperature, preferably overnight (4 to 18 hours). the biga should rise to triple size and become a thick batter.

DOUGH: Sprinkle yeast over biga and then add all the water and stir vigorously to break it up entirely. Transfer to a large bowl. I always mix and knead by hand; a stand mixer could be used at this point with a dough hook and a shorter mix/knead time.

Add the flakes and corn meal and mix thoroughly. Add the whole wheat flour a half-cup at a time while stirring to develop the gluten. Add the sesame or flax seed, the nuts and the honey and stir. Then slowly add in the bread flour until the dough just begins to come together. Add the salt and stir slightly to mix and then turn out wet dough on the counter while you knead in the remaining bread flour. Continue to knead for 8 to 10 minutes. Dough will be slightly sticky and never smooth and shiny, but will become springy and stretchy and easy to knead.

Rise two hours in a lightly oiled, covered bowl with room to double, although it's more likely to increase about 1-1/2 times in size.

Do not punch down; divide dough in half. Shape each half into a tight round or shape into a cylinder if you will be baking in a loaf pan. Proof wrapped in a cloth

(linen couche) or on a proofing board covered with a damp towel and enclose entirely in a plastic bag for 1 to 1-1/2 hours.

At least 30 minutes before baking, pre-heat oven to 425 degrees; include a steam pan if you have one or put an empty pan on the bottom rack. Unwrap loaves. Score the tops with a sharp knife and transfer to oven. Carefully add up to 1 cup water to steam pan or open pan. Bake 55 minutes or until deep brown and sounds hollow when bottom of loaves are tapped. Cool on a rack at least 1 hour before eating.

Lucky Lemon Clovers

Liz Luxem

YIELD: 24 ROLLS

INGREDIENTS

1 package dry yeast

1/4 cup warm water

1/2 cup sugar

2 teaspoons salt

1/2 teaspoon nutmeg

1/2 teaspoon cinnamon

1/2 teaspoon mace

1 teaspoon lemon extract

1/2 cup Crisco

1 cup scalded milk

2 large eggs, slightly beaten

5 to 5-1/2 cups flour

zest of 1 lemon

2 cups sugar

1 teaspoon nutmeg

1/4 cup butter, melted

Soften yeast in warm water. In a large mixing bowl combine 1/2 cup sugar, shortening, salt, spices, lemon extract and scalded milk. Cool to lukewarm. Stir in eggs and yeast. Mix in 1 cup flour and continue adding flour to form dough. Knead on floured surface until smooth and satiny. Place in a greased bowl, cover and let rise in a warm place until doubled in bulk (1-1/2 to 2 hours).

Punch down. Divide dough in half. Let rest 15 minutes. Combine lemon zest, 2 cups sugar and nutmeg. Set aside. Spray muffin tins with non-stick spray.

Shape dough into a oblong roll about 12 inches. Divide into 12 pieces. Form into balls. Repeat with remaining dough.

Dip the balls into butter and sugar mixture and place in muffin tin. Spray scissors with non-stick spray and cut each ball in half almost to the bottom and then cut into quarters. Separate the quarters slightly. Let rise.

Sprinkle the rolls with remaining sugar mixture. Bake at 375 degrees for 15 to 20 minutes. Immediately remove rolls from muffin tins. Serve warm.

TIP: The day before, prepare the rolls as far as rolling in butter and sugar mixture. Cover with aluminum foil and refrigerate. Then a few hours before serving, remove the aluminum foil, cut rolls into quarters and add remaining sugar mixture on top. Cover with a clean white towel to come to room temp and rise.

Barrett's Rolls

Lorraine Morton,
Former Evanston Mayor

YIELD: 18 TO 24 ROLLS

Lorraine Morton was Evanston's longest serving mayor. Beloved by all, Lorraine guided the city for 16 years, after having served as the first African-American school principal in Evanston at Haven Middle School. After her retirement, the Evanston Civic Center was named in her honor.

INGREDIENTS

2 packages self-rising yeast

1/2 cup warm water

1-1/2 cups butter, melted

2/3 cup sugar

2 teaspoons salt

1 cup milk, scalded

2 eggs, beaten

1 teaspoon vanilla extract

4-1/2 cups flour

Soften yeast in warm water. Mix melted butter, yeast mixture, sugar, salt and scalded milk. Allow to cool. Then add two beaten eggs and vanilla. Gradually mix in flour or use electric mixer to mix.

Allow dough to rise. If the dough is ready before you are, just punch it down with a knife until it deflates. Let it rise again and place on a floured board and roll out. Cut in the shape of your choice (biscuit cutter works well) and put into lightly buttered baking pan in a 400 degree oven. Bake 15 to 20 minutes. For super tasty rolls, take the rolls out of the oven and pour melted butter over them while still in the pan. Serve hot.

Overtime

Desserts

BASEBALL/ SOFTBALL

Men's Baseball:

Head Coach Paul Stevens (1988–present)
– *26th head coach*

• First game played in 1869 vs. La Purissimas.

• 1st intercollegiate year: 1871 with a record of
5 wins and 2 loses. They were called "the finest
bunch of ball tossers in any part of the farming
country adjacent to Chicago."

• Since 1983 there have been 59 Cats drafted or
signed by the Majors with 7 in the big leagues
including Joe Girardi, Mark Loretta and J.A.
Happ.

• There were 176 Academic All-BigTen honorees
in the years 1980–2011.

• The famous evangelist Billy Sunday coached the
team in 1888. He attended NU as well and
played for the Cubs (Chicago White Stockings).

Women's Softball:

Head Coach Kate Drohan (2002–present)
– *3rd head coach*

• It has been a varsity sports since 1976.
Mary Conway was the first coach (1976–78).

• Coach Sharon Drysdale was the head coach for 23 years (1979–2002).
She had a record of 640-512-3. The Wildcats play on Drysdale Field,
renamed in 2001.

• The Purple Cow… represents "be remarkable in all that you do!"

• There were 11 All-Americans and 148 Academic All-Big Ten honorees in the
years 1983–2011.

bars

Wally's Almond Squares

Sandy White,
Women's Fencing Mom — Whitney

YIELD: 9x13 INCH PAN

INGREDIENTS

1/2 pound almond paste at room
    temperature

2 cups sugar

1/2 pound butter, softened

2 large eggs

2 cups flour

2 tablespoons lemon juice

*Be sure to get almond paste, not almond
pastry filling.*

Creme the almond paste, sugar and
butter (at room temperature). Add eggs,
flour and lemon juice (fresh is best). Put
batter in a 9x13 inch baking pan and
bake for 30 minutes at 325 degrees or
until the dessert is slightly brown. Cut
into squares before it completely cools.

Surfer Squares

Beth Trumpy,
Football Mom — Mike #29

YIELD: 9x13 INCH PAN

INGREDIENTS

12 ounces butterscotch chips

1/2 cup brown sugar

1/2 cup butter

2 eggs

1-1/2 cups flour

2 teaspoons baking powder

1/2 teaspoon salt

2 teaspoons vanilla extract

12 ounces semi-sweet chocolate chips

2 cups miniature marshmallows

In a large mixing bowl, melt butterscotch
chips, brown sugar and butter in
microwave. Add eggs and mix well. Blend
in flour, baking powder and salt. Stir in
vanilla. Let mixture cool before adding
next ingredients.

Fold in chocolate chips and marshmallows. Spread in greased 9x13 inch pan.
Bake at 350 degrees for 20 to 25 minutes
until edges begin to brown. Cool before
cutting in squares.

Long Bomb Bars

Laura & Jim Phillips,
Director of Athletics and Recreation

YIELD: 9x13 INCH PAN

INGREDIENTS

1 cup light corn syrup

1 cup sugar

1 cup peanut butter

6 cups crisped rice cereal

6 ounces chocolate chips

1 package (6 ounces)
    butterscotch chips

Spray a 9x13 inch baking dish with non-stick spray. In large saucepan (large enough to mix 6 cups of cereal), combine syrup and sugar over medium heat, stirring frequently until mixture begins to boil. Remove from heat. Stir in peanut butter followed by cereal. Press into prepared baking dish.

Melt chocolate and butterscotch chips in a bowl or double boiler over boiling water stirring constantly until smooth. Alternatively, use microwave oven for melting; times vary based on oven power. Spread evenly over cereal base. Chill until firm, about 15 minutes.

Cut into desired servings. Store in a cool place.

Wonder Bars

Megan Anderson, 1976

YIELD: 9x13 INCH PAN

INGREDIENTS

16 Kraft caramels

1 cup chopped nuts

3/4 cup melted butter

2/3 cup evaporated milk, divided

1 cup peanut butter chips

1 package German chocolate cake mix

Preheat oven to 350 degrees. Melt caramels and stir in 1/3 cup of the milk. Combine mix, butter and remaining milk and nuts. Press 1/2 of the dough into a 9x13 inch greased pan. Bake for 6 minutes. Sprinkle chips over dough and pour on caramel mixture. Dot top with the remaining dough. Bake 10 to 12 minutes until dough tests done. Cool in refrigerator. Take out 30 minutes before cutting.

Pizza Fruit Platter

Joanne & Coach Mick McCall,
Offensive Coordinator, Football

YIELD: 12 PIECES

INGREDIENTS

1 package yellow cake mix

2 tablespoons water

2 tablespoons brown sugar, packed

1 egg

2 tablespoons butter

1/2 cup chopped pecans or walnuts, optional

12 ounces cream cheese, softened

1/2 cup sugar

1 teaspoon vanilla extract

1 pint fresh strawberries, halved

1 can (20 ounces) pineapple tidbits drained or fresh, bite sized

2 bananas, sliced

24 seedless green grapes, halved

1/2 cup apricot preserves

You can substitute mandarin oranges or peaches, canned or fresh if you like.

CRUST: Combine first five ingredients. Mix well, then fold in nuts. Pour batter onto heavily greased and floured 12 inch pizza pan. Bake at 375 degree 12 to 15 minutes. Let cool.

Mix cream cheese with sugar and vanilla, blend thoroughly. Spread over cooled crust.

FRUIT: Arrange fruit in circular pattern over cream cheese mixture.

GLAZE: Heat preserves and 2 tablespoons water until preserves are melted. Remove from heat and brush glaze over fruit. Cool and cut in 12 pie shaped wedges. Refrigerate until needed.

Cherry Delight

Candee Nustra

YIELD: 6 SERVINGS

INGREDIENTS

1-1/4 cups graham cracker crumbs

1/4 cup brown sugar

1/3 cup margarine

8 ounces cream cheese

1/2 cup powdered sugar

4 tablespoons milk

1 can (15 ounces) cherry pie filling

1 package (5 ounces) Dream Whip

Mix together graham cracker crumbs, brown sugar and soft margarine. Pat evenly in bottom of 9x9 inch pan.

Mix cream cheese, powdered sugar and milk. Spread on crust.

Mix Dream Whip according to package directions and spread over cream cheese layer.

Spoon cherry pie filling over Dream Whip layer. Chill until ready to serve.

Hello Dollies

Marjo Kraft,
**Wife of NU Hall of Fame
Wrestling Coach Ken Kraft**

INGREDIENTS

1/4 pound butter
1-1/2 cups graham cracker crumbs
8 ounces butterscotch chips
8 ounces chocolate chips
2/3 cup coconut
1/2 cup chopped nuts
1 can Eagle Brand sweetened
    condensed milk

Preheat oven to 350 degrees. Melt butter in 8x8 inch baking pan. Add graham cracker crumbs and press on bottom and sides. Layer the butterscotch chips, chocolate chips, coconut and chopped nuts. Drip condensed milk over entire top. Bake 20 to 25 minutes until the chips are melted. Cut in small squares when cooled.

Congo Bars

Miriam Marie Toelke

YIELD: 9x9 INCH PAN

INGREDIENTS

2-3/4 cups flour
2-1/2 teaspoons baking powder
1/2 teaspoon salt
2/3 cup shortening
2-3/4 cups light brown sugar
3 large eggs

OPTIONAL INGREDIENTS:

1/2 cup chopped nuts
1 package (12 ounces) semisweet
    chocolate chips or a mixture of
    chocolates, partially melted
1 cup crushed graham crackers
1 cup dried cranberries or sour
    cherries

Preheat oven to 350 degrees. Add flour, baking powder and salt to a bowl; stir to blend and set aside.

Melt shortening and stir in brown sugar. Mix well and let cool.

Transfer sugar mixture to a mixing bowl. Beat in eggs one at a time. Add all dry ingredients and mix well. If desired, add nuts and chocolate chips. Grease and flour a 9x9 inch pan. If desired, spread the cracker crumbs in the pan. Add and spread the batter mixture in the pan. Bake for 25 to 30 minutes. Cool slightly prior to cutting into squares.

Golden S'mores

Rev. Julie Windsor Mitchell,
Campus Minister,
University Christian Ministry

YIELD: 9X13 INCH PAN

INGREDIENTS

8 cups Golden Grahams Cereal
6 cups mini marshmallows, divided
1-1/2 cups milk chocolate chips
1/4 cup corn syrup
5 tablespoons butter
1 teaspoon vanilla extract

Microwave 5 cups marshmallows, chocolate chips, corn syrup and butter for 2 to 3 minutes, stirring every minute, until melted. Stir in vanilla. Add cereal and mix well. Add remaining 1 cup marshmallows, mix well. Press in buttered 9x13 pan and let stand 1 hour. Store loosely covered at room temperature up to two days.

Note: if you add the last cup of marshmallows to the hot mixture, they will melt into the mixture. If you prefer to see the marshmallows, wait a few minutes after mixing in the cereal before adding.

Best Ever Almond Bars

Kim & Coach Tim Cysewski,
Associate Head Coach, Wrestling

YIELD: 9X13 INCH PAN

INGREDIENTS

4 whole eggs
2 cups sugar
1/4 teaspoon salt
1 cup melted butter
2 cups flour
2-1/2 teaspoons almond extract
sliced almonds
1 to 2 tablespoons sugar

Preheat oven to 325 degrees. Beat all ingredients together, except nuts, and spread in greased 9x13 inch pan. Sprinkle top with sugar and sliced almonds. Bake for 30 to 35 minutes.

COACHES QUOTES

Jimmy Tierney,
Women's Swimming & Diving:

"Ability may get you to the top, but it takes character to keep you there."
—John Wooden

Wilma's Chocolate Mess

Joanne & Coach Mick McCall,
Offensive Coordinator, Football

YIELD: 12 TO 14 SERVINGS

INGREDIENTS

CRUST:
1/2 cup butter, melted
1-1/3 cups flour
1 cup chopped walnuts or pecans

FIRST LAYER:
8 ounces cream cheese
2 packages Cool Whip (15 ounces each), divided
1 cup powdered sugar

SECOND LAYER:
1 package instant chocolate pudding (3 ounces)
1 package instant vanilla pudding (3 ounces)
3-1/2 cups milk
chopped almonds, optional
shaved chocolate, optional

CRUST: Mix melted butter and flour together until soft and crumbly. Add chopped nuts and mix; press into bottom of 9x13 inch pan. Bake 15 minutes at 350 degrees. Let cool.

FIRST LAYER: Whip together cream cheese, 1 package of Cool Whip and powdered sugar; pour over crust.

SECOND LAYER: Mix puddings and milk. Spread over cheese layer.

THIRD LAYER: Cover with remaining package of Cool Whip. If desired, top with almonds and shaved chocolate.

Chill.

Toffee Bars

Marjorie Brumitt

YIELD: 9x13 INCH PAN

INGREDIENTS

1 cup butter
1 cup brown sugar
1 teaspoon vanilla
2 cups flour
6 ounces chocolate chips
1 cup chopped nuts

Preheat oven to 350 degrees. Cream the butter, brown sugar and vanilla. Then add flour, chocolate chips and chopped nuts; mix. Place in an ungreased 9x13 inch pan and bake for 20 minutes. Cut while still warm and allow to cool in the pan.

Wildcat's Caramel Bars

Tim Hayden,
Athletics Compliance

INGREDIENTS

2 cups quick-cooking oats
2 cups flour
1-1/2 cups firmly packed brown sugar
1 teaspoon baking soda
1/2 teaspoon salt
1 cup margarine or butter, melted
10 ounces semisweet chocolate chips
1 cup pecans or walnuts, coarsely chopped
1 cup caramel sauce

Preheat oven to 350 degrees. Spray bottom and sides of 9x13 inch pan with non-stick cooking spray.

In bowl stir together oats, flour, sugar, baking soda and salt. Add melted butter and mix well. Distribute half of the mixture in prepared pan and press gently with your fingertips to form an even layer. Reserve the remaining half for later.

Bake for 8 to 10 minutes, just until set.

Remove pan from oven. Sprinkle chocolate chips and nuts evenly over crust, then drizzle evenly with caramel sauce. Distribute the reserved oat mixture over the top and press gently with your fingertips to form an even layer. Return pan to oven and continue baking until topping is golden brown, about 25 minutes longer.

Remove pan to a wire rack and cool completely. Then cut into bars. Store at room temperature, tightly covered.

Special K Bars

Carol Lovett,
Lacrosse Mom — Emily 2007

YIELD: 9x13 INCH PAN

INGREDIENTS

1 cup white Karo Syrup
1 cup white sugar
1 cup peanut butter
6 cups Special K cereal
6 ounces chocolate chips
6 ounces butterscotch chips

Bring Karo Syrup and sugar to a boil. Add peanut butter and stir until peanut butter is melted. Add Special K and stir until coated. Pat down into a buttered 9x13 inch pan. For the frosting, melt the chocolate and butterscotch chips and pour over Special K mixture.

Peanut Butter Swirl Bars

Patsy Emery,
Director, FA Operations — retired.

YIELD: 4 DOZEN

INGREDIENTS

1/2 cup peanut butter
1/3 cup softened butter
3/4 cup light brown sugar, firmly packed
3/4 cup granulated sugar
2 eggs
2 teaspoons vanilla extract
1 cup flour
1 teaspoon baking powder
1/4 teaspoon salt
12 ounces semisweet morsels

Preheat oven to 350 degrees.

In large bowl, combine the peanut butter, softened butter, brown sugar and granulated sugar; beat until creamy. Gradually beat in eggs and vanilla extract and mix until light and fluffy.

In small bowl, combine flour, baking powder and salt; blend into peanut butter mixture.

Spread into greased (or spray with nonstick spray) 9x13 inch baking pan.

Sprinkle with semisweet morsels; place in oven for 5 minutes. Remove; run knife through to marbleize. Return to oven and bake for approximately 20 minutes or until golden brown.

Baby Ruth Bars

Joanie Alley,
Lacrosse Mom — Abby, 2005 and Hilary, 2008

YIELD: 9X13 INCH PAN

INGREDIENTS

1 cup white corn syrup
1/2 cup brown sugar
1/2 cup white sugar
1 cup peanut butter
6 cups corn flakes
1 cup peanuts (salted Spanish)
1-1/2 cups chocolate chips

Combine corn syrup, white and brown sugar and bring almost to a boil, but not quite. Add the peanut butter, corn flakes and peanuts and spread in a 9x13 inch dish. Wet hands and pat down. Melt the chocolate chips and spread on top. Cut in squares and store in refrigerator.

Peanut Butter Rice Krispie Squares

Joanie Alley,
Lacrosse Mom — Abby, 2005 and Hilary, 2008

YIELD: 9X13 INCH PAN

INGREDIENTS

1 stick butter
1 cup sugar
1 cup light corn syrup
1 cup peanut butter
6 cups Rice Krispies cereal
12 ounces chocolate chips

In a large pot, bring the butter, sugar and corn syrup to a rolling boil stirring continuously. Add the peanut butter and mix well. Remove from heat, add the Rice Krispies and mix until well coated. Spread in a buttered 9x13 inch pan. Melt the chocolate chips and spread over the Rice Krispie mixture. Cool several hours in the refrigerator before cutting.

Twix Cookie Bars

Ellen Watkins,
Football Mom — Evan #18

YIELD: 9X13 INCH PAN

INGREDIENTS

3/4 cup sugar
3/4 cup brown sugar
1/3 cup milk
1/2 cup margarine or butter
2/3 cup peanut butter
1 cup graham crumbs
1 cup chocolate chips
1 cup peanut butter
1 box Keebler Club Crackers

Boil the first six ingredients together.

Layer crackers in a greased 9x13 inch pan. Pour mixture over crackers. Add a second layer of crackers.

Melt together the chocolate chips and peanut butter and pour over top of crackers. Refrigerate until set.

Paul's Pumpkin Bars

Kenan & Coach Paul Stevens,
Head Coach, Baseball

YIELD: 10x15 INCH PAN

INGREDIENTS

4 eggs
1-2/3 cups white sugar
1 cup vegetable oil
1 can (15 ounces) pumpkin purée
2 cups all-purpose flour
2 teaspoons baking powder
1 teaspoon baking soda
2 teaspoons ground cinnamon
1 teaspoon salt

FROSTING:
3 ounces softened cream cheese
1/2 cup softened butter
1 teaspoon vanilla extract
2 cups sifted confectioners' sugar

BARS: Preheat oven to 350 degrees. In a medium bowl, mix the eggs, sugar, oil and pumpkin until light and fluffy. Sift together the flour, baking powder, baking soda, cinnamon and salt. Stir into the pumpkin mixture until thoroughly combined. Spread the batter evenly into an ungreased 10x15 inch jellyroll pan. Bake for 25 to 30 minutes. Cool before frosting.

FROSTING: Cream together the cream cheese and butter. Stir in vanilla. Add confectioners' sugar a little at a time, beating until mixture is smooth. Spread evenly on top of the cooled bars. Cut into squares.

Raspberry Walnut Crumble Bars

Debbie Hinchcliff Seward, 1974

YIELD: 16 TO 24 BARS

INGREDIENTS

1-3/4 cups all-purpose flour
1/2 teaspoon kosher salt
1/2 teaspoon ground cinnamon
1/4 teaspoon ground nutmeg
3/4 cup unsalted butter,
     at room temperature
1 cup sugar
2 large egg yolks
1 teaspoon pure vanilla extract
2/3 cup raspberry jam
1 cup chopped walnuts

Preheat oven to 350 degrees. Spray an 8 inch square baking pan with cooking spray. Line the pan with a piece of parchment, leaving an overhang on two sides: spray parchment with the cooking spray.

In a medium bowl, whisk together the flour, salt, cinnamon and nutmeg.

Using an electric mixer, beat the butter and sugar on medium-high speed until fluffy, 2 to 3 minutes. Beat in the egg yolks and vanilla. Reduce speed to low and gradually add the flour mixture, mixing until just combined (do not overmix).

Transfer two-thirds of the dough to the prepared pan and press in evenly; spread the jam on top. Crumble the remaining dough over the jam and sprinkle with the walnuts. Bake until golden, 35 to 45 minutes. Cool completely in the pan.

Holding both sides of the paper overhang, lift cake out of the pan, transfer to a cutting board, and cut into 16 to 24 bars. Store bars in an airtight container at room temperature for up to 5 days.

brownies

Turtle Brownies

Brian Leahy, 1994,
Football

YIELD: 9X13 INCH PAN

INGREDIENTS

1 cup evaporated milk, divided

14 ounces Kraft caramels

1 box Betty Crocker German
    Chocolate Cake mix

3/4 cup melted butter

12 ounces semisweet chocolate chips

1 cup pecans, optional

Combine the dry cake mix, butter and 1/2 cup evaporated milk. Mix until well-blended. Pat 1/2 batter into well-greased 9x13 inch pan. Bake at 350 degrees for 10 minutes.

Melt caramels with 1/2 cup of evaporated milk. Stir well to get rid of lumps.

Remove pan from oven. Sprinkle chocolate chips evenly over bottom layer. Trickle caramel mixture over chocolate chips. Add pecans if desired.

Take remaining batter and drop dollups over caramel.

Return pan to oven at bake and additional 15 to 20 minutes. Easiest to cut if chilled.

Grandma Betty's Brownies

Betty & Fred Ruben, 1957

YIELD: 10X15 INCH PAN

INGREDIENTS

1 tub soft Imperial margarine

2 cups sugar

2 teaspoons vanilla

6 eggs

1 cup Wondra (instant) flour

1 teaspoon baking powder

1/2 teaspoon salt

1 cup chopped walnuts, divided,
    optional

4 envelopes pre-melted Nestlé's
    chocolate

1 cup chopped nuts, divided, optional

Pre-melted chocolate can be replaced by 4 ounces unsweetened chocolate, melted and cooled.

In a large mixing bowl, cream margarine and sugar. In a separate bowl, gently beat eggs with vanilla; add to sugar mixture. Add dry ingredients. Blend about 1 minute. Add chocolate and blend; if using nuts, mix in one-half cup. Pour in greased and flour-dusted 10x15 inch pan; top with remaining nuts. Bake for 20 to 25 minutes. Dust with confectioners' sugar when cool.

Oreo Brownies

Julie Swieca, 1994,
WNUR

YIELD: 9x13 INCH PAN

INGREDIENTS

BROWNIES:

1 cup butter, softened

2 cups sugar

4 eggs

2 teaspoons vanilla extract

1-3/4 cups all-purpose flour

6 tablespoons baking cocoa

1 teaspoon baking powder

1/4 teaspoon salt

12 Oreo cookies, coarsely crushed

FROSTING:

4 Oreo cookies, finely crushed

1 pound powdered sugar

1/2 cup butter, softened

1 teaspoon vanilla

3 to 4 tablespoons milk

The number of Oreos can be varied, based on taste.

Preheat oven to 350 degrees.

In a large mixing bowl, cream butter and sugar. Add eggs, one at a time, beating well after each addition. Beat in vanilla.

Combine in a separate bowl the flour, cocoa, baking powder and salt; gradually add to creamed mixture and mix well. Stir in the coarsely-crushed cookies. Spread into a greased 9x13 inch pan. Bake for 25 to 30 minutes or until a toothpick inserted near the center comes out clean. Cool in pan on a wire rack.

FROSTING: In a mixing bowl, beat the powdered sugar and butter. Add vanilla. Gradually add the milk until desired consistency is achieved. Frost the cooled brownies with the buttercream and sprinkle with the finely-crushed Oreo crumbs.

Butterscotch Brownies

Jimmy Tierney,
Director, Fitness/Wellness, NUDAR

YIELD: 9x13 INCH PAN

INGREDIENTS

2 cups light brown sugar

1/2 cup butter, melt and cool

2 medium eggs

1-1/2 cups flour, sifted

1-1/2 teaspoons baking powder

1 cup nuts, optional

1 pinch salt

1 teaspoon vanilla extract

Chocolate frosting can be used on top, if desired.

Preheat oven to 300 degrees. Mix cooled butter with brown sugar. Add remaining ingredients in order given, mixing after each addition. Makes a stiff dough. Spread into a greased 9x13 inch pan. Bake for 40 to 45 minutes until edges begin to crisp.

Outrageous Brownies

Lisa & Jeff Weiss, 1990

YIELD: 12X18 INCH PAN

With one pound butter and over two pounds chocolate, what could go wrong?

INGREDIENTS

1 pound unsalted butter
1 pound plus 12 ounces semi-sweet
    chocolate chips, divided
6 ounces unsweetened chocolate
6 extra large eggs
3 tablespoons instant coffee granules
2 tablespoons pure vanilla extract
2-1/4 cups sugar
1-1/4 cups all-purpose flour, divided
1 tablespoon baking powder
1 teaspoon salt
3 cups chopped walnuts

Preheat oven to 350 degrees. Butter and flour a 12x18 inch baking sheet (jelly roll pan).

Melt together the butter, 1 pound of chocolate chips and the unsweetened chocolate in a medium bowl over simmering water. Allow to cool slightly. In a large bowl, stir (do not beat) together the eggs, coffee granules, vanilla and sugar. Stir the warm chocolate mixture into the egg mixture and allow to cool to room temperature.

In a medium bowl, sift together 1 cup of the flour, baking powder and salt. Add to the chocolate mixture. Toss the walnuts and 12 ounces of chocolate chips in a medium bowl with 1/4 cup of flour, then add to the chocolate batter. Pour into the baking sheet.

Bake for 20 minutes, then rap the baking sheet against the oven shelf to force the air to escape from between the pan and the brownie dough. Bake for about 15 minutes, until toothpick comes out clean. Do not over bake! Allow to cool thoroughly, refrigerate, and cut into squares.

Chocolate Chip Brownie Double Deckers

Mary Pat Watt,
Football Mom — Kevin #42

YIELD: 24 BARS

INGREDIENTS

CHIP LAYER:
3/4 cup unsalted butter, melted
1 cup packed light brown sugar
1 large egg
1 teaspoon vanilla extract
1-1/2 cups flour
1/2 teaspoon baking soda
1/4 teaspoon salt
1 cup (6 ounces) semi-sweet
    chocolate chips

BROWNIE LAYER:
3/4 cup unsalted butter, melted
3/4 cup unsweetened Dutch process
    cocoa powder
1-1/2 cups granulated sugar
1/4 teaspoon salt
2 large eggs
1-1/2 teaspoons vanilla extract
3/4 cup all-purpose flour

Preheat oven to 325 degrees. Line a 9x13 inch pan with foil, letting foil extend above pan on both ends. Spray non-stick spray on foil.

BROWNIE LAYER: Whisk cocoa into butter until smooth. Whisk in sugar and salt, then add eggs one at a time. Add vanilla. Stir in flour with a rubber spatula just until blended. Spread evenly in prepared pan.

CHOCOLATE CHIP LAYER: Whisk brown sugar in butter until smooth. Cool, then whisk in egg and vanilla. Stir in flour, baking soda and salt until blended. Stir in chocolate chips. Drop spoonfuls over brownie batter; spread to cover. Bake 35 to 40 minutes until the top is set and a wooden toothpick inserted in center comes out with moist crumbs. Cool in pan on a wire rack. Lift foil by ends onto cutting board. Cut in 6 rows crosswise and 4 lengthwise.

If you prefer a drier brownie, cook a little longer until toothpick comes out dry.

Marble Brownies

Donna Chlopak,
Lacrosse Mom — Shelby 2005

INGREDIENTS

1 box Brownie mix
        (preferably Duncan Hines) or
        make from scratch
8 ounces cream cheese softened
3/4 cup sugar
2 tablespoons butter
1 egg

Make brownie mix as per package (make chewy variety) and set aside 3/4 cup. Put rest of batter in the baking pan. Cream together the cream cheese, butter and sugar. Add in the egg and blend well. Spread the cream cheese mixture over the brownie mix in the pan. Spoon the remaining brownie batter over the cream cheese mixture in dollops. Blend/marble

the mixture with a knife. Bake according to the package instructions; toothpick when inserted into center should come out fairly clean.

Nancy Reagan's Brownies

Ona Puzinauskas,
Microbiology, retired

YIELD: 12x18 INCH PAN

The former First Lady's step father, Loyal Davis was a noted neurosurgeon on the faculty of Northwestern. At many events, Mrs. Davis' Brownies, as they were known then, were a favorite of the students. This recipe is from Officers' Wives Club Cookbook.

INGREDIENTS

3 ounces semisweet chocolate
2 ounces unsweetened chocolate
1-1/2 cups butter
6 large eggs
2 cups white sugar
2/3 cup cake flour
1-1/2 teaspoons salt
1 teaspoon baking powder
1 tablespoon vanilla extract
2 cups chopped pecans

Melt both chocolates and butter; set aside to cool. Preheat oven to 350 degrees. Beat eggs; add sugar and beat until light and fluffy. Add the cooled chocolate. Sift the dry ingredients together, add to the butter mixture and stir to incorporate. Add the vanilla and pecans. Fold to incorporate.

Pour the mixture into a buttered and floured 12x18 inch pan. Bake for 30 to 35 minutes or until a toothpick comes out clean. Cool and sprinkle with confectioners' sugar. Cut into squares.

Blonde Brownies

Janie Varley

INGREDIENTS

2-1/2 cups graham cracker crumbs

1 teaspoon vanilla

1 can (14 ounces) sweetened
    condensed milk

1 teaspoon baking powder

6 ounces chocolate chips

Preheat oven to 350 degrees. Mix to-gether all ingredients. Batter is very thick. Spray a 9x9 inch pan with non-stick spray; pour in batter. Bake for 25 to 30 minutes. Loosen edges when cooled.

cakes— cheesecake

Robin's Cheesecake

Robin Voigt,
Volleyball

YIELD: 8 INCH CAKE

INGREDIENTS

2 pounds cream cheese

1 teaspoon vanilla

1/4 teaspoon almond extract

1-3/4 cups sugar

4 eggs

1/3 cup graham cracker crumbs

Fresh fruit for garnish, optional

Beat cream cheese until smooth; add fla-vorings. Add sugar and beat well. Add eggs, one at a time, beating well after each egg.

Butter an 8 inch by 3 inch deep round pan (a soufflé pan). Pour batter into pan. Place pan in a pan filled with hot water.

Bake (steam) at 350 degrees for 90 min-utes. Cool completely, about 5 hours. Invert onto a greased plate. Sprinkle with graham crackers crumbs. Invert again onto serving plate and refrigerate for 5 to 6 hours. Serve with fruit if desired.

Mary DiNardo's Ricotta Cheese Cake

Gerry DiNardo,
Big Ten Network

Yield: 1 cake

Ingredients

1 pound ricotta cheese

1 pound cream cheese

1-1/2 cups sugar

1/4 pound softened butter

2 teaspoons fresh lemon juice

1 tablespoon vanilla extract

4 eggs

2 tablespoons corn starch

2 tablespoons flour

16 ounces sour cream

Preheat oven to 325 degrees. Butter and flour a large springform cake pan.

Combine in mixing bowl: ricotta, cream cheese, sugar, butter, lemon juice, vanilla, eggs, corn starch, flour and sour cream. Beat for one hour. (The step to beat for an hour is the subject of many family debates. Some stick to an hour; others beat until very creamy, perhaps 5 minutes. In Mary's memory, we included the recipe the way Mary made it.) Pour into prepared pan and bake for one hour. Turn oven off and let cake sit in oven for one hour. Remove from pan and place on serving platter in refrigerator to chill. Serve chilled. Serve plain or with cherry, caramel or other toppings.

Kathy's Cheesecake

Kathy Quinlan,
Director, Operations & Strategy, NAA

Yield: 1 cake

Ingredients

CRUST:

1/3 cup butter (about 5 tablespoons)

1/4 cup sugar

1-1/4 cups graham cracker crumbs

FILLING:

1 pound cream cheese, softened

1 cup sugar

3 large eggs

1 pint sour cream

1 tablespoon vanilla extract

Preheat oven to 375 degrees.

In a small saucepan, melt the butter over low flame. In a medium mixing bowl, combine the graham cracker crumbs, sugar and melted butter; mix until thoroughly combined. Transfer the crumb mixture to an 8 inch springform pan; using the back of the spoon, press the crumbs against the bottom and sides of the pan. Place in the oven and bake for 6 to 8 minutes, or until the crust is lightly browned. Remove from the oven and allow to cool before filling.

Reduce oven temperature to 350 degrees.

In a large mixing bowl, combine the cream cheese and sugar; mix. Add the eggs, one at a time, and continue mixing. Stir in the sour cream and the vanilla; mix until thoroughly blended. Spoon the cheese mixture into the crust. Smooth the top with a spatula.

Bake for 30 minutes. Turn off the oven and allow the cake to remain in the oven for an additional hour, then remove and allow to cool. Refrigerate for at least 6 hours, preferably overnight, before serving.

To serve, slide a knife around the side of the cake to separate it from the pan. Release the pan's spring and carefully remove.

Pumpkin Cheesecake

Shon Morris, 1988,
Senior Associate AD (Development), Basketball

YIELD: 9-INCH PIE

INGREDIENTS

2 packages (8 ounces each) cream cheese, softened

1/2 cup cooked pumpkin purée

1/2 cup sugar

1/2 teaspoon vanilla extract

1/2 teaspoon cinnamon

dash each cloves and nutmeg

1 graham cracker pie crust

2 eggs

Preheat oven to 350 degrees.

Mix cream cheese, pumpkin, sugar, vanilla and spices at medium speed. Add eggs and mix. Pour into crust. Bake for 40 minutes or until center is almost set. Refrigerate 3 hours or overnight.

cakes—layer

Carrot Cake

Betsy Jaeschke,
Women's Basketball Mom — Amy #22

YIELD: ONE 9-INCH CAKE

INGREDIENTS

CAKE:

2 cups sugar

1-1/2 cups oil (Crisco or Mazola)

4 eggs

2 cups flour

3 teaspoons cinnamon

2 teaspoons baking soda

1 teaspoon salt

2 teaspoons vanilla extract

3 cups grated carrots

1/2 cup chopped pecans

FROSTING:

8 ounces cream cheese, softened

1/4 pound butter

2 teaspoons vanilla extract

1 pound confectioners' sugar
(sift if desired)

Preheat oven to 350 degrees. Combine sugar and oil, add eggs. Beat well. Sift flour, soda, salt and cinnamon together. Add to sugar mixture. Beat well. Add vanilla and stir in grated carrots and nuts. Pour into two 9 inch round cake pans that have been well greased. Bake for 45 minutes. The cakes will look like hockey pucks. Do not fear. Cool on wire racks.

FROSTING: Combine cheese and butter, beat well. Add vanilla and beat. Add powdered sugar and beat well.

Frost cake after it has cooled.

Pumpkin Roll

Shon Morris, 1988,
**Senior Associate AD (Development),
Basketball**

YIELD: 1 CAKE

INGREDIENTS

CAKE:

3 eggs, beaten

1 cup sugar

2/3 cup cooked pumpkin purée

3/4 cup flour

1 teaspoon salt

1 teaspoon cinnamon

1 teaspoon baking soda

FILLING:

1 package (8 ounces) cream cheese

2 teaspoons margarine

1 teaspoon vanilla extract

1 cup powdered sugar

CAKE: Preheat oven to 350 degrees. Combine eggs, sugar, pumpkin, flour, salt, cinnamon and baking soda. Beat until smooth. Grease a rimmed 10x15 inch cookie sheet or line with waxed paper. Pour batter into pan and bake for 15 minutes.

FILLING: Combine filling ingredients and beat until smooth. set aside.

ASSEMBLY: When roll has cooled, dampen a towel and lay over pan and invert. Peel off wax paper if used. Roll dough with towel in it. Let stand 15 minutes. Unroll and remove towel. Spread filling to 1/2 inch from the edges. Roll back, wrap in foil and freeze.

Seven Minute Frosting

Evelyn Berning

YIELD: 1 CAKE

Especially good on devil's food cake!

INGREDIENTS

2 egg whites (1/3 cup)

1-1/2 cups sugar

1/4 teaspoon cream of tartar

1/3 cup water

1-1/2 teaspoons vanilla extract

Combine egg whites, sugar, cream of tartar and water in a double boiler over low heat. Beat until stiff peaks form. Fold in vanilla.

Frost your cooled cake.

cakes—loaf

Grandma T's Raisin Cake

Lorriane Burke

YIELD: 1 LOAF

This is a dark, rich, heavy spice cake good any time, but especially during the winter holidays. When covered it stays moist and fresh for over a week. Add a white frosting if desired.

INGREDIENTS

3 cups raisins

1-1/2 cups sugar

2 eggs

2 cups flour

1 cup raisin water

2 teaspoons baking soda

1 teaspoon cinnamon

1 teaspoon nutmeg

3/4 teaspoon allspice

3/4 teaspoons cloves

5 ounces butter

In a small pot, cover raisins with water, bring to a boil; then cool. Save water. Combine flour, baking soda and spices; set aside. Cream butter and sugar until fluffy, add eggs, then alternate raisin water and flour mixture. Add raisins. Beat 100 strokes by hand. Bake in a loaf pan at 350 degrees for 1 hour or more, until toothpick comes out clean.

NU Carrot Cake

Eileen Boege,
Lacrosse Mom — Kristen 2007

YIELD: 1 LOAF

This recipe multiplies well. I multiply the cake by 8 to fill a huge turkey roasting pan.

INGREDIENTS

1 cup flour

1 teaspoon baking powder

1 teaspoon baking soda

1 teaspoon cinnamon

1/2 teaspoon salt

2/3 cup oil

1 teaspoon vanilla extract

1 cup sugar

2 eggs

1-1/2 cups grated carrots

1/2 cup chopped walnuts, optional

FROSTING:

3 cups confectioners' sugar

6 ounces cream cheese, softened

6 tablespoons softened butter

1-1/2 teaspoons vanilla

CAKE: Preheat oven to 350 degrees. In a bowl, mix together flour, baking powder, baking soda, cinnamon and salt. In another bowl, mix together oil, vanilla, sugar and eggs. Combine the two bowls and blend together. Add the carrots and nuts, if using; mix. Pour into greased and floured (or parchment lined) loaf pan. Bake for 35 to 40 minutes, testing with toothpick. Cool on rack.

FROSTING: In a large bowl at low speed, mix all ingredients until blended. Increase speed to medium and beat until frosting is smooth and fluffy, about 1 minute. If desired, slice loaf horizontally and use as filling and frosting.

Carrot Cake

Sandy Eszes

YIELD: 1 LOAF

INGREDIENTS

CAKE:

2 cups all-purpose flour

2 teaspoons baking powder

2 teaspoons baking soda

2 teaspoons cinnamon

1 teaspoon salt

1-1/4 cups oil

2 cups sugar

2 to 3 cups ground carrots
      (use finest blade)

4 eggs

1/2 to 1 cup chopped nuts

FROSTING:

1/4 pound butter or margarine,
      room temperature

3 ounces cream cheese, softened

2 teaspoons vanilla extract

1 pound confectioners' sugar

Preheat oven to 350 degrees.

CAKE: Mix oil and eggs together. Put all dry ingredients together and mix with oil and eggs. Add carrots and nutmeats last. Bake in a 10x13 inch loaf pan about 45 minutes or in 2 layers in 9 inch pans, for 35 minutes.

FROSTING: Blend butter and cheese; add vanilla and powdered sugar. The more you stir the creamier it gets; mix to your liking. If you like a lot of frosting, you may need more cream cheese.

cakes—mini

Black Bottoms

Jayne Donohoe,
Lacrosse Mom — Casey 2009

INGREDIENTS

CAKE:

3 cups flour

2 cups sugar

1/2 cup cocoa

2 teaspoons baking soda

1/2 teaspoon salt

2 cups water

2/3 cup oil

2 tablespoons vinegar

2 teaspoons vanilla extract

FILLING:

16 ounces cream cheese

2 eggs, beaten

2/3 cup sugar

1/4 teaspoon salt

2 cups chocolate chips

Preheat oven to 350 degrees.

CAKE: Combine flour, sugar, cocoa, soda and salt in a bowl. Add water, oil, vinegar and vanilla, beating after each addition.

FILLING: Beat cheese until smooth. Add egg and mix. Add sugar and salt and beat well. Fold in chocolate chips.

Fill mini cupcake liners about 2/3 full with cake mixture. Place 1 teaspoon of the filling mixture on top of batter in each liner. Bake for about 20 minutes. These freeze well.

Hot Chocolate Lava Cake

Dave & Cindy Gaborek,
Owners, Let's Tailgate,
the official merchandiser for
Northwestern University

Yield: 4

Ingredients

granulated sugar for coating ramekins
1/4 pound unsalted butter
1 cup confectioners' sugar
1/2 teaspoon Godiva dark chocolate
    liqueur
2 whole large eggs
3 large egg yolks
vanilla ice cream

Preheat oven to 350 degrees. Coat inside of each ramekin with butter, then sprinkle with granulated sugar; tap out the excess; set aside.

Sift together flour and sugar; set aside.

Combine butter and chocolate in top of a double boiler, place over simmering water. Stir until the butter and chocolate have melted and mixture is smooth. Stir in the chocolate liqueur; set aside.

Combine the whole eggs and egg yolks in the bowl of an electric stand mixer. Beat at medium-low speed until thoroughly mixed, 1 to 2 minutes. Add the chocolate/butter mixture and mix until completely incorporated. Add the flour mixture, increase the speed and mix until smooth, 3 minutes.

Pour the batter into prepared ramekins, dividing it evenly. Bake until the tops are slightly puffed and have begun to crack, the edges are firm and set, and the center is still, about 22 to 24 minutes. Remove from oven and let cool 5 minutes. Serve hot with vanilla ice cream.

cakes—pan

Pineapple Angel Food Cake

Liz Kerr, 1981

Yield: 1 cake

Ingredients

1 box angel food cake mix
1 large can (15 ounces) crushed
    pineapple

In a 9x13 inch pan, pour the angel food mix. Add crushed pineapple and stir to mix thoroughly (it will foam up a bit). Follow baking instructions on cake mix box—be sure that it bakes through. Cut into squares and serve.

Applesauce Cake

Mary Ann Graham

YIELD: 9X13 INCH PAN

INGREDIENTS

CAKE:

2 cups flour

1 teaspoon baking soda

1/4 teaspoon salt

1 teaspoon cinnamon

1/2 cup butter

1 egg

1 cup nuts, coarsely broken

1 cup thick applesauce

1/4 teaspoon cloves

1/2 teaspoon nutmeg

1 cup raisins, optional

1 cup of sugar

PENUCHE ICING:

1/2 cup butter

1 cup firmly packed light brown sugar

1/4 cup milk

1-3/4 to 2 cups sifted confectioners'
    sugar

CAKE: Preheat oven to 350 degrees. Sift flour, baking soda and spices 3 times. Cream butter well; gradually add sugar, beating well after each addition. Add the egg and beat well. Alternately add dry ingredients and applesauce, about 1/3 at a time, beating until smooth. Add nuts and raisins.

Turn into a greased 9x13 inch pan. Bake for 30 minutes until toothpick inserted in center comes out clean. Cool in pan on wire rack. When cooled, spread icing on the cake and serve.

ICING: Melt butter in saucepan; stir in brown sugar. Boil and stir over low heat for 2 minutes. Stir in milk. Bring to boil, stirring constantly. Cool to lukewarm. Gradually stir in confectioners' sugar. Place pan in ice water and stir until thick enough to spread

Upside Down German Chocolate Cake

Liz Kerr, 1981

YIELD: 9X13 INCH PAN

INGREDIENTS

1 box German Chocolate Cake mix

1 cup chopped pecans

1 cup shredded sweetened coconut

1 pound powdered sugar

1/4 pound butter

8 ounces softened cream cheese

In a 9x13 inch pan, layer the pecans and coconut to cover bottom of pan. Mix German Chocolate cake mix per the box directions and pour over nuts/coconut mixture. Mix powdered sugar, butter and cream cheese. Drop spoonfuls on cake batter. Bake at 350 degrees for 40 to 45 minutes until edges are crisp. Test with toothpick half-way into cake. Cool in pan and serve slices upside down. Or cool 15 minutes in pan, then remove from pan and cool on rack.

Crumb Cake

Denise Munday,
Lacrosse Mom — Lindsey 2006

YIELD: 9x13 INCH PAN

INGREDIENTS

1 box yellow cake mix
3/4 pound butter
1 cup sugar
3 cups flour
3 to 4 tablespoons cinnamon

Preheat oven and mix cake batter according to box directions. Butter and flour an 11x17 inch baking pan. Place batter in pan and bake till almost done, about 12 to 15 minutes.

Meanwhile, mix the butter, sugar, flour and cinnamon till crumbly. Put on top of cake and bake for an additional 12 to 15 minutes. Top with confectioners' sugar when completely cooled.

Note: may use a 9x13 inch baking pan but cake with be thicker. Cooking time may differ.

West Haven Cake

Nancy Lee

YIELD: 9x13 INCH PAN

Great for tailgating since it transports well.

INGREDIENTS

12 ounces dates
1 teaspoon baking soda
1 cup hot water
1/2 cup softened butter
1 cup sugar
2 large eggs
1-3/4 cups flour
1 tablespoon cocoa
1 pinch salt
3/4 cup pecan halves
1 large (about 4 ounces)
    milk chocolate bar

Preheat oven to 350 degrees. Spray a 9x13 inch pan with non-stick spray and dust lightly with flour.

Chop dates and place in small bowl. Sprinkle baking soda over top of dates and then add hot water. Let stand.

Cream butter and sugar. Add eggs and then beat mixture thoroughly.

Mix or sift together flour, cocoa and salt. Add flour mixture to wet ingredients and mix well. Add dates (with water) and blend.

Pour into pan. Crack up Hershey Bar into bite-sized pieces and sprinkle pieces and whole pecans over top.

Bake for 30 to 40 minutes, until toothpick comes out clean. Serve with whip cream or ice cream, if desired.

Texas Sheet Cake

Liz Luxem

YIELD: 24 SERVINGS

INGREDIENTS

CAKE:

2 cups flour

2 cups sugar

1/2 teaspoon salt

1 teaspoon baking soda

1 cup butter

1 cup water

4 tablespoons unsweetened cocoa

2 large eggs

1 cup sour cream

FROSTING:

1/2 cup butter

4 tablespoons unsweetened cocoa

6 tablespoons milk

1 teaspoon vanilla

1 pound confectioners' sugar

1 cup chopped walnuts or pecans

Preheat oven to 375 degrees. Grease and flour a jelly roll pan.

CAKE: Combine flour, sugar, salt and baking powder in a large mixing bowl and set aside. Bring butter, water and cocoa to a boil. Remove from heat and add to the dry ingredients. Mix well. Beat in eggs and sour cream. Pour batter into the prepared jelly roll pan. Bake 20 to 25 minutes. Cool slightly.

FROSTING: Put confectioners' sugar in a mixing bowl. Bring butter, cocoa, milk and vanilla to a boil. Remove from heat and add to powdered sugar; beat. Stir in nuts. Pour frosting on slightly warm cake and spread. If the cake is too hot the frosting will run off. Refrigerate frosted cake to keep frosting from melting.

cakes—tube

Ginger Pound Cake

Mary Pat Watt,
Football Mom — Kevin #42

YIELD: 1 CAKE

INGREDIENTS

3/4 cup milk

1 jar (2.7 ounces) crystallized ginger or 18 pieces of Trader Joe ginger chunks

2 cups butter, softened

3 cups sugar

6 large eggs

4 cups flour

1 teaspoon vanilla extract

Preheat oven to 325 degrees. Finely mince crystallized ginger. Cook milk and minced ginger in a saucepan until thoroughly heated but not boiling. Remove from heat and set aside for 10 to 15 minutes.

Beat butter until creamy. Gradually add sugar, beating 5 to 7 minutes. Add eggs, one at a time, beating after each addition just until the yellow disappears.

Add flour to the butter mixture alternately with milk mixture, beginning and ending with the flour. Beat at low speed until blended after each addition. Stir in vanilla. Pour batter into a greased and floured 10 inch tube pan.

Bake for 1 hour and 25 minutes or until a tester comes out clean. Cool in pan on wire rack for 10 minutes. Remove from pan and cool completely on a wire rack.

Serve with vanilla ice cream and garnish with crystallized ginger.

Lila's Lower-In-Fat Chocolate Bundt Cake

Mindy & David Kaplan,
WGN Sports Broadcaster

YIELD: 1 BUNDT CAKE

INGREDIENTS

1 box chocolate cake mix
   (without pudding)
1 box sugar-free instant
   chocolate pudding
4 eggs
1/2 cup no sugar added apple sauce
1/2 cup water
8 ounces light sour cream
6 ounces chocolate chips

Preheat oven to 350 degrees. Mix ingredients together until well blended. Spray Bundt pan with cooking spray and pour batter into pan. Bake for 50 to 60 minutes until toothpick comes out clean. When cool, flip upside down on cake plate. Sprinkle with powdered sugar just before serving. If desired, serve with lower-in-fat ice cream.

Vanilla Wafer Cake

Janie Varley,

YIELD: 8 TO 10 SERVINGS

This is very good as a coffee cake also.

INGREDIENTS

1-1/2 sticks butter
2 cups sugar
6 eggs
1/2 cup milk
1 package (14 ounces) vanilla wafers
1 package (6 ounces) coconut
1 cup pecans, optional

Preheat oven to 300 degrees. Cream butter and sugar. Add one egg at a time. Add milk and crushed vanilla wafers. Stir in coconut and pecans. Bake in well greased tube pan 1-1/2 hours or until toothpick comes out clean.

Angel Food Cake Frosting

Janie Varley,

YIELD: FROSTS ONE CAKE

Great for birthday cakes — no need for ice cream.

INGREDIENTS

1 angel food cake (baked or bought)
1 pint whipping cream
1 cup sugar
3 heaping tablespoons cocoa
pinch salt
1 teaspoon vanilla extract

Mix all frosting ingredients, but do not beat. Set in refrigerator over night. Three hours (or more) before serving, whip frosting and spread on cake. Keep in refrigerator until ready to serve. ◪

Alice Bay Carrot Cake

Abbey Boudreau,
Daughter of Tammy and the late Coach Randy Walker

YIELD: 1 BUNDT CAKE

This recipe is a favorite of many friends, including a few who previously said they didn't like carrot cake!

INGREDIENTS

CAKE:

2 cups sugar

1-1/2 cups vegetable oil

4 eggs

2 cups unbleached all-purpose flour

1 teaspoon salt

2 teaspoons baking soda

3 teaspoons cinnamon

3 cups grated carrots (packed)

1/2 cup chopped nuts, optional

FROSTING:

8 ounces cream cheese, softened

3/4 cup butter, softened

1-1/2 pounds confectioners' sugar

2 teaspoons vanilla extract

1/2 cup chopped nuts

Preheat oven to 350 degrees.

CAKE: In a large bowl mix sugar, oil and eggs. Sift flour, salt, baking soda and cinnamon together and gradually add to wet mixture. Stir in grated carrots and nuts. Pour into a greased and lightly floured

Bundt pan. Bake for 45 to 60 minutes until toothpick comes out clean; cool in pan about 10 minutes, then remove and cool completely before frosting.

FROSTING: Combine cream cheese and butter, then slowly add powdered sugar and vanilla, mixing on low constantly. Add powdered sugar to desired consistency. ◪

Sherbet Angel Food Cake

Liz Luxem,

YIELD: 1 CAKE

INGREDIENTS

1 prepared angel food cake

1 pint orange or lime sherbet

1 pint raspberry sherbet

8 ounces Cool Whip

toasted coconut, optional

Freeze cake for 30 minutes. Let sherbet stand at room temperature about 20 minutes or until softened.

Slice the cake horizontally into 3 layers (Freezing makes it easier to cut into layers). Place the bottom layer on a cake plate, add a layer of sherbet, another layer of cake. Follow with the other flavor of sherbet and top with the final layer of cake. Freeze just to set.

Frost with Cool Whip and top with coconut, if using; freeze. Remove from freezer 30 minutes before serving. ◪

Greg's Island Rum Cake

Greg Lutzen, 2005

YIELD: 10 SERVINGS

INGREDIENTS

CAKE:

4 eggs

1/2 cup cold milk

1/2 cup vegetable oil

1/2 cup dark rum (Myers, Appleton Estate)

1 package (18-1/2 ounces) yellow cake mix

1 package (1-3/4 or 2 ounces) instant vanilla pudding mix

GLAZE:

1/2 cup butter

1/4 cup water

1 cup sugar

TOPPING:

1 cup chopped toasted walnuts or pecans, optional

CAKE: Preheat oven to 325 degrees. Grease a 12-cup Bundt pan with flour and olive oil. Combine all cake ingredients. Beat for 3 minutes on high with electric mixer. Pour into prepared pan. Bake for 1 hour. Cool in pan.

Flip the pan over on serving plate. Drizzle glaze over top of cooled cake. Use brush or spoon to put extra dripping back on cake. If desired, use a toothpick or skewer to poke holes in top of cake before pouring glaze so glaze will seep into cake.

GLAZE: Melt butter in saucepan. Stir in water and sugar. Boil 6 minutes, stirring constantly. Remove from heat and stir in rum.

Tailgate Favorite Carrot Cake

Joe Slowik

YIELD: 1 BUNDT CAKE

INGREDIENTS

CAKE:

2 cups granulated sugar

2 teaspoons vanilla

4 large eggs

1 cup vegetable oil

2 teaspoons baking soda

1 teaspoon salt

2 cups all-purpose flour

3 teaspoons cinnamon

3 to 4 cups grated carrots

FROSTING:

1/2 cup butter or margarine

8 ounces cream cheese

2 cups powdered sugar

1 cup chopped pecans

CAKE: Preheat oven to 350 degrees. Grease and flour a Bundt or tube pan.

Cream together sugar, vanilla and eggs until thick. Blend in oil. In a separate bowl, sift soda, salt, flour and cinnamon. Gradually mix dry ingredients into egg mixture; fold in carrots. Pour into prepared pan. Bake for 40 to 50 minutes until toothpick inserted in center comes out clean; edges will be crisp. Cool in pan 15 minutes; remove and cool completely on rack. Frost or sprinkle with powdered sugar.

FROSTING: Cream butter and cream cheese. Add 1 cup of sugar, mix, then gradually add more and beat to desired consistency. Fold in pecans, if desired, and frost cake. May also top with pecans rather than fold into frosting.

candy

Chocolate Caramel Candy

Clare Jorgensen,
Football Mom — Paul #78

YIELD: 30 PIECES

Several steps but worth it!

INGREDIENTS

BASE:
1 cup (6 ounces) milk chocolate chips
1/4 cup butterscotch chips
1/4 cup creamy peanut butter

FILLING:
1/4 cup butter or margarine
1 cup sugar
1/4 cup evaporated milk
1-1/2 cups marshmallow creme
1/4 cup creamy peanut butter
1 teaspoon vanilla extract
1-1/2 cups chopped salted peanuts

CARAMEL:
1 package (14 ounces) caramels
1/4 cup whipping cream

ICING:
1 cup (6 ounces) milk chocolate chips
1/4 cup butterscotch chips
1/4 cup peanut butter

BASE: Combine chocolate and butterscotch chips and peanut butter in small saucepan. Stir over low heat until melted and smooth (or melt in microwave). Spread into bottom of lightly greased 9x13 inch pan. Refrigerate until set.

FILLING: Melt butter over med-high heat. Add sugar and milk and bring to a boil. Boil and stir for 5 minutes. Remove from heat. Stir in marshmallow creme, peanut butter and vanilla. Add peanuts. Spread over 1st layer. Refrigerate until set.

CARAMEL: Combine caramels and cream in saucepan. Stir over low heat until melted and smooth. Spread over the filling; refrigerate until set.

ICING: Combine chocolate and peanut butter chips and peanut butter and melt. Pour over the caramel layer. Refrigerate at least one hour. Cut into one inch squares. Keep refrigerated. **N**

Peanut Butter Pretzel Bites

Tarresha Poindexter, 2011,
Cheerlerleading

YIELD: 20 TO 24 PIECES

INGREDIENTS

1 cup creamy peanut butter
2 tablespoons softened butter
3/4 cup powdered sugar
3/4 cup brown sugar
1 bag (12 ounces) semi-sweet
  chocolate chips
48 mini-pretzels

Combine peanut butter and butter in a large bowl. Add the sugars; mix to combine. At this point if the mixture will roll easily into balls without sticking to your hands, it is ready. If not, add a little more of each sugar until you reach a consistency that is easy to roll.

Use a teaspoon measure to scoop the filling. Roll each portion into a small ball, then sandwich them between two whole pretzels. When all the balls are rolled and successfully sandwiched, stick the whole tray in the freezer for about half an hour.

Pour the chocolate chips into a micro-wave safe bowl and heat at 30-second intervals, stirring occasionally until completely melted. Remove the pretzel sandwiches from the freezer and quickly dip each half-way into the melted choco-late. Return to the tray and repeat with remaining sandwiches. When all are dipped, return the tray to the freezer to set up completely. Store the sandwiches in the refrigerator until serving time.

White Chocolate Party Mix

Coach April & Craig Likhite,
Head Coach, Cross Country

INGREDIENTS

16 cups popped popcorn
    (about 8 ounces)

3 cups frosted Cheerios

1-1/2 cups pecan halves

14 ounces milk chocolate M&Ms
    preferably purple and white

1 package (10 ounces) pretzel sticks

1 package (10 ounces) English toffee
    bits

2 packages (10 ounces each) white
    chocolate chips

2 tablespoons vegetable oil

In a very large bowl combine first 6 ingre-dients. Melt chips and oil and pour over popcorn. Toss to coat.

Spread into 2 or 3 baking sheets. Let stand to dry for 2 hours. Store in an air-tight container.

This makes the perfect snack for your NU Tailgate!

White Chocolate Cereal Clusters

Julie Kent

YIELD: 5 TO 6 CUPS

INGREDIENTS

4 cups honey graham cereal

1-1/2 cups honey roasted peanuts

2 cups vanilla chips

1 cup dried cranberries, optional

In a large bowl combine cereal and peanuts. In a microwave safe bowl, melt chips at 30% power for 3 minutes, stir-ring every minute until smooth. Pour over cereal mixture; stir until well coated. Spread onto a waxed paper-lined baking sheet. Let stand until chocolate is set. Break into small pieces.

Wildcat Chow

Bonnie & Dan Wefler,
Bonnie 1950 and Dan 1950

INGREDIENTS

1 box Crispix cereal (about 18 cups)

2 cups chocolate chips

2 cups peanut butter

1/4 pound butter

2 tablespoons powdered sugar or more
    as needed

Melt chips, butter and peanut butter in saucepan. Put cereal in a very large bowl. Pour chocolate mixture over cereal. Put mixture in a paper bag with powdered sugar. Shake to coat. Spread on waxed paper to cool. Store in airtight container.

Chocolate Peanut Clusters

Stacy & Coach Pat Fitzgerald,
Head Coach, Football

YIELD: 25 TO 30 PIECES

INGREDIENTS

12 ounces milk chocolate chips
12 ounces peanut butter chips
12 ounces Heath Bar chips
1 container (7 ounces or more)
    honey-roasted peanuts

In a large pot, melt milk chocolate and peanut butter chips. Stir in Heath Bar chips. Remove from heat, stir in honey roasted peanuts.

Place wax paper on cookie sheet. Spoon quarter size clusters onto wax paper. Place cookie sheet into refrigerator for 10 to 15 minutes. Remove clusters from wax paper.

Almond Graham Crunch

Carri Martin, 2004,
Softball

YIELD: 1 PAN

INGREDIENTS

1/2 pound butter
1 cup brown sugar
1 bag sliced almonds
1 box (14-1/2 ounces)
    graham crackers

Preheat oven to 350 degrees. Line cookie sheet with aluminum foil. Line cookie sheet with one layer of graham crackers. In sauce pan melt butter, brown sugar and almonds. Boil 2 minutes.

Spread over graham crackers. Bake for 10 minutes. Cut immediately. Let cool.

Buckeye Bites

Jennifer Vierneisel

YIELD: ABOUT 200 PIECES

INGREDIENTS

2 pounds peanut butter
1 pound margarine
3 tablespoons vanilla
3 pounds powdered sugar
12 ounces chocolate chips

I have used dipping chocolate and Ghirardelli chocolate chips; both are delicious.

Mix together peanut butter, margarine and vanilla. Work in the powdered sugar until it is thoroughly mixed. Roll the peanut butter mixture into small balls (about 1 inch). Place the balls on a baking sheet covered with waxed paper and freeze for 15 to 20 minutes.

Melt the chocolate in a slow cooker or double boiler. Using a toothpick, dip the balls one at a time in the chocolate leaving a small circle undipped to resemble a buckeye. Place on waxed paper to set. Voila — buckeyes for Wildcat fans to devour!

Store in a covered container in the refrigerator.

Cat Caramel Corn

Liz Meyers

YIELD: 15 TO 20 SERVINGS

Serve after a Wildcat win!

INGREDIENTS

6 quarts popped popcorn

1/4 teaspoon cream of tarter

2 cups light brown sugar

1/2 cup light corn syrup

1/2 pound butter

1/2 teaspoon baking soda

Add peanuts or other nuts if desired.

Bring to a boil the cream of tarter, brown sugar, corn syrup and butter in saucepan. Add baking soda while stirring constantly.

Pour over popcorn and mix thoroughly. Spread on greased cookie sheets.

Bake for one hour at 200 degrees.

Homemade Toffee Grahams

Debby Zirin

YIELD: 3 TO 4 CUPS

This is an incredibly popular, crowd-pleaser dessert and it takes minutes to make!

INGREDIENTS

2 sleeves of honey graham crackers (any brand, but not low fat or generic)

1/2 pound butter

1 cup brown sugar

16 ounces Nestlé Tollhouse Morsels

8 ounces Heath Bits 'O Brickle Toffee bits or chocolate covered toffee bits

Preheat oven to 350 degrees. Melt butter and brown sugar in a saucepan on low. Cook 2 minutes (don't boil). Line a jelly roll pan with aluminum foil, spray with non-stick spray, then line with graham crackers. Pour the butter/sugar mixture over the graham crackers. Bake in oven for 10 minutes. Take it out and pour the chocolate chips over it while hot. Spread the chocolate as it melts to cover the entire pan. Sprinkle the toffee bits over the chocolate. Refrigerate for a few hours until firm. Cut or break into toffee-sized pieces.

Prize Fudge

Sandy Eszes

YIELD: 24 PIECES

INGREDIENTS

4 cups sugar

1 can (12 ounces) evaporated milk

1 cup butter or margarine

12 ounces semisweet chocolate pieces

1 jar (7 ounces) marshmallow creme

1 teaspoon vanilla extract

1 cup broken walnuts

Butter sides of heavy 3 quart sauce pan. In it combine sugar, milk and butter. Cook over medium heat to softball stage (236 degrees or 5 to 10 minutes after it starts boiling), stirring frequently. Remove from heat, add chocolate, marshmallow creme, vanilla and nuts. Beat until chocolate is melted and blended. Pour into a buttered 9x9 inch or 9x13 inch pan.

cobbler

Grandma's Peach Cobbler

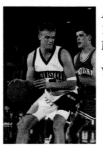

Evan Eschmeyer, 1998, Men's Basketball

YIELD: 8 TO 10 SERVINGS

INGREDIENTS

1-1/2 cups sugar

1-1/2 cups flour

1/2 teaspoon baking powder

2 eggs

1 can (30 ounces) sliced peaches in juice

1 tablespoon butter

1 tablespoon cinnamon

1/8 teaspoon salt

Preheat oven to 375 degrees (350 if using a glass dish). Butter 9x9 inch baking pan. Add peaches with juice. Sprinkle with half the cinnamon. In a separate bowl mix flour, salt, baking powder and sugar. Add eggs and mix until crumbly. Spread mixture over peaches. Dot with butter and remaining cinnamon. Bake for 30 to 45 minutes.

Giants' Peach Cobbler

Barry Cofield, 2005,
Football/NY Giants

Yield: 10 to 12 servings

Ingredients

3 cans (15 ounces each) Del Monte
 Sliced Peaches in
 100% Real Fruit Juice

2 cups sugar, divided

1/2 cup water

8 tablespoons butter

1-1/2 cups self-rising flour

1-1/2 cups milk

cinnamon, optional

Also try making with sweet cherries in syrup.

Preheat oven to 350 degrees. Combine the peaches with juice, 1 cup of the sugar and water in a saucepan and mix well. Bring to a boil and simmer for 10 minutes. Remove from heat.

Put butter in a 3-quart baking dish and place in oven to melt. Mix remaining sugar with flour, then slowly add milk, stirring to prevent clumping. Pour mixture over melted butter. Do not stir.

Spoon fruit on top, gently pouring in syrup. Sprinkle top with cinnamon. Bake for 30 to 45 minutes until the dough in the center tests done.

To serve, scoop onto a plate and serve with your choice of whipped cream or vanilla ice cream.

Easy Peach Cobbler

Bonnie & Dan Wefler,
Bonnie 1950 and Dan 1950

Yield: 9x13 inch pan

Ingredients

1/2 cup unsalted butter

1 cup all-purpose flour

1 tablespoon baking powder

2 cups sugar, divided

pinch salt

1 cup milk

4 cups fresh or frozen peach slices

1 tablespoon lemon juice

ground cinnamon, optional

Preheat oven to 375 degrees. Melt butter in 9x13 inch baking dish. Combine flour, 1 cup sugar, baking powder and salt; add milk stirring just until dry ingredients are moistened. Pour batter over butter (do not stir). Bring remaining 1 cup sugar, peach slices and lemon juice to a boil over high heat stirring constantly; pour over batter (do not stir). Sprinkle cinnamon if desired. Bake for 40 to 45 minutes or until golden brown. Serve warm or cool.

cookies

Cake Mix Chocolate Chip Cookies

Megan Anderson, 1976

INGREDIENTS

1 box chocolate cake mix

1 cup mayonnaise

2 eggs

1 cup chocolate chips

1/2 cup chopped walnuts

Preheat oven to 350 degrees. Mix all ingredients together and drop by tea-spoonful on cookie sheet. Bake 5 to 10 minutes.

Soft Lemon Cookies

David Wuellner

YIELD: 3 TO 4 DOZEN

INGREDIENTS

1 box lemon cake mix

1 egg

8 ounces whipped topping, thawed

1 cup powdered sugar, sifted

Use other flavors of cake mixes — chocolate, yellow, spice, carrot, etc. for variety. Easy but good!

Preheat oven to 350 degrees.

Place whipped topping in a mixer bowl, add cake mix and egg and mix. In another bowl sift the powdered sugar. Using 2 spoons, drop 3 or 4 tablespoon-sized cookies into the powdered sugar. Roll to coat with sugar and place on a cookie

sheet sprayed with non-stick spray. Bake for 10 to 12 minutes then let cool on sheets for 2 minutes. Remove and cool on a wire rack.

Chewy Flourless Cookies (gluten-free)

Robin Studlien,
Football Mom — Will #56

YIELD: 15 COOKIES

INGREDIENTS

1-3/4 cups confectioners' sugar

1/2 cup Dutch processed unsweetened cocoa powder

2 teaspoons cornstarch

1/4 teaspoon salt

2 egg whites

1 cup coarsely chopped pecans or walnuts, toasted

Preheat oven to 300 degrees. Line a baking sheet pan with parchment.

Mix together the sugar, cocoa, cornstarch and salt. Gradually add the egg whites, stirring with a wooden spoon until the mixture forms a glossy dough. The dough should be thick enough to form balls; if not, add more sugar and cocoa. Stir in nuts.

Form dough into 1-1/2 inch balls, about 15. Arrange on the baking sheet, spacing 3 inches apart. Bake 16 to 19 minutes or until glossy and top is crackled. Cool completely on baking sheet.

Chocolate Nut Christmas Wreaths

Julie Wood, 1982

YIELD: 48 COOKIES

INGREDIENTS

12 ounces Tollhouse semi-sweet morsels

12 ounces Tollhouse milk chocolate morsels

3 to 4 cups salted mixed nuts, Brazil nuts removed

red and green sprinkles

24 cherry licorice strings, separated

For your first attempt, allow some extra time to shape the wreaths.

First, tie the licorice strings into bows. Then melt the chocolate chips together in the microwave in a large bowl for approximately 2 minutes or until melted. Stir in the nuts until they are well-coated. Drop by tablespoonful onto waxed or parchment paper. Using the tip of the handle of a wooden spoon, shape the mixture into wreaths. While the candy is still warm, sprinkle with red and green sprinkles and press licorice bows into place. Allow to harden overnight.

Chocolate Mint Layer Cookies

Janie Varley

YIELD: 9x9 INCH PAN

INGREDIENTS

2 squares (1 ounce each) unsweetened chocolate

1/2 cup butter

2 eggs

1 cup sugar

1/2 cup flour

1-1/2 cups powdered sugar

3 tablespoons butter, softened

2 tablespoons milk

3/4 teaspoon peppermint extract

4 ounces sweet cooking chocolate

2 tablespoons butter

1 teaspoon vanilla extract

Add food coloring as desired, red for Valentines, orange for Halloween, red/blue for NU games.

Melt unsweetened chocolate and butter. Cool. Beat eggs and sugar until light and thick; stir in flour and melted chocolate. Spoon mixture into a greased 9x9 inch (or bigger) pan. Bake at 350 degrees for 25 minutes. Cool.

Combine powdered sugar, butter, milk, mint extract and food coloring; beat until smooth. Spread over the baked brownie layer, cover and cool in the refrigerator.

Melt sweet chocolate and butter, stir in vanilla and drizzle over the mint layer. Cover and chill an hour or until firm.

Irresistibly Perfect Chocolate Chip Cookies

Harvey Blender, 1973

YIELD: 24 COOKIES

INGREDIENTS

1 teaspoon vanilla

1/2 pound butter at room temperature

2 eggs at room temperature

1 cup white sugar

1 cup brown sugar

2-1/2 cups uncooked oatmeal

2 cups flour

12 ounces chocolate chips

1/2 teaspoon salt

1 teaspoon baking soda

1 teaspoon baking powder

1 teaspoon vanilla extract

I prefer quick oats — easier to blend

Preheat oven to 375 degrees. Cream butter and sugars; add eggs and stir till smooth. Blend the oatmeal to a powder; add 1/3 of the chocolate chips and blend again for a few seconds. Add salt, baking powder, baking soda and vanilla. Stir in flour, then stir in the rest of chocolate chips. Make 1-1/2 to 2 inch balls; put on ungreased cookie sheets. Bake for 9 to12 minutes. Let cool for few minutes on the pan then cool completely on a rack.

The Brennan Family Chocolate Chip Cookie

Christine Brennan, 1980, 1981, USA Today sports columnist, ABC News and NPR commentator

YIELD: 3 TO 4 DOZEN

Recipe adapted to include eating the dough

INGREDIENTS

2-1/4 cups all-purpose flour

1 teaspoon baking soda

1 teaspoon salt

1 cup butter, softened

3/4 cup granulated sugar

3/4 cup packed brown sugar

1 teaspoon vanilla extract

2 large eggs

1 to 2 cups chocolate chips, as desired

Preheat oven to 375 degrees. Combine flour, baking soda and salt in a small bowl. Set aside.

Combine butter, granulated sugar and brown sugar in a larger bowl. Once creamy, add the vanilla, or, before you do that, have a taste.

Don't eat too much or you'll throw off the entire recipe. If you've eaten too much, you might want to throw in more sugar or butter.

Then add the eggs, one at a time, beating well. Gradually mix in the flour mixture. Stir in the chips. If you eat the dough at this point, with the raw eggs included, you do so at your own risk, but it certainly has been done. Drop by rounded tablespoon onto ungreased cooking sheets.

Bake for 9 to 11 minutes or until golden brown. Cool on cooking sheets for 2 minutes, then move to a rack to cool.

Chocolate Rum Balls

Beverly Roitman

YIELD: 45 TO 50 PIECES

INGREDIENTS

1 package (6 ounces) Nestlé
    semi-sweet chocolate morsels
3 tablespoons corn syrup
1/2 cup rum
2-1/2 cups vanilla wafer crumbs
1/2 cup sifted confectioners' sugar
1 cup finely chopped nuts
1/2 cup (approximately) granulated
    sugar

Melt chocolate morsels over hot (not boiling) water. Remove from heat. Add corn syrup and rum; set aside. In large bowl, combine vanilla wafer crumbs, confectioners' sugar and nuts. Add chocolate mixture; mix well. Let stand 30 minutes. Form into 1 inch balls. Roll in granulated sugar. Let season in a cool place in a covered container for several days.

Oreo Balls

Janis Ziffer

YIELD: 10 TO 12 SERVINGS

INGREDIENTS

8 ounces cream cheese (whipped is
    better) at room temperature
1 package (15 ounces) Oreo cookies
10 to 12 ounces baking chocolate,
    milk, dark or white

Pound the Oreo cookies until very smashed (easier to do half the package at a time) or crush using a food processor. Mix cookies and cream cheese in a bowl and mix until smooth. Then make into balls about 1-1/2 to 2 inches in diameter. Put balls into freezer for approximately 2 to 3 hours on waxed paper.

Melt chocolate and dip balls into the chocolate, letting excess drain. Let cool on waxed paper.

Midnight Meringues

Bonnie & Dan Wefler,
Bonnie 1950 and Dan 1950

YIELD: ABOUT 4 DOZEN

INGREDIENTS

2 egg whites
3/4 cup sugar
1/2 teaspoon cream of tartar
pinch salt
6 ounces mint or regular chocolate
    chips

Preheat oven to 375 degrees. Beat egg whites with salt and cream of tartar until foamy. Gradually add sugar, beating until stiff and shiny. Fold in chips. Cover 2

COACHES QUOTES

Pat Fitzgerald, Football:

*"Wildcat Attitude – "Kaizen" –
Constant and consistent
improvement."*

cookie sheets with parchment paper. Place cookies by teaspoonfuls (or desired size) on sheet. Put in oven and turn oven off. Leave 8 hours or overnight, until cookies are dry and crisp.

Monster Cookies

Abby Kurz

YIELD: 3 DOZEN

The cookies are very peanut buttery.

INGREDIENTS

3 eggs

1 cup granulated sugar

1/2 teaspoon salt

1/2 teaspoon vanilla extract

1 jar (12 ounces) creamy peanut butter

1/4 pound butter, softened

1/4 cup milk chocolate M&Ms

1/2 cup chocolate chips

3/4 cup Reese's Pieces

1/4 cup raisins, optional

2 teaspoons baking soda

4-1/2 cups quick cooking oats (not instant)

1-1/4 cups packed light brown sugar

Preheat oven to 350 degrees. Line cookie sheets with parchment paper or nonstick baking mats. In a very large mixing bowl, combine eggs and sugars. Mix well. Add the salt, vanilla, peanut butter and butter. Mix well. Stir in the M&Ms, chips, Reese's Pieces and raisins if using. Add baking soda and oatmeal; mix well. Drop by tablespoons 2 inches apart onto the prepared cookie sheets.

Bake 8 to 10 minutes until edges start to brown. Let cool on pans for about 3 minutes before transferring to wire racks to cool.

Willie's Purple Pride Cookies

Arlene Sunkel, 1956

YIELD: 48 COOKIES

INGREDIENTS

2 cups sifted flour

1/2 teaspoon salt

1 cup butter (no substitutes)

1/2 cup sugar

1-1/2 teaspoons vanilla extract

1/2 teaspoon almond extract

1/2 cup (approximately) Smucker's concord grape jam

1/2 cup sifted confectioners' sugar

Sift together flour and salt. Set aside. Cream butter until light and fluffy. Add extracts. Mix in flour, 1/2 cup at a time, until blended. Handle dough as little as possible otherwise it will be soft, mushy and difficult to handle. Chill dough for 1 to 2 hours.

Preheat oven to 325 degrees. Quickly shape dough into 1 inch balls. Place 2 inches apart on ungreased baking sheets. Make a deep thumbprint into the center of each cookie and fill with jam. (I use Smucker's Grape for an N.U. effect.) Bake for 15 minutes until cookies are the color of pale sand.

Transfer to cooling racks. When completely cooled, lightly dust with confectioners' sugar. Store cookies in tins between layers of waxed paper. They keep for weeks in a cool place.

Christmas Biscotti

Wendy Mathewson,
Associate University Chaplain

YIELD: 25 PIECES

INGREDIENTS

2-1/4 cups flour

1-1/2 teaspoons baking powder

3/4 teaspoon salt

6 tablespoons butter, softened

1/2 cup sugar

1 teaspoon lemon extract or grated
lemon peel

2 teaspoons vanilla extract

1-1/2 teaspoons ground allspice

1 cup dried cranberries

3/4 cup pistachios

*I have used both salted and unsalted
pistachios and they are both good. If you
like the salty/sweet combination, try the
salted ones.*

Preheat oven to 325 degrees. Line a large
baking sheet with parchment paper. Sift
flour, baking soda and salt into medium
bowl. Beat butter and sugar in large bowl
to blend well. Beat in eggs, 1 at a time.
Mix in lemon extract, vanilla and allspice.

Beat in flour mixture just until blended.
Stir in cranberries and pistachios (dough
will be sticky). Turn dough out onto
lightly floured surface. Divide dough in
half. Roll each half into 15 inch long log,
about 3 inches wide, depending on how
big you want the biscotti. Log should be
somewhat flattened. Transfer logs to
prepared baking sheet, spacing 3 inches
apart.

Bake logs until almost firm to touch but
still pale, about 28 minutes. Cool logs on
baking sheet 10 minutes. Maintain oven
temperature.

Transfer logs still on parchment to cutting board. Using very sharp knife and
gentle sawing motion, cut logs crosswise
into generous 1/2 inch thick slices. Place
slices upright, half an inch apart, on the
baking sheet. Bake until firm and pale
golden, about 18 minutes. Transfer
cookies to racks and cool.

Washington Cookies

Janie Varley,

YIELD: 6 DOZEN

Kurz/Varley family favorite cookies

INGREDIENTS

1-1/2 cups flour

1 teaspoon baking soda

1 teaspoon salt

1 cup margarine

3/4 cup brown sugar

3/4 cup granulated sugar

2 eggs

1 teaspoon vanilla extract

1 cup chopped walnuts, optional

2 cups rolled oats

12 ounces chocolate bits

Preheat oven to 350 degrees. Sift flour
soda and salt. Cream margarine with
both sugars. Beat eggs into margarine-
sugar mixture. Add vanilla. Stir in dry
ingredients. Add nuts, oats and bits and
mix all thoroughly. Drop on greased
cookie sheet. Bake 12 to 15 minutes until
light brown.

Oatmeal Toffee Cookies

The NU Women's Lacrosse Team

Yield: 2 dozen

Ingredients

1-1/2 cups all-purpose flour

1 teaspoon baking soda

1 cup unsalted butter, room temperature

3/4 cup granulated sugar

3/4 cup light brown sugar

1 egg

1 teaspoon pure vanilla extract

1-1/2 cups oatmeal

1 cup bittersweet chocolate, coarsely chopped

1 cup toffee pieces (5-1/2 ounces)

This dough can be baked immediately, refrigerated for up to two days, or frozen up to a month.

Heat oven to 350 degrees. Sift together flour and baking soda; set aside. In a mixing bowl, cream butter and sugars on medium-high speed until light and fluffy, 2 to 3 minutes. Scrape down the sides of the bowl once or twice during mixing. Add egg and mix on high speed to combine. Add vanilla extract; mix to combine. Scrape down the sides of the bowl. Add the sifted flour a bit at a time on a low speed until well combined. Add oatmeal, chocolate and toffee pieces; mix to combine. Divide dough into three equal portions and using plastic wrap roll into logs, approximately 1-1/2 inches in diameter. To bake, cut logs into 3/4 inch pieces. Bake on parchment lined baking sheets until golden brown, 8 to 10 minutes. Remove from oven and transfer to a baking rack to cool.

Whitney's Florentine Cookies

Whitney White, 2010, Women's Fencing

Yield: 3-1/2 dozen sandwich cookies

Ingredients

COOKIE:

2/3 cup butter

2 cups quick oats, uncooked

1 cup sugar

2/3 cup all-purpose flour

1/4 cup corn syrup

1/4 cup milk

1 teaspoon vanilla extract

1/4 teaspoon sea salt

FILLING:

2 cups semisweet or dark chocolate morsels

COOKIES: Preheat oven to 375 degrees. Melt butter in medium saucepan over low heat. Remove from heat. Stir in oats, sugar, flour, corn syrup, milk, vanilla extract and sea salt; mix well. Drop by level teaspoonfuls, about 3 inches apart, onto foil lined cookie sheets. Spread thin with rubber spatula. Bake for 5 to 7 minutes. Cool completely. Peel foil away from cookies.

FILLING: Melt the chocolate morsels in a bowl over hot (not boiling) water (or microwave); stir until smooth.

Spread chocolate on flat side of 1/2 the cookies. Top with remaining cookies.

Worlds Best Oatmeal Chocolate Chip Cookies

Hillary Fratzke,
Assistant Coach, Lacrosse

INGREDIENTS

1 cup softened butter
1 cup packed light brown sugar
1/2 cup white sugar
2 eggs
2 teaspoons vanilla extract
1-1/2 cups all-purpose flour
1/2 teaspoon baking soda
1 teaspoon salt
3 cups quick cooking oats
1 cup Ghirardelli milk chocolate chips

Preheat oven to 325 degrees. Mix butter, brown sugar and white sugar. Beat in eggs, one at a time. Stir in vanilla.

In a separate bowl combine flour, baking soda and salt, then add to the butter/sugar mixture. Mix in oats and chocolate chips.

Bake for 12 minutes. Cool on pan for 5 minutes before transferring to wire rack.

Chocolate Chip Oatmeal Cookiesp

Kim & Coach Tim Cysewski,
Associate Head Coach, Wrestling

YIELD: 3 DOZEN

INGREDIENTS

1 cup unsalted butter
3/4 cup sugar
3/4 cup brown sugar
2 eggs
1 teaspoon vanilla extract
2 cups flour
2 cups oatmeal
1 teaspoon salt
1 teaspoon baking powder
1 teaspoon baking soda
12 ounces semi-sweet chocolate chips
8 ounces Hershey bar, chopped
1 cup chopped toasted walnuts

Preheat oven to 350 degrees. Measure oatmeal and blend in blender to a fine powder. In a large bowl, cream the butter and both sugars. Add eggs and vanilla to creamed mixture and blend well.

In a separate bowl, combine together flour, oatmeal, salt, baking powder and baking soda. Stir to mix dry ingredients and slowly add to creamed mixture. Mix well. Stir in chocolate chips, chopped Hershey bar and nuts. Roll into balls and place two inches apart on a cookie sheet. Bake for 10 minutes.

Grandma Berning's Oatmeal Candy Cookies

Bonita Paynter, 1972, 1974

YIELD: ABOUT 30 2 INCH COOKIES

These cookies are easy to make and take little time to prepare.

INGREDIENTS

4 tablespoons cocoa
3 cups quick oatmeal
1 teaspoon vanilla
1/2 cup crunchy peanut butter
1 cup chopped nuts, optional
2 cups sugar
1/2 cup milk
1/2 cup butter or margarine

Place cocoa, oats, vanilla, peanut butter and nuts in a large mixing bowl. Combine the sugar, milk and butter in a saucepan; bring to a full rolling boil. Boil for one FULL minute. Quickly combine the hot mixture with the cocoa and oatmeal mixture; stir well. Working quickly, drop by spoonfuls onto waxed paper. Cool.

No-Bake Cookies

Laura & Coach Joe McKeown, Head Coach, Women's Basketball

YIELD: 40 COOKIES

INGREDIENTS

2 cups sugar
1/4 pound butter
1/4 cup cocoa
1/2 cup milk
1/2 cup creamy peanut butter
1 teaspoon vanilla extract
1 pinch salt
3 cups uncooked oatmeal

Can substitute 12 large marshmallows for the peanut butter.

Boil first 4 ingredients for 1 minute or until shiny. Add next 4 ingredients into hot mixture. Spoon onto wax paper in bite-sized circles. Let cool.

Wally's Oatmeal Cookies

Walt White,
Fencing Dad — Whitney 2010

YIELD: 48 SMALL OR 24 LARGE COOKIES

INGREDIENTS

1/2 pound butter
1 cup firmly packed dark brown sugar
1/2 cup granulated sugar
2 large eggs
1 teaspoon vanilla extract
1-1/2 cups all-purpose flour
1 teaspoon baking soda
1 teaspoon cinnamon
1/2 teaspoon sea salt
3 cups oats (old fashion or quick
    uncooked)
1 cup raisins
1 cup chopped walnuts
1 cup semi-sweet or dark chocolate
    chips

Preheat oven to 350 degrees.

Beat together butter and sugar until creamy. Add eggs and vanilla; beat well. Add combined flour, baking soda, cinnamon and sea salt; add to batter and mix well. Stir in oats, raisins, chips and walnuts. Drop by rounded teaspoonfuls onto ungreased cookie sheets. If you prefer large cookies, double the teaspoonfuls. Bake 10 to 12 minutes or until golden brown. Cool on wire baking rack.

Frango Mint Cowboy Cookies

Sue Ryan,
Basketball Mom — Jeff #5

YIELD: 24 COOKIES

INGREDIENTS

2 cups flour
2 cups oatmeal (uncooked)
1 teaspoon baking soda
1/2 teaspoon baking powder
1/2 teaspoon salt
1/2 pound butter at room temperature
3/4 cup + 2 tablespoons dark brown
    sugar (packed)
3/4 cup granulated sugar
2 large eggs
1 teaspoon vanilla extract
12 ounces coarsely chopped Frango
    Mints

Whisk first 5 ingredients in medium bowl to blend. Using electric mixer, beat butter and both sugars in large bowl until light and fluffy. Add eggs and vanilla, beating to combine. Add dry ingredients and beat until just blended. Stir in chopped Frango Mints. Cover dough and chill 1 hour.

Preheat oven to 350 degrees and put rack in the middle. Form dough into 24 balls. Flatten with hand to approximately 3 inch rounds. Bake 14 minutes or until golden brown and firm in the center. Cool on baking sheets for 2 minutes; remove to wire rack to cool completely.

Oatmeal Cookies

Marge & Tom Kennedy,
**Football Grandparents —
Kevin Watt #42**

We have made these cookies for Kevin since he was a freshman football player at Northwestern. They are his favorite.

INGREDIENTS

1 cup white sugar

1/2 cup brown sugar

1 cup butter, softened

1 large egg

1-1/2 cups flour

1 teaspoon baking soda

1 teaspoon cinnamon

1 teaspoon vanilla extract

3/4 cup chopped pecans

1-1/2 cups raw, quick cooking oatmeal

These are a flatter, thinner cookie than a traditional oatmeal cookie.

Cream sugars and butter. Add egg and beat until blended. Add vanilla and nuts. Stir in sifted dry ingredients. Stir in oatmeal until well blended. Chill dough in refrigerator for about an hour.

Preheat oven to 375 degrees. Drop rounded teaspoons, 2 inches apart, on greased cookie sheet. Butter bottom of drinking glass and dip in sugar and flatten each cookie, dipping in sugar for each cookie.

Bake 5 minutes then turn cookie sheet for another 4 or 5 minutes.

Pretzel Yummies

Arlene Koester,
Lacrosse Mom — Courtney 2005

YIELD: 25 PIECES

Dipping and rolling definitely works best with two people. Lloyd and I usually start the dipping and rolling after 5 to 10 minutes of cooling; otherwise the caramel cools and thickens to the point of breaking the pretzels.

INGREDIENTS

2 cups pecans

1 cup peanut butter pieces candy

1 cup milk chocolate chips

1 cup brown sugar

1/2 cup light corn syrup

1/4 cup butter

2/3 cup sweetened condensed milk

1/2 teaspoon vanilla

25 pretzel rods

Process pecans, peanut butter pieces and milk chocolate chips until coarsely chopped. Set aside. Combine brown sugar, corn syrup and butter. Bring to a boil over medium heat. Stir in sweetened condensed milk. Return to boiling. Reduce heat to medium-low; continue cooking until mixture reaches 236 degrees (soft ball stage) on candy thermometer. Remove from heat. Add vanilla and cool 5 minutes until slightly thick. Dip pretzel rods into caramel mixture covering two-thirds of pretzel. Roll pretzel in chopped mixture pressing slightly with back of spoon. Let stand on non-stick foil until caramel is set. Store in airtight container between layers of wax paper in refrigerator up to 4 days or freeze up to 1 month.

Special K Peanut Butter Cookies with Nuts

Sally Madden Hayward, 1961

Great for tailgating.

INGREDIENTS

1 jar (12 ounces) Skippy Super
    Crunch peanut butter
1 cup sugar
1 cup white Karo syrup
4 to 5 cups Special K cereal
12 ounces Nestlé's Toll House Morsels
12 ounces Nestlé's Butterscotch
    Morsels
1/2 cup chopped pecans

Melt in top of double boiler Karo syrup, peanut butter and sugar until sugar is dissolved. Remove top of double boiler from hot water, stir until blended. Add cereal 1 cup at a time; stir with wooden spoon. Add enough cereal to absorb the sauce. Spread mixture on large sided cookie sheet. Cover with waxed paper and flatten with palm of hand. Set aside. On very low heat, melt Toll House and butterscotch morsels, stirring until creamy. Pour over peanut butter mixture and spread evenly. Immediately, sprinkle chopped pecans on top while mixture is hot. Place cookie sheet in refrigerator until mixture hardens 1/2 to 1 hour. Cut into squares. Can be frozen, defrosts quickly.

Special K Peanut Butter Cookies

Tammy Walker,
**Athletic Department; Widow of
NU Football Coach Randy Walker**

YIELD: 40 TO 50 COOKIES

When I made treats each week for the football players, this was the most requested cookie.

My mother created this recipe by adapting a similar recipe that used Rice Krispies cereal. I modified it a little, using chocolate kisses instead of chocolate stars. Then, my daughter, Abbey Boudreau, added her twist by forming balls around the kisses, creating a chocolate center surprise.

INGREDIENTS

1 cup sugar
1 cup light corn syrup
2 cups creamy peanut butter
6 cups Special K cereal
1 bag Hershey chocolate kisses
    (about 50 kisses)

Stir sugar and corn syrup in a large saucepan over medium heat until small bubbles cover the bottom of the pan and they start to rise. Add the peanut butter and turn off the burner. Mix thoroughly and then add the Special K cereal.

Drop by rounded tablespoons onto waxed paper and immediately top with a chocolate kiss, pushing it down into the cookie. As an alternative, you can form a ball of the cereal mixture around the kiss, so that there is a chocolate center in the cookie. The cookie and chocolate will harden a little as they cool.

Bon Bon Cookies

Sandy Kwiatkowski

YIELD: 80 TO 100 COOKIES

INGREDIENTS

7 cups Rice Krispies (slightly crushed)

1/4 pound margarine

7 cups powdered sugar

3 pounds of peanut butter

1/2 slice paraffin wax (2 ounces)

12 ounces semisweet chocolate chips

Mix Rice Krispies, peanut butter and powdered sugar together. Melt margarine and pour over Rice Krispies mixture. Make round balls with the palms of your hands and set aside on waxed paper.

In top of double boiler, melt chips and wax. Drop balls into chocolate mixture, remove with teaspoons and place on waxed paper covered cookie sheet. Only place 3 to 4 balls in mixture at a time. Place in refrigerator to cool.

Double Peanut Butter Cookies

Joe Slowik

YIELD: 4 DOZEN COOKIES

The very best peanut butter cookies!

INGREDIENTS

1/4 cup butter or margarine

1/4 cup shortening

1/2 cup smooth peanut butter

1/2 cup granulated sugar

1/2 cup packed light brown sugar

1 egg

1-1/4 cups all-purpose flour

3/4 teaspoon baking soda

1/2 teaspoon baking powder

1/4 teaspoon salt

2 cups peanut butter chips
    (12 ounce package)

sugar for dipping

Preheat oven to 375 degrees. Cream butter, shortening, peanut butter, sugar, brown sugar and egg in a large bowl. In a separate bowl, mix flour, baking soda, baking powder and salt. Add dry ingredients to butter mixture, mixing until blended. Stir in peanut butter chips. Shape into 1-inch balls. Place on an ungreased cookie sheet. Flatten in a criss-cross pattern with a fork dipped in sugar. Bake for 8 to 10 minutes or until set. Cool for several minutes before moving from cookie sheet to a wire rack to cool.

Impossible Peanut Butter Cookies

Amy Backus,
Former Women's Basketball Assistant Coach and current Yale Head Coach, Women's Basketball

YIELD: 2 DOZEN

INGREDIENTS

1 cup sugar
1 cup peanut butter
1 egg, lightly beaten

Mix all ingredients in bowl. Drop by spoonful onto a non-stick cookie sheet.

Flatten with a wet fork. Bake 10 to 12 minutes at 300 degrees.

Wildcat Cookies

Clem West, 1973,
Women's Swimming

YIELD: 4 DOZEN

Use a regular bag of M&Ms for BigTen cookies.

INGREDIENTS

2-1/4 cups flour
1 teaspoon baking soda
1 cup butter, softened
3/4 cup brown sugar (firmly packed)
1/4 cup granulated sugar
1/2 cup instant vanilla pudding mix
1 teaspoon vanilla extract
2 large eggs
12 ounces purple & white M&Ms

Preheat oven to 375 degrees. Mix flour with baking soda and set aside. Combine butter, sugars, pudding mix and vanilla in a large bowl. Beat until smooth and creamy. Beat in eggs. Gradually, add flour mixture, then fold in M&Ms. Batter will be stiff. Drop from teaspoon onto ungreased baking sheet about 2 inches apart. Bake for 8 to 10 minutes.

Purple Pride

Snickerdoodles

Jean Yale, 1957,
Athletic Development/Special Events

YIELD: 3 TO 4 DOZEN

INGREDIENTS

1 cup butter
1-1/2 cups sugar
2 large eggs
2-3/4 cups flour
2 teaspoons cream of tartar
1 teaspoon baking soda
1/2 teaspoon salt
2 tablespoons sugar
2 teaspoons cinnamon

Cream butter and sugar, add eggs and mix thoroughly. Mix dry ingredients together and fold into butter/egg mixture until mixture is uniform. Combine sugar and cinnamon in a small bowl. Roll into balls then in sugar/cinnamon mixture.

Place two inches apart on ungreased cookie sheet and bake at 400 for 8 to 10 minutes.

Ginger Cookies

Marian Kurz, MSJ

YIELD: 4 DOZEN

INGREDIENTS

3/4 cup margarine or butter
2 cups flour
1 cup sugar
1/2 teaspoon ground ginger
1/2 teaspoon cloves
1/2 teaspoon salt
1/4 cup molasses
2 teaspoons baking soda
1 teaspoon cinnamon
1 egg
granulated sugar

Preheat oven to 375 degrees. Melt butter in saucepan over low heat. Remove from heat and allow to cool. Add sugar, molasses and egg; beat well. Sift together flour, soda, cloves, ginger, salt and cinnamon. Add to sugar/molasses mixture, mix well and chill thoroughly. Divide dough in half; keep half refrigerated while working on first piece. Form into one inch balls, roll in granulated sugar. Place on greased cookie sheet 2 inches apart. Bake for 8 to 10 minutes. Store in airtight container.

COACHES QUOTES

Tracey Fuchs,
Women's Field Hockey:

"Dream Big!"

Ginger Snaps

Katie Braun, 2008,
Women's Swimming

YIELD: 24 COOKIES

INGREDIENTS

3/4 cup butter
1 cup sugar
1/4 cup molasses
1 egg
2 cups sifted flour
1/2 tablespoon salt
2 teaspoons baking soda
1 teaspoon cinnamon
1 teaspoon cloves
1 teaspoon ginger
sugar for rolling

Cream together butter and sugar. Add molasses; mix. Add egg; mix. In a separate bowl, sift together the dry ingredients.

Add sifted dry ingredients to sugar/butter batter and mix. Chill.

Shape into 1 inch balls; roll in a small dish of granulated sugar. Place 2 inches a part on a greased cookie sheet.

Bake 10 minutes at 365 degrees. Cookies become crisp when cool.

Snickers Cookies

Ling & Ed Albrecht,
Lacrosse parents — Hilary 2006

YIELD: 20 COOKIES

INGREDIENTS

1 cup butter, softened
1 cup creamy peanut butter
1 cup light brown sugar
1 cup sugar
2 eggs
1 teaspoon vanilla extract
3-1/2 cups flour, sifted
1 teaspoon baking soda
1/2 teaspoon salt
1 package (13 ounces) Snickers miniatures
1 package (11 ounces) milk chocolate

Combine the butter, peanut butter and sugars using a mixer on medium to low speed until light and fluffy. Slowly add eggs and vanilla until thoroughly combined. Then mix in flour, salt and baking soda. Cover and chill for 2 to 3 hours.

Unwrap all Snickers Miniatures (or Fun-size cut in half). Remove dough from refrigerator. Lightly flour work surface. Divide dough into 1 tablespoon pieces and flatten. Place a Snickers in the center of each piece of dough. Form the dough into a ball around each Snickers. Place on a greased cookie sheet and bake at 325 degrees for 10 to 12 minutes. Let cookies cool on baking rack or waxed paper. After cooling, drizzle melted milk chocolate over the top of each cookie.

Pecan Tassies

Harriet Skiba

YIELD: 2 DOZEN

INGREDIENTS

1/2 cup butter
3 ounces cream cheese
1 cup flour
3/4 cup brown sugar
1 large egg
1 teaspoon vanilla extract
1 cup chopped pecans

Soften butter and cream cheese to room temperature. Mix well. Add flour and mix well. Chill dough at least 1 hour or overnight.

Grease mini muffin tins. Once the dough is chilled, divide into 24 pieces, roll into balls and shape into mini muffin tins.

Preheat oven to 350 degrees. Mix brown sugar, eggs, vanilla and chopped nuts. Mix well. Fill tarts 3/4 full. Bake for 15 minutes. Reduce heat to 250 degrees and bake an additional 30 minutes until brown. Dust tops of cookies with powdered sugar. Remove from muffin tins and cool.

fruit

Lemon Curd

Marian Kurz, MSJ

YIELD: 1-1/2 CUPS

INGREDIENTS

2 large eggs plus 2 large egg yolks
6 tablespoons unsalted butter
1 cup sugar
6 tablespoons fresh lemon juice
2 teaspoons grated lemon zest
dash salt

Whisk egg and yolks in medium bowl. Melt butter over simmering water. Whisk in sugar, lemon juice, lemon zest and salt. Gradually add egg mixture and whisk until thick. Cover and chill for a few hours.

Fill store-purchased meringues, use for parfaits alternating fruit and curd, dollop on a cookie or eat it right out of the container.

Pineapple Vanilla Rounds

Top Chef Stephanie Izard,
**Top Chef (Season 4) and
chef/owner of the
Girl and the Goat Restaurant, Chicago**

YIELD: 8 TO 10 SLICES

INGREDIENTS

1 whole pineapple
1 vanilla bean (this gives the flavor)
1/3 to 1/2 cup sugar
1 cup water

Purchase sliced pineapple or cut a fresh pineapple into slices. Combine sugar, water and fresh vanilla bean broken into 4 to 5 pieces to cover pineapple slices. Adjust sugar amount based on the sweetness of the pineapple. Add additional sugar/water if needed so that the pineapple cooks, not burns. Cook at 375 degrees for about an hour or until tender. Pour off remaining liquid and remove vanilla bean bits. Serve warm with a scoop of vanilla ice cream or gelato. **N**

Yummy Baked Apples

Debby Zirin

YIELD: 6 SERVINGS

INGREDIENTS

6 Rome Beauty baking apples
2 tablespoons sugar
1 to 2 tablespoons cinnamon
1/2 cup raisins
3 tablespoons butter, cut in 6 pieces

Preheat oven to 400 degrees. Core apples well but don't go through the bottom of the apple. Peel apple skin around the top of the core opening for about 1/2 inch. Fill each cavity to the top with a mixture of sugar, cinnamon and raisins. Top each cavity with a pat of butter. Fill bottom of baking dish with approximately 1 inch of cold water. Add filled apples. Bake uncovered for 45 to 60 minutes, basting often with liquid from the bottom of baking dish. **N**

Baked Apples

Randy Toelke

YIELD: 8 TO 10 SERVINGS

INGREDIENTS

10 to 12 large Macintosh apples
1/4 cup granulated sugar
1/2 cup brown sugar
2 tablespoons flour
2 teaspoons cinnamon
4 tablespoons butter

Preheat oven to 325 degrees. Peel and slice apples. In a bowl, combine brown sugar, granulated sugar, flour and cinnamon. Mix well. Add apples to the dry ingredients and mix to coat.

Place apple mixture in a greased 9x13 inch pan. Cut butter into thin slices and place over apples. Bake for 45 minutes or until golden brown.

pastry

Marie's Cannoli Filling

Sandy Orlandino,

YIELD: FILLS 30 MINI CANNOLI SHELLS

INGREDIENTS

1 pound ricotta, whipped
1 cup powdered sugar
6 ounces Cool Whip
2 teaspoons vanilla extract
12 ounces mini semisweet chocolate chips

Mix all ingredients together stirring by hand until combined; refrigerate for at least 8 hours to set. Spoon into pre-made cannoli shells (can be purchased from Italian bakery), or mini ice cream cones.

Apple Dumplings

Arlene Koester,
Lacrosse Mom — Courtney 2005

YIELD: 12 SERVINGS

INGREDIENTS

SYRUP:

2 cups white sugar

2 cups water

1/4 teaspoon cinnamon

1/4 teaspoon nutmeg

1/4 cup butter or margarine

FILLING:

6 to 7 apples

Cinnamon and sugar for sprinkling

6 pats of butter for finish or
        butter-flavored cooking spray

DOUGH:

2 cups flour

1 teaspoon salt

2 teaspoons baking powder

*Instead of wedges, cut the dough into 5
to 6 inch squares and pinch together at
the top.*

SYRUP: Combine sugar, water, cinnamon, nutmeg and butter. Heat and stir occasionally until sugar dissolves.

DOUGH: Combine flour, salt, baking powder. Cut in shortening. Moisten with milk, adding one tablespoon at a time to form a smooth dough. With rolling pin, roll out into a large circle, approximately 16 inches. Cut into 6 pie wedges.

ASSEMBLY: Preheat oven to 375 degrees. Peel and slice apples. Place slices in the middle of each dough wedge. Sprinkle with the additional cinnamon and sugar. Fold the dough over the mound of apples. Carefully place the dumplings, folded side down in a 9x13 inch baking dish. Chop any remaining apple and place the pieces around the dumplings. Pour the syrup over the dumplings. Place a pat of butter on each dumpling. Bake for about 35 minutes or until golden brown.

pie

Easy Breezy Blueberry Pie

Bonnie & Dan Wefler,
Bonnie 1950 and Dan 1950

YIELD: ONE 9-INCH PIE

INGREDIENTS

2 pints fresh blueberries,
    washed and air dried

1 jar (12 ounces) currant jelly

16 ounces sour cream

1 unbaked graham cracker crust
    pie shell, 9 inches

Bake crust as directed and cool. Melt jelly in saucepan on medium low heat. Put blueberries into cooled pie crust reserving a few for decoration. Pour melted jelly over berries. Refrigerate until ready to serve. Just before serving, spread sour cream over berries using all or part of the container, to taste. Decorate with re-served berries.

Summer Blueberry Pie

Arlene Sunkel, 1956

YIELD: ONE 9-INCH PIE

INGREDIENTS

1 baked 9-inch pie crust, cooled

3/4 cup sugar

2-1/2 tablespoons cornstarch

1/4 teaspoon salt

2/3 cup water

3 cups large fresh blueberries, divided

2 tablespoons butter

1 cup heavy cream, divided

1-1/2 tablespoons freshly squeezed
    lemon juice

2 tablespoons confectioners' sugar,
    divided

1/2 teaspoon vanilla extract, divided

The larger the berries, the better.

Combine sugar, cornstarch and salt in saucepan. Add water and 1 cup of the blueberries. Bring to a boil and cook stir-ring constantly until thick. Stir in butter and lemon juice. Cool for about 45 min-utes. Fold in the remaining blueberries and chill for 1 hour.

Beat 1/2 cup cream until thick. Stir in 1 tablespoon confectioners' sugar and 1/4 teaspoon vanilla. Spread over bottom of pie shell. Top with blueberry filling. Chill at least 2 hours.

Beat second 1/2 cup of cream until thick. Stir in 1 tablespoon confectioners' sugar and 1/4 teaspoon vanilla. Mound over top center of pie. Chill until ready to serve.

Cherry Sauce or Pie Filling

Helene Bak Slowik, 1973

YIELD: 2 CUPS

This makes a great pie or can be served with crepes, waffles, ice cream or cake such as angel food or pound cake. Red food coloring is optional but makes the sauce more appealing.

INGREDIENTS

2 cans (16 ounces each) tart
    red cherries
1 cup sugar
1/3 cup flour
1/8 teaspoon salt
2 tablespoons butter
1/2 teaspoon almond extract
1/4 teaspoon red food coloring,
    optional

Drain the cherries, reserving the syrup. Add 1 cup syrup to a medium saucepan. Combine sugar, flour and salt. Stir into syrup. Over medium-high heat, bring to a boil while stirring. Reduce heat to simmer and cook about 5 minutes, stirring frequently. Stir in butter. If too thick, stir in remaining syrup, about a tablespoon at a time. Add almond extract and food coloring, stir. Add cherries.

If using for a pie, cool, covered with plastic wrap directly on surface. Bake according to pie dough recipe.

Chocolate Chip Walnut Pie

Megan Anderson, 1976

YIELD: ONE 9-INCH PIE

INGREDIENTS

1 unbaked 9 inch pie shell
2 large eggs
1/2 cup flour
1/2 cup sugar
1/2 cup brown sugar
1 cup melted butter
1 tablespoon vanilla extract
6 ounces semisweet chocolate chips
1 cup chopped walnuts
whipped cream or vanilla ice cream

Preheat oven to 325 degrees.

Beat eggs in large mixing bowl until foamy. Gradually beat in flour and sugars. Beat until well blended. Add melted butter and vanilla; beat until smooth. Fold in chocolate chips and nuts. Pour into unbaked pie shell. Bake until golden and toothpick inserted in center comes out clean, about 50 minutes. Cool completely on wire rack. Serve topped with whipped cream or vanilla ice cream.

Whitehouse Chocolate Chip Pie

Whitney White, 2010,
Women's Fencing

Yield: 8 to 10 servings

Ingredients

2 large eggs
1/2 cup all-purpose flour
1/2 cup sugar
1/2 cup firmly packed brown sugar
1 cup butter, melted and cooled to
    room temperature
1 cup Nestle Toll House semi-sweet or
    dark chocolate morsels
1 cup chopped walnuts
1 unbaked pie shell, 9 inch

Preheat oven to 325 degrees. In large bowl, beat eggs until foamy. Add flour, sugar and brown sugar; beat until well blended. Blend in melted butter. Stir in chocolate morsels and chopped walnuts. Pour into pie shell and bake for one hour. Serve warm with whipped cream.

Lemonade Pie

Liz Kerr, 1981

Yield: 10 to 12 servings

Ingredients

1 can (6 ounces) frozen pink
    lemonade concentrate
1 can (14 ounces) sweetened
    condensed milk
12 ounces Cool Whip
1 whole graham cracker pie crust

Mix condensed milk and Cool Whip together, then add defrosted lemonade. Pour into prepared graham cracker crust. Chill in refrigerator until set. Can garnish with lemon and/or lime slices and strawberry slices.

COACHES QUOTES

Kelly Amonte-Hiller,
Women's Lacrosse:

"One phrase that I live by is 'You're only as good as your last game.' My dad used to say it to us Amonte kids all the time. It would help ground us and constantly push to get to the next level. I think this mentality has helped my program achieve continued success. We are continuing to focus on getting better all of the time!"

Wildfire's Homemade Key Lime Pie

Executive Chef Joe Decker,
Wildfire Restaurant, multiple locations

YIELD: 9 INCH PIE

INGREDIENTS

2 cups graham cracker crumbs
1 tablespoon granulated sugar
4 tablespoons butter, melted
1/2 cup egg yolks (about 5)
1-1/2 cups sweetened condensed milk
3 tablespoons granulated sugar
1/2 cup key lime juice (about 5 limes)
1-1/2 teaspoons fresh lemon juice
1 pinch table salt
whipped cream for topping, optional
grated lime zest for topping, optional

CRUST: For the crust, combine the first three ingredients together. Place mixture into 9 inch pie pan. Form a shell, using an empty pie tin to push down; make the crust even. Bake shell for 5 minutes in 350 degree oven.

TOPPING: In a stainless bowl, whisk together the next six custard ingredients until smooth and place into the pre-baked shell. Bake for 15 to 18 minutes in 300 degree oven. Custard should be slightly loose in center of pie. Let cool and enjoy with whipped cream and grated lime zest.

Grasshopper Pie

Allison McCormick, 1999

YIELD: 2 PIES

INGREDIENTS

1 package crushed regular Oreos
(about 30 cookies)
3/4 cup melted butter
1-1/3 cups scalded milk
48 large marshmallows
1 pint whipping cream
4 ounces green Creme De Menthe
liquor
2 ounces clear Creme De Cocoa liquor

SHELL: Mix crushed Oreo cookies and melted butter. Pat into two pie tins and put in freezer.

FILLING: To scalded milk, add marshmallows. Stir until dissolved. Cool to room temperature. Add liquors to mixture. Whip cream until stiff. Fold into green mixture with a spatula. Pour into crust. Freeze.

Can be served with whipped cream or grated chocolate, but tastes amazing plain.

Snickers Pie

NU Women's Lacrosse Team

Yield: 9 inch pie

Ingredients

5 Snickers candy bars
    (2.07 ounces each)
1 baked 9 inch pastry shell
12 ounces cream cheese, softened
1/2 cup sugar
2 eggs
1/3 cup sour cream
1/3 cup peanut butter
2/3 cup semisweet chocolate chips
2 tablespoons heavy whipping cream

Preheat oven to 325 degrees.

Cut the candy bars into approximately 1/4 inch pieces. Place candy bar pieces and all scraps in the pastry shell; set aside.

In a mixing bowl, beat cream cheese and sugar until smooth. Add eggs, sour cream and peanut butter; beat on low speed just until combined. Pour into pastry shell. Bake for 35 to 40 minutes or until set. Cool on a wire rack.

In a small heavy saucepan, melt chocolate chips with cream over low heat until smooth. Spread over filling. Refrigerate for 2 hours or overnight. Cut with a warm knife.

Strawberry Pie

Ella Anderson

Yield: 8 servings

Ingredients

1 quart strawberries
1 cup sugar
3 tablespoons cornstarch
1 pinch salt
1 cup boiling water
4 tablespoons Strawberry Jell-O
1 pie shell, baked
whipped cream or Cool Whip,
    optional

Wash and slice strawberries. Add sugar, salt and cornstarch to boiling water. Cook until thickened. Remove from heat and stir in Jell-O until dissolved. Let the mixture cool a little; pour over the strawberries. Refrigerate. Top with whipped cream if desired.

pudding

Triple Chocolate Mess

Ruth Anne Velaer-Wheeler, 1988

YIELD: 10 TO 12 SERVINGS

INGREDIENTS

1 package chocolate cake mix

1 pint sour cream

1 package chocolate pudding mix
(3 ounces)

12 ounces Ghirardelli semi-sweet
chocolate chips

3/4 cup vegetable oil

4 eggs

1 cup water

Spray slow cooker with non-stick cooking spray. Mix all ingredients together, and pour into the slow cooker. Cook on low 4 to 5 hours. Less cooking time produces a gooey dessert, longer cooking time produces a cake-like dessert.

Serve in bowls topped with ice cream.

Dirt Pudding

AnnMarie Finch,
Lacrosse Mom — Christy 2008

YIELD: 9x13 INCH PAN

INGREDIENTS

1-1/4 packages (about 24 ounces)
Oreo Cookies

1/4 pound butter or margarine

1 package (8 ounces) cream cheese

2 packages (3 ounces each) instant
vanilla pudding

3 cups milk

12 ounces Cool Whip

1 package gummy worms, optional

Crush cookies in plastic bag and place 2/3 of the bag in 9x13 inch pan. Soften butter and cream cheese and blend together. Add pudding and milk to creamed mixture; mix well. Fold in Cool Whip and gummies. Pour mixture over cookies and top with remaining cookies. Refrigerate.

Espresso Crème Brûlée

Suzanne Calder

INGREDIENTS

2 cups 2% milk

1 cup whole espresso coffee beans

3/4 cup nonfat dry milk

3 tablespoons sugar, divided

1 teaspoon vanilla extract

dash salt

4 large egg yolks

1/4 cup sugar, divided

Preheat oven to 300 degrees.

Combine milks, espresso beans and 2 tablespoons sugar in a medium saucepan. Heat over medium heat to 180 degrees or until tiny bubbles form around edge (do not boil), stirring occasionally. Remove from heat, cover and steep 30 minutes. Strain mixture through a sieve into a bowl; discard solids. Stir in vanilla.

Combine 1 tablespoon sugar, salt and egg yolks in a medium bowl, stirring well with a whisk. Gradually add milk mixture to egg mixture, stirring constantly with a whisk. Divide the mixture evenly among 4 (4 ounce) ramekins, custard cups or 2 inch deep baking dishes. Place ramekins in a 9x13 inch baking pan and add hot water to pan to a dept of 1 inch. Bake at 300 degrees for 25 minutes or until center barely moves when ramekin is touched. Remove ramekins from pan, cool completely on a wire rack. Cover and chill at least 4 hours or overnight.

Sift 1 tablespoon sugar evenly over each custard. Holding a kitchen blow torch about 2 inches from the top of each custard, heat the sugar, moving the torch back and forth until sugar is completely melted and caramelized. Serve immediately or within 1 hour (otherwise the sugar will dissolve into the custard).

Or if no torch, place 1/4 cup sugar and 1 tablespoon water in a small heavy saucepan. Cook over medium heat 5 to 8 minutes or until golden. Resist the urge to stir since doing so may cause the sugar to crystallize. Immediately pour the sugar mixture evenly over cold custards, spreading to form a thin layer. **N**

Cheater Bread Pudding — Yet Compliance-approved!

Mike Polisky,
Senior Associate Director of Athletics (External Affairs)

YIELD: 12 SERVINGS

INGREDIENTS

1 loaf (1 pound) cinnamon raisin
    bread

1 quart milk

3 eggs, beaten

1-1/2 cups sugar

2 tablespoons vanilla extract

3 tablespoons margarine
    (or non-stick spray)

Alternatives: 1) Add dark chocolate chips to the mixture before baking. 2) Garnish with Cool Whip. 3) Top with bourbon sauce. Bourbon sauce recipe: Cream 1 cup of sugar and 1 egg until well mixed. Add 1 stick of melted margarine and mix well. Add Jim Beam bourbon, to taste and to make a smooth sauce. Go Cats!

Preheat oven to 350 degrees. Soak bread in milk. Crush with hands until well mixed. Add eggs, sugar and vanilla. Stir well. Pour margarine (or spray Pam) into the bottom of a 9x13 inch baking dish. Pour the bread mixture into the pan and bake for 30 minutes or until firm.

Perfect Blocker Bread Pudding

Brian Kardos, 1996,
Football, Rose Bowl Team

YIELD: 12 TO 14 SERVINGS

Brian said we could name this whatever we wanted. He just didn't want any references to holding penalties in the title!

INGREDIENTS

1/2 cup butter

1 cup sugar

5 eggs

2-1/4 cups heavy cream

1 tablespoon pure vanilla extract

1 teaspoon ground cinnamon

1/2 cup yellow golden raisins (make
    sure to use the yellow raisins)

1/2 cup sliced almonds

2 tablespoons confectioners' sugar

1 tablespoon amaretto

2 large loaves sourdough bread,
    cut off crusts and pull apart into
    small pieces

SAUCE:

1 cup heavy cream

1 cup sugar

1/4 teaspoon cinnamon

1 tablespoon butter

1 tablespoon cornstarch

1 tablespoon water

2 tablespoons amaretto

1 dash of vanilla extract

1 cup chopped almonds

PUDDING: Preheat oven to 350 degrees. Cream butter and sugar; add eggs, heavy cream, vanilla, amaretto and cinnamon. Place liquid ingredients and half of the bread into the bowl of an electric mixer and begin mixing on slowest speed, gradually increasing speed and adding bread to the bowl until the mixture becomes mush. You may need to add a little more cream to keep it extremely moist. Add yellow golden raisins and almonds and place all into a greased casserole dish, put the casserole in a pan; fill pan with water to half the height of the casserole (in a water bath) and bake covered for 45 minutes. Uncover and bake another 15 minutes until a toothpick stuck into the center comes out clean. Dust the bread pudding with confectioners' sugar.

AMARETTO SAUCE: Bring cream, sugar, cinnamon and butter to a boil and stir until sugar dissolves. Separately, dissolve the cornstarch and water. Add the cornstarch mixture to the hot sauce and cook until thickened. Add almonds. Place on very low heat, add the amaretto and vanilla; stir. Remove from heat. Sauce may be used on top of bread pudding or as a side sauce. Sauce stores well in refrigerator and may be reheated.

OPTIONAL SAUCE: 1 pound (3-1/2 cups) sifted confectioners' sugar, 1/2 cup melted butter and 1 tablespoon milk.

Mix ingredients together. You may add more milk or butter to make the sauce more of a liquid state if preferred.

sauce

Hot Fudge Sauce

Mary Pat Watt,
Football Mom — Kevin #42

Serve with ice cream

Ingredients

1/2 cup butter or margarine

2-1/4 cups confectioners' sugar

2/3 cup evaporated milk
(one small can)

4 squares unsweetened chocolate

Mix butter and sugar in top of double boiler; add evaporated milk and chocolate, broken into pieces. Cook over hot water for 30 minutes. Do not stir while cooking. Remove from heat and beat by hand until smooth and thickens a bit (this takes a few minutes). May be stored in refrigerator and reheated as needed.

Go! U Northwestern!

Grandma Nev's Chocolate Sauce

Joann Skiba

This is a delicious sauce for ice cream or chocolate milk.

INGREDIENTS

7/8 cup Hershey's unsweetened cocoa
1-3/4 cups granulated sugar
1-1/2 cups boiling water
dash salt

Combine cocoa, sugar, water and salt in a saucepan. Bring to a boil and cook for 5 minutes. Remove sauce to a double boiler and cook for 1/2 hour. Cool completely. Store in covered bowl or jars in the refrigerator.

World's Best and Easiest Hot Fudge Sauce

Janie Varley

INGREDIENTS

4 squares (1 ounce each) unsweetened chocolate, melted
2 cups confectioners' sugar
2/3 cup evaporated milk (not sweetened)
3 tablespoons butter
1/4 teaspoon salt
1/2 teaspoon vanilla extract

Gradually add sugar to chocolate and stir in milk. Cook over low heat until smooth, stirring often. Add butter and salt and continue cooking till butter is melted. Add vanilla. Store in refrigerator and reheat in microwave as needed.

Me-Me's Hot Fudge Sauce

Julie Rachlis, 1960

YIELD: ABOUT 1-1/2 CUPS SAUCE

INGREDIENTS

4 ounces unsweetened chocolate
1 tablespoon butter
1 cup sugar
3/4 cup cream
1 dash salt
1 teaspoon vanilla extract

Melt chocolate and butter in a double boiler over hot water. Add sugar, salt and cream. Bring to boil over direct heat. Turn heat to low and stir. Cook for 10 minutes without stirring. Remove from heat, cool five minutes and add vanilla. Serve over ice cream.

Time Out

VOLLEYBALL

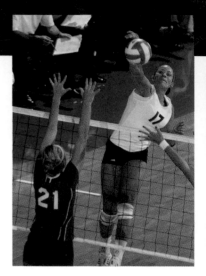

Head Coach Keylor Chan (2000–present)
– 5th head coach

- It became a varsity sport in 1976 under Coach Mary Conway.

- Through 2009, their record was 572-572-5. (The 2010 record was 20-13, breaking the tie!)

- There were 137 Academic All-Big Ten honorees in the years 1986–2010.

Christmas Scent

Megan Anderson, 1976

YIELD: 1 QUART

INGREDIENTS

3 bay leaves

3 sticks cinnamon

1/4 cup whole cloves

3 orange peels

2 lemon sections

1 quart water

Bring to a boil and just let it sit on the back burner of the stove with very low heat. Or, you can turn off the heat and reheat when the scent fades. Add more water as necessary to keep the wonderful aroma.

How to Make a Roux

Helene Bak Slowik, 1973

YIELD: DEPENDS ON THE INGREDIENTS

Roux is a thickening agent that is the base for many soups and sauces. Roux is a mix of fat and flour. There are three basic types: white, blond and brown. The longer the roux is cooked, the darker the color, the more intense the flavor and the less its thickening power. Any fat can be used to make a roux.

INGREDIENTS

desired amount of fat

about the same amount of
    all-purpose flour

Start by heating the fat over medium low heat, stirring to avoid browning. Add flour until the mixture thickens, like a pourable paste. Equal parts fat and flour

are often noted in recipes, but the amount of flour needed may be more or less. For a white roux, cook the mixture for 1 to 2 minutes, just enough to cook the flour. For blond, cook for 3 to 5 minutes, until the mixture is a light peanut color. For brown roux, cook on a higher heat until the mixture has a light brown color and a nutty smell.

Willie's Play Dough

Tammy Walker,

Athletic Development, and Widow of NU Football Coach Randy Walker

YIELD: ABOUT 2 CUPS

INGREDIENTS

2 cups flour

1 cup salt

2 tablespoons oil

3 tablespoons cream of tartar

2 cups water

food coloring, optional

Combine all ingredients in a medium saucepan. Add your choice of food coloring, but why would you want any color but purple? (If you don't have purple food coloring, combine red and blue). Mix over low to medium heat, stirring constantly until the mixture is the consistency of dough. Cool and store in sealed plastic bag.

How to Make a Simple Syrup

Helene Bak Slowik, 1973

YIELD: ABOUT 2-1/2 CUPS

Simple Syrup is a staple bar ingredient but is also used in cooking when a touch of sweetness is needed.

INGREDIENTS

2 cups sugar
1 cup water

A batch of Simple Syrup can be stored in the refrigerator in a tightly sealed bottle for up to 6 months.

Raw sugar can be used for a different flavor, but it will also give color to the syrup. Syrup can be infused with flavors such as vanilla, ginger, jalapeño, etc. Add the desired flavoring item (vanilla bean, chunk of fresh ginger, etc.) and let sit for at least 3 hours.

This recipe makes a rich syrup, so you may use less than a recipe specifies. Or make a syrup that has a 1 to 1 ratio.

Bring the water to boil. Add the sugar to the boiling water, stirring constantly. As soon as the sugar is dissolved completely, after about 5 minutes, remove the pan from the heat. Do not let the syrup boil too long or it will be too thick. Allow to cool, then bottle.

To prolong the shelf-life, add 2 tablespoons of unflavored vodka.

How to Roast Peppers

Joe Slowik

Most recipes specify bell peppers, but you can roast many other fresh peppers such as poblano, jalapeño, etc.

INGREDIENTS

whole peppers
vegetable oil

Set oven to broil. Coat each pepper with a thin layer of oil, then arrange peppers on a baking sheet. Place tray on the highest rack in your oven. Roast the peppers until the skins are blistered and black spots appear (5 to 7 minutes). Remove tray from oven and turn the peppers with a set of tongs. Roast on the other side until skin is blistered and blackened.

When the peppers are blistered and blackened evenly, remove from oven. Place peppers in a large bowl and cover with plastic wrap. Let sit for 20 minutes. After the peppers are done steaming, scrape off the scorched skin and remove the stem and seeds. Use only the inner flesh of the pepper in your dish.

Cat Food

FACTS

FIELD HOCKEY

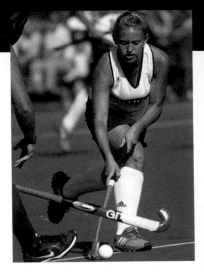

Head Coach Tracey Fuchs (2009–present)
– *9th head coach*

• The program began in 1975 with Coach Mary Ann Kelling. It became a varsity status sport in 1980.

• Field Hockey student-athletes from NU have been chosen for the U.S. National Team, the U.S. Olympic Team and the U.S. World Cup Team.

• There were 170 Academic All-Big Ten honorees in the years 1984–2010.

Willie's Wildcat Food

Grilled Lion Steaks

Toasted Buckeye Nuts

Wolverine Fricassee

Barbecued Spartan Spare Ribs

Hoosier Sugar Daddies

Boilermakers

Orange Crush Soda

Skewered Badger Bites

Baked Gopher Meatloaf

Fried Hawkeye Wings

Creamed Corn

Pregame Meals

Jose Alfaro, Catering Chef for Sodexo Sports & Leisure, suppliers of all the food at Northwestern University, says this is what he traditionally prepares for the NU Football and Basketball Teams for a pregame meal:

Football

30 gallons of Clam Chowder served in a bread bowl

250 pieces of Grilled Salmon with a Lemon Butter Sauce

100 pounds of Beef Tenderloin with Au Jus

225 potatoes at a Baked Potato Bar with Sour Cream, Cheddar Cheese and Green Onions

65 pounds of Rice Pilaf

Men's & Women's Basketball

25 – 5 ounce Grilled Chicken Breasts

25 – 5 ounce Grilled Salmon or Tilapia

25 – 5 ounce Lean Sirloin Steaks (Men's Team)

8 pounds Herbed (Rosemary, Parsley) Roasted Potatoes

8 pounds Steamed Mix Vegetables

Home & Away

Cooking & Tailgating Tips

WRESTLING

Head Coach Drew Pariano (2010–present)

• Coach Pariano is a 2000 graduate of NU.

• Became a varsity sport in 1924.

• There are 22 men on the team.

• Since 2005: 3 individual NCAA championships, 14 All-Americans, 7 Individual Big Ten championships, and 8 Midlands championships.

• There were 16 Academic All-Big Ten honorees in the years 1987–2011 and 25 NWCC All-Academic team members.

- A roast with the bone in will cook faster than a boneless roast — the bone carries the heat to the inside of the roast.

- Let raw potatoes stand in cold water for at least half an hour before frying to improve the crispness of French-fried potatoes.

- Lettuce keeps better if stored in refrigerator without washing so that the leaves are dry. Wash the day you are going to use.

- It's important to let a roast, whether beef, pork, lamb or poultry, sit a little while before carving. The wait allows the juices to retreat back into the meat. If you carve a roast too soon, much of its goodness will spill out onto the carving board.

- Microwave a lemon for 15 seconds before squeezing to get double the juice.

- Microwave garlic cloves for 15 seconds and the skins slip right off.

- When slicing a hard-boiled egg, try wetting the knife just before cutting. If that doesn't do the trick, try applying a bit of cooking spray to the edge.

- Rescue stale or soggy chips and crackers: Preheat the oven to 300 degrees. Spread the chips or crackers in a single layer on a baking sheet and bake for about 5 minutes. Allow to cool, then seal in a plastic bag or container.

- The best way to store fresh celery is to wrap it in aluminum foil and put it in the refrigerator—it will keep for weeks.

- Store freshly cut basil on your kitchen counter in a glass with the water level covering only the stems. Change the water occasionally. It will keep for weeks this way, and will even develop roots! Basil hates to be cold, so NEVER put it in the refrigerator. Also, regular cutting encourages new growth and healthier plants.

- A dampened paper towel or terry cloth brushed downward on a cob of corn will remove every strand of corn silk.

- When working with dough, don't flour your hands; coat them with olive oil to prevent sticking.

- Use a gentle touch when shaping ground beef patties. Over handling will result in a firm, compact texture after cooking. Don't press or flatten with spatula during cooking.

- Never heat pesto sauce — the basil will turn black and taste bitter.

- If your cake recipe calls for nuts, heat them first in the oven, then dust with flour before adding to the batter to keep them from settling to the bottom of the pan.

- Noodles, spaghetti and other starches won't boil over if you rub the inside of the pot with vegetable oil.

- When taking foods off the grill, put them on a clean plate, not the same platter that held raw meat.

- A quick way to give barbeque fare a garlic flavor is to toss garlic cloves on the coals while the food grills.

- It's a good idea to use a separate cooler for drinks, so the one containing perishable food won't be constantly opened and closed.

- A cooler chest can also be used to keep hot food hot. Line the cooler with a heavy kitchen towel for extra insulation and place well wrapped hot foods inside. It's amazing how long the foods will stay not only warm, but hot. Try to use a cooler that is just the right size to pack fairly tightly with hot food so less heat escapes.

- Whenever barbecuing, use tongs to turn the meat. A fork should never be used since it will punch holes in the flesh and allow the natural juices to escape, loose flavor and become chewy.

- Tomato and/or sugar based BBQ sauces should be added only at the end of the grilling process. These products will burn easily and are seldom considered an internal meat flavoring. Once added, the meat should be turned often to minimize the possibility of burning.

- Coat portable grill with heavy duty foil for easy cleanup and disposal of charcoal.

- Warm outside? Freeze bottled water – pop it into the cooler the day of the game. When it's hot out you can take it out and drink as it melts. Also serves as ice packs for the cooler and won't water down like ice.

- It's always a good idea to bring a "jumbo" cup. Less trips to fill it on up. Make sure that your cup sticks out like a sore thumb or has distinguishable markings so that you know it's yours.

- Oh, where would we be without the large storage bins? These magnificent totes keep your tailgating gear and equipment organized. It's easy in and easy out all season long.

- Whenever possible, pack your food in zip lock bags for easy packing of leftovers and little or no clean up.

- If cooking burgers, make in advance and freeze between waxed paper. Burgers should be 3/4 inch thick. You can cook them frozen for 3 to 4 minutes each side.

- Bring large plastic trash bags for easy clean-up.

Tailgate Must-haves

- **Jumper Cables.** The one time you don't bring 'em is the time you'll need 'em. You may also be the hero when someone's battery decides to go kaput.

- **Plastic Trash Bags.** Make sure that you bring extras. Don't get caught short because keeping your tailgating area clean after you're done results in great future tailgating karma.

- **Extra Ice.** Just bring an extra chest filled with ice. You never want to run out of ice.

- **First Aid Kit.** Bumps, burns and cuts can happen.

- **Antacid.** Defense wins championships. And sometimes, we need a little extra help to keep us on our game.

- **Tent** – stay dry or avoid the sun.

- **Laminated checklist** – as you pack for the game, simply check items with a dry erase marker. When done, simply erase and you are ready for the next game.

- **Music** – the music you play will be the energy you feed off for the best of the day.

- **Antacid.** Defense wins championships. And sometimes, we need a little extra help to keep us on our game.

- **Comfy shoes.**

- **Paper towels, wet naps.**

- **Bottle and can opener.**

United States Standard Measurements

60 drops	1 teaspoon	1/6 ounce
1 teaspoon	1/3 tablespoon	1/6 ounce
3 teaspoons	1 tablespoon	1/2 ounce
4 tablespoons	1/4 cup	2 ounces
8 tablespoons	1/2 cup	4 ounces
16 tablespoons	1 cup	8 ounces
1 cup	16 tablespoons	8 ounces
2 cups	1 pint	16 ounces
1 quart	2 pints or 4 cups	32 ounces
1 gallon	4 quarts	128 ounces

FENCING

Head Coach Laurence "Laurie" Schiller
(1978–present)
– *2nd head coach*

• First NCAA season was in 1977. They have never finished lower than fourth in the conference.

• Charlotte Remenyik was the 1st head coach in 1977.

• Their matches include Epee, Foil and Sabre.

• During his time with fencing, Coach Schiller has won over 1,000 matches.

• There were 100 Academic All-Big Ten honorees in the years 2003–2011.

Additional copies of this cookbook are available through
NUSports.com.

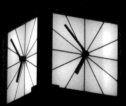

Hail to Purple
Hail to White
Hail to thee Northwestern